Mailer's America

Published for University of Connecticut by
University Press of New England
Hanover and London, 1987

Mailer's America

Joseph Wenke

© 1987 by the Trustees of the University of Connecticut

Printed in the United States of America

LIBRARY OF CONGRESS CATALOGING-IN-PUBLICATION DATA
Wenke, Joseph.
    Mailer's America.
    Bibliography: p.
    Includes index.
    1. Mailer, Norman—Criticism and interpretation.
2. United States in literature.   3. National
characteristics, American, in literature.   I. Title.
PS3525.A4152Z954   1987   813'.52   86–40389
ISBN 0–87451–393–6

5   4   3   2   1

For Lori

How much America becomes the character, no, the protagonist of that novel no genius is large enough to write. Shakespeare would grow modest before America.

NORMAN MAILER,
Some Honorable Men

Contents

Acknowledgments

I would like to thank Jack Davis and Joseph Cary for their critical readings of the manuscript. I would especially like to thank John Wenke for his reading of the manuscript and for his much appreciated comments and suggestions. In particular, I would like to thank Milton Stern for encouraging me to write this book on Mailer and for lending this project his constant and most eloquent support. Above all, I would like to thank my wife, Lorraine Giampa, for her critical and imaginative contributions, which helped shape so much of the manuscript, and for her understanding and patience during the many hours that I spent working on this book.

Mailer's America

Introduction

There is no better subject for a serious American writer than America itself. "In the beginning," said John Locke, "all the world was America."[1] And at America's beginning the land stretched out like a geographic *tabula rasa* upon which the European mind could write its dreams, having discovered at last a reality that was "commensurate to" its "capacity for wonder." Out of that limitless capacity for wonder was born the idea of America, "the last and greatest of all human dreams."[2] It is an idea that has continued to be expressed throughout American history with an astonishing constancy of vision, for despite significant differences in values and attitudes, conquistadors and Puritans, deists and transcendentalists, liberal Democrats and conservative Republicans have all shared one central belief: in America anything is possible.

Indeed, from the beginning both the light and the dark sides of the questing spirit, at times inextricably bound, have sought to project themselves upon the image of America as millennium so that, for example, in the Spanish imagination the country could represent both the epitome of romantic aspiration that is the land of the heart's desire and an elusive treasure-trove that could tantalize an insatiable greed for gold. Likewise, from the beginning millennial America has encouraged the identification of religious and political purposes so that imperialistic expansion might serve the united purpose of God and king (or president) and patriotic addresses seem curiously incomplete without some earnest reference to America's unique place in the divine plan. Thus America was and is the New World ever waiting to be discovered, an unknown territory whose possibilities continue to live in the imagination in the form of countless millennialistic ideas: America as El Dorado, the seventeenth-century city on a hill, the eighteenth-century agrarian New Eden, the mid-nineteenth-century embodiment of transcendentalist cosmic democracy, and the late nineteenth-century nation of Manifest Destiny. In the twentieth century, the influence of millennialism is reflected not only in the idea of America as the savior nation of Wilson's Fourteen Points and the redemptionist nation of the Marshall Plan but also in our most notable political slogans, which have conceived of America as a land of power and opportunity that can make the world safe for democracy and promise its citizens new life through participation in the New Deal, the New Frontier, or the Great Society.

At this late date cynicism is virtually an intellectual birthright. So it would seem in the light of Vietnam, Watergate, and increasing economic polarization that such political promises have proven empty. It would seem, in short, that the reality of America has failed to live up to the dream. Yet, as Milton R. Stern has noted, this view expresses only part of the truth. For "America, in the fantastic quality of its actualities, has always outgrown those who envision it, just as, equally, it has never been as great as the vision."[3] As our most powerful works of literature suggest over and over again, the crucial problem of American experience emerges out of the relationship between vision and actuality, for what is most remarkable about America, the belief that we are God's Chosen People engaged in realizing in our own lives a vision of ever-expanding possibilities, has actually inspired much of what is most dangerous. As Melville knew, when transcendent vision becomes absolute, the questing spirit takes the shape of an Ahab, and everything is lost. Indeed, there is nothing more inimical to morality or more threatening to humanity than the unquestioned assumption of one's own moral supremacy. What is self-righteousness in a person manifests itself as cultural chauvinism in a nation, and this attitude on the part of some Americans has fostered a debased millennialism that has transformed the belief that God's Country, America, is the New Jerusalem into the knowledge that God's Country, America, is The-Greatest-Little-Ol'-Country-In-The-World.

The relationship that I am describing between American myth and American history establishes the proper context for discussing Norman Mailer's work. For Mailer's subject is preeminently America: throughout his work he is involved in trying to discover our identity as a nation by relating the promise and the debasement of the millennial idea of America to the complexities of the contemporary American scene. In so doing, he has pursued through his writing what he believes to be the highest purpose of literature, which is to "clarify a nation's vision of itself."[4] In the case of America, clarity is possible only through a continuing engagement of ambiguities, for, as Mailer has stated, "America is the most dialectical of nations . . . and the best of our history is coupled as in no other nation with much of our worst."[5]

Mailer dramatizes both the best and the worst of American life by connecting the lives of his characters to the life of the nation. At the heart of this drama is the importance of risktaking, for which Mailer finds a paradigm in the myths as histories of such American figures as the pioneer, the outlaw, the inventor, the early industrialist, the boxer, and the movie star as well as in the transcendentalist quester of Emerson, Thoreau, and Whitman. The ethic that Mailer derives from these figures is quite clear: when a person thrusts himself into a situation in which the "end is unknown"[6] rather than planned or routine, he enters into conflict with himself and the world and tests the limits of his personality. If he is able to meet the challenge, he extends his freedom in an act that is an exercise of moral courage and redeems himself from being little more than a manifestation of biological and social forces. In other words he grows: he becomes capable of greater expression and more intense experience, a capability that will allow him in the future to exert his will in situations of increased danger and complexity. Thus risktaking is the means to achieving psychological, social, and political power. On the other hand, failure of nerve in the risktaking situation can have the gravest of consequences. When one's nerve fails, when one shrinks from the bold and heroic assertion of oneself, one actually becomes less like oneself, a personality that says I choose to be what I am and nothing else, and more like an impersonal embodiment of moral cowardice, which constitutes the lowest common denominator of twentieth-century "mass man" (PP 38). Mailer believes that such cowardice is perverse. It goes against nature, because according to Mailer, growth is a natural imperative, and conflict is the fundamental condition of existence. Thus moral courage is an absolute necessity, while cowardice is a fundamental violation of the self that literally causes one's body to rebel against itself in an insane multiplication of cancerous cells.

That these are Mailer's beliefs will not be news to anyone familiar with Mailer's work. In fact, it is Mailer's insistence on the importance of risktaking and his preoccupation with the idea of growth through conflict, which is an existential idea precisely because it describes a dynamic that expresses the nature of existence, that have led to so much discussion of Mailer's existentialism as a subject in and of itself.[7] Unfortunately, more than a few critics have used Mailer's existentialism, his notoriety— whether sought after or not—or his inclusion in his works of various personae of himself as justifications for placing a great deal of critical emphasis on Mailer's life.[8]

I believe that such an approach is misconceived. A critic should not unreflectively take his cues from an artist on how to perform the act of criticism, and he should never argue that an artist ought to be judged "by his own standards,"[9] for those standards must also be subject to a critic's judgment. Establishing a focus is the first and most crucial critical judgment. By now it should be clear that far too much space and ingenuity have been devoted to discussing Mailer's personality. Certainly Mailer's importance depends ultimately upon his art rather than on the force of his personality. And in the final analysis, what Mailer does in his own life to enable him to write better is really beside the point when it comes to the consideration of his work.[10] Just as insisting that language is self-referential and that art has no relation to life trivializes language and art, overemphasizing the importance of a writer's personality can distract that writer's audience from seriously considering his work. In the case of Norman Mailer, it is time to concentrate on that work and treat his existentialism as a conceptual preoccupation and a mode of action rather than as an end in itself. Indeed, as Samuel Hux has argued, and as I am arguing here, the source of Mailer's existentialism is actually traceable to Mailer's own absorption of American myth.[11] Mailer's Americanness therefore subsumes his existentialism while providing him with both a locus of values and a purpose that are outside the limits of the self.

Thus one realizes that in order to establish a proper focus for an extended study of Mailer's work, one must first make the necessary connection between Mailer's existentialism and his continuing attempt to define the meaning of America and then concentrate on that attempt, which has always been his central purpose as a writer. One also realizes that Mailer's books are "best considered" not as "one large work"[12] in progress but as separate, finished works that try to dramatize through the relationship of American myth and history what America was, is, and may soon become. In other words, his books try to relate "the American image to American experience."[13] As works of literature they are, of course, involved in the attempt to enlarge the possibilities for expression in America. And undeniably Mailer would like his books to influence thought and action. But placing too great an emphasis on the possible influence of the books has the disadvantage of making them seem to be primarily the polemical instruments of a visionary existentialist. Though Mailer does say in *Advertisements for Myself* that he is "imprisoned with a perception which will settle for nothing less than making a revolution in the consciousness of our time,"[14] there is no reason why a critic must be imprisoned by this statement. After all, Mailer has not been. His revolutionary persona is only one of several fictive creations of himself, very different, for example, from the comic Mailer of *The Armies of the Night* or the Acolyte of *The Prisoner of Sex*, who wonders "whether the revolution" is "the most beautiful or diabolical idea of man,"[15] very different too from Mailer as Aquarius, the detached observer in *Of a Fire on the Moon* and *St. George and the Godfather*. Nor is the attempt to revolutionize consciousness the most compelling aspect of any of his works of fiction or his impressive and disturbing nonfiction novel, *The Executioner's Song*. Clearly, the revolutionary potential of Mailer's work does not suggest the most accurate or fruitful critical approach.

Concentrating on the possible influence of Mailer's books succeeds paradoxically in exaggerating the effect that Mailer's work can have on life while at the same time shifting attention from that work to Mailer's personal ambitions.[16] On the other hand, in discussing America as Mailer's subject, one goes right to the center of Mailer's work. Nevertheless, no critic has yet chosen to develop the implications of this material in anything approaching rigorous detail throughout the course of a book-length study. In doing so myself, I will, in fact, be involved in writing a thematic analysis of Mailer's individual major works. But my purpose will not be to focus primarily on Mailer's existentialism as an autonomous body of thought, his personality, or his revolutionary persona. Instead I will show that Mailer's ideas and self-creations derive ultimately from his Americanness and that this Americanness is manifested most significantly in his continuing concern with the relationship between the idea and the actuality of America. It is this concern that identifies the dimensions and energies of his existentialism, his sense of his books as public acts, and his belief in the revolutionary power of his work.[17]

Mailer's American focus also reveals the close relationship between his philosophy and his politics, a relationship that previous thematic studies of Mailer's works have not closely examined.[18] This relationship is evident, however, throughout his career, and it is especially striking from the time of *The Armies of the Night* onward. During the late 1960s, Mailer's left radicalism evolved into what he has termed left conservatism, a paradoxical ideology that combines a commitment to leftist activism with a deeply felt conservative concern for preserving dialectical distinctions and culturally nourishing traditions. Mailer's left conservatism represents the political expression of a syncretic philosophy that integrates such disparate elements as existential risktaking, nihilistic rebelliousness, and a transcendentalist faith that affirms the primacy of the self and the life of the spirit. Clearly, in view of the close relationship between Mailer's philosophy and politics, it is only by studying both that one can truly understand either. In the course of this book, I will try to provide such an understanding while extending the discussion of Mailer's work to his most recent books, including *The Executioner's Song*, *Ancient Evenings*, and *Tough Guys Don't Dance*.

Throughout this book I hope to show that, in making America his subject, Mailer is following in the best tradition of American literature, and I will attempt to define his place within that tradition and so demonstrate the ways in which Mailer is truly original. I will also suggest a possible direction not only for Mailer's work but for the contemporary American novel as well and conclude by evaluating Mailer's place among American prose writers.

Chapter 1

The Threat of Totalitarianism

The threat of totalitarianism sits like an evil presence over Norman Mailer's early work. Throughout his career Mailer has written much about what he considers to be the totalitarian aspects of American life, and in forthcoming works he will no doubt continue to brood upon this problem. But it is clear that until Mailer was able to write "The White Negro," totalitarianism was a particularly intimidating and intimate enemy of his art. In addition to representing an external political threat, it presented itself to Mailer as an immediate, almost insuperable aesthetic problem that insinuated itself into the very creation of his first three novels. What is more, the problem revealed itself in two separate stages, the second stage proving to be even more perplexing and debilitating than the first.

Ironically, the first part of the problem actually had its source in one of Mailer's great strengths. From the beginning of his career Mailer has understood the workings of power and violence and enjoyed a talent for dramatizing them. Unfortunately, the very nature of these subjects suggested that they were available as prerogatives only to characters who embodied totalitarian attitudes and objectives, a suggestion that left Mailer with rather limited access to two of his most attractive subjects. As a result, in *The Naked and the Dead* the totalitarians, General Cummings and Sergeant Croft, prove to be the novel's most dynamic characters. Their essential amorality frees them from considerations that might inhibit them from taking risks to gain more power, while their understanding of the weaknesses of human nature makes them the only characters in the novel who are capable of vision: because they know the power of evil and are able to use fear to manipulate men, they can often succeed in altering present circumstances to move closer to achieving an ideal, which for each of them is total power.[1] On the other hand, much of what is interesting about Mailer's protagonist, Lieutenant Hearn, derives from his immersion in the question of how to formulate a significant response to Cummings and Croft in particular and to totalitarianism in general, a question that neither Hearn nor the novel satisfactorily answers.

In noting these aesthetic problems, I am not pursuing the argument, familiar to Mailer critics, that *The Naked and the Dead* is a novel that fails to provide a satisfactory conclusion to a liberal thesis or that the conclusion is an attempt to salvage such a thesis. As I will show, the novel clearly rejects liberalism as an adequate response to totalitarianism. But Mailer's inability to dramatize an alternative political response confirms the aesthetic problem that I am describing, a problem that sets Mailer's talent for creating powerful and violent characters at odds with the thematic necessity of placing some limits on the success of totalitarians. After all, one does not have to be a liberal to want to avoid writing a first novel in which ruthlessness is rewarded with total power. Unfortunately, Mailer's aesthetic dilemma forces him in the conclusion of the book to fall back upon the resources of his naturalistic heritage to thwart the totalitarians, with the result that he overdramatizes the extent of human impotence. And as we should all know by now, impotence is not the theme with which Mailer would finally wish to be identified.

The conclusion of the novel does succeed rather nicely, though, in suggesting Mailer's view of the kind of bureaucratic world that will emerge after the war. For there is a species of revolution and counterrevolution within totalitarianism itself. Though a totalitarian movement may well have its origin in a powerful and charismatic personality committed to risktaking as a way of achieving power, totalitarian institutions gravitate inexorably toward a consolidation of power and an elimination of personality. Cummings believes that "'for the past century the entire historical process has been working toward greater and greater consolidation of power.'"[2] Accordingly, he sees the purpose of World War II as "'power concentration'" (177) and the subordination of man to machine. But he initially fails to understand that he will also become a victim of this process.

One realizes then that war is Cummings' only element. Only in war can he give full play to his talent for daring, eccentric manipulations of men. Without war Cummings loses his chief reason for being. He becomes an anachronism and a liability to an institution that thrives on orderly process and lack of imagination. Correspondingly, it is only in a war that Croft's murderousness can find sanction. His brutality is the essentially apolitical force that impels totalitarianism. And his is the face behind the facelessness of the institution. Consequently, nothing is more important to the institution than denying its implicit connection with Croft. After the war, he too becomes the outsider, as alienated from the source of real power as anyone on the political left, his violence apparently limited to expressing itself in acts of criminality.

Thus, in transforming itself from a movement into an institution, totalitarianism rejects dynamism and becomes less interesting as novelistic material. And in this way the second stage of Mailer's aesthetic problem begins. As the bureaucratic Major Dalleson, with his relish for routine and his talent for banality, is elected by Mailer's view of American history to inhabit the seat of power, Mailer is deprived by the logic of that history of any credible foundation for creating dynamic totalitarian characters. Having dramatized the right wing's bureaucratic masking of evil while he was as yet unable to create a significant literary expression of commitment on the left, Mailer arrived at an impasse in characterization and in his treatment of America as a subject. Undoubtedly, the most serious aspect of this problem involved Mailer's characterization of his protagonists, for they would have to carry the greatest part of the thematic burden in his treatment of America.

Both *Barbary Shore* and *The Deer Park* reflect this fundamental problem. As many critics have noted, the novels' respective protagonists, Mikey Lovett and Sergius O'Shaugnessy, are remarkably undefined. Of course, it is important to point out that the protagonist's lack of definition is an assumption of both novels. Each of the young men is a would-be writer who is trying to discover a way of writing and acting that would represent a significant response to the totalitarian aspects of American life. Correspondingly, each is educated in great part through his relationship to an older man so that finally each protagonist restores through his sense of vocation something of the original integrity of the badly compromised idealism of the previous generation.

Unfortunately, neither Lovett nor O'Shaugnessy is able to hold the dramatic center of his story. In *Barbary Shore* such elements as the shabby, claustrophobic setting and the odd, airless atmosphere, which help create the paranoid sense of a strangely skewed world always verging on the openly sinister, are certainly more compelling than Mailer's characterization of Lovett. Indeed, as I will argue, despite the fact that he is considerably less interesting than his totalitarian counterparts in *The Naked and the Dead*, the undercover agent Hollingsworth comes much closer to working as a character than does Mikey Lovett. Similarly, in *The Deer Park*, almost everyone else is more interesting than Sergius O'Shaugnessy; Charles Francis Eitel, Elena Esposito, and Marian Faye are the most notable examples.

I am convinced that Mailer found Lovett and O'Shaugnessy to be of sufficient dramatic interest at least partly because of his own attraction to the idea of the alienated romantic hero, an attraction that is evident in his characterization of Hearn and indeed even earlier in his portrayal of Bowen Hilliard in *A Calculus at Heaven*, the war novella that he wrote when he was nineteen years old. Moreover, the posture of the romantic hero, who stands as "the simple genuine self against the whole world,"[3] might also have suggested that Lovett and O'Shaugnessy were satisfactory literary expressions of political engagement. It is as if the romantic tradition itself had *a priori* charged with meaning the fact of a protagonist's opposition to society and made it necessarily compelling. Actually, the tradition places the greatest possible demands on the characterization of the alienated protagonist, who must embody in his own identity and through his own actions the values denied by the culture that he opposes. Otherwise, his act of protest is empty, announced, as it were, in a narcissistic vacuum. Perhaps this dependency on tradition in the absence of personality is what Richard Poirier is suggesting, with some exaggeration in the case of Hearn, when he writes that Mailer's early heroes display only "a rhetoric of engagement."[4]

In making these criticisms, I have been emphasizing Mailer's belief in his characterizations of Mikey Lovett and Sergius O'Shaugnessy. But paradoxically, balanced against that belief, there must have been an undeniable dissatisfaction with them and the novels in which they appear. One thinks not only of Mailer's own criticism of *Barbary Shore* but also of his self-advertised obsession with the materials of *The Deer Park*, particularly the character of Sergius, which suggest the situation of a writer who is involved with materials that refuse to fulfill their ultimate promise.[5] And, of course, Mailer's decision in *Advertisements for Myself* to commit himself to a radical departure from the narrative techniques of his earlier books bears dramatic testimony to a deep-seated dissatisfaction with the points of view of those works. But perhaps it is only by examining some of Mailer's later statements on the nature of totalitarianism that one can get an adequate sense of exactly what he felt he was up against in trying to solve the aesthetic problem that I am describing.

For Mailer, totalitarianism is not limited in its expression to despotic governments and dictatorial leaders such as Hitler, Mussolini, and Stalin. Instead it is a "*geist*, a spirit, which takes many forms" (PP 126). It is manifested in any attempt at reducing complexity, minimizing expression, or eliminating differences in personality and culture. For the "essence of totalitarianism is that it beheads. It beheads individuality, variety, dissent, extreme possibility, romantic faith, it blinds vision, deadens instinct, it obliterates the past" (PP 184). Thus for Mailer, women's liberationists are totalitarians when they insist with a "dull, moral, abstract force" (PP 126) that there is no essential difference between men and women and demand that women be liberated from their wombs. And liberal technologues assume a similar totalitarian position when they act and speak as though the machine were now the quintessential work of art and language purely functional.

One might say then that for Mailer the perfect metaphor for totalitarianism is the monolith, the single undifferentiated stone face that insists in its blankness of expression on the absolute importance of its own existence while at the same time concealing precisely what its specific function or ultimate purpose is. As Mailer notes, much of the architecture of contemporary America is a manifestation of the totalitarian mentality that intentionally divorces form from function. We do indeed "design edifices which reveal no more than the internal structure of a ten-million-dollar bill" (PP 181). "So we have housing projects which look like prisons and prisons which look like hospitals which in turn look like schools, schools which look like luxury hotels, luxury hotels which seem to confuse themselves with airline terminals, and airline terminals which cannot be told apart from civic centers." And as a sign of our confusion of purpose and our disdain for definition, "even the new churches look like recreation centers at large ski resorts" (PP 179).

The immediate effect of such architecture and one of the major objectives of totalitarianism, as Mailer defines it, is to divorce human beings from their connection to the past. Both history and the myths that would express the culture's origin, values, and purpose are denied, reduced to cliché, or turned into forms of nationalistic propaganda, leaving all of us rootless, our attention fixed only upon the ephemeral pleasures and pains of the present. In fact, because of our passion for mobility and expansion and our addiction to the fast and the new, "the plastic shacks, the motels, the drive-in theatres, the highway restaurants and the gas stations proliferate year by year until they are close to covering the highways of America with a new country which is laid over the old one the way a transparent sheet with new drawings is set upon the original plan" (PP 178).

In this way experience itself is rendered discontinuous; life appears to be inconsequential, and, as we become separated from our actions and their effects, responsibility disappears. This attempt to avoid responsibility is manifested most dramatically in the totalitarian denial of the eschatological view of death. For if death is nothingness, if death is simply extinction rather than the divine revelation of the moral value of one's life, then the conduct of one's life does not finally matter. Morality becomes both subjective and passé, a quaint human construction whose purpose—maintaining a semblance of order in social relations—is now superseded by the amoral exercise of power. According to Mailer then,

the crucial characteristic of modern totalitarianism is that it is a moral disease which divorces us from guilt. It came into being as a desire to escape the judgments of the past and our responsibility for past injustice—in that sense it is a defense against eternity, an attempt to destroy that part of eternity which is death, which is punishment or reward. . . . In our flight from the consequence of our lives, in our flight from adventure, from danger, and from the natural ravages of disease, in our burial of the primitive, it is death the Twentieth Century is seeking to avoid. (PP 176).

If death is annihilation, there would seem to be no recourse but to desire more life, whatever the cost. As Mailer insists, however, the cost has been very great. For the attempt to deny the eschatological view of death expresses an utter contempt for mystery and a callous disregard for the sacredness of organic growth through the natural cycle of death and rebirth. In attempting to eliminate death, we are actually revealing our opposition to life and nature. And in our desire to discover simple solutions to complex problems, we are succeeding only in creating problems which are more complex and which threaten the very balance of nature, a process demonstrated, as Mailer points out, in the fact that our dependency on antibiotics to avoid "the natural ravages of disease" actually produces contagious diseases without definition.

According to Mailer this predicament is a result of our perverse relation to both life and death. In trying to avoid death, we spread it, while in attempting artificially to prolong life, we deaden it. For Mailer then, totalitarianism is essentially opposition to nature: human beings and institutions become totalitarian when they try to subvert the sacred relation between life and death, substitute inorganic growth through duplication for organic growth through conflict, or seek to limit the existential freedom of others for the sole purpose of gaining more power. If, as Mailer believes, organic growth through conflict is the way that one creates an identity that can give coherence to the conflicting parts of one's personality for at least as long as one can continue to act with courage, then the totalitarian rejection of risk represents a cowardly denial of identity. This cowardice and the need to deny identity suggest yet another reason for totalitarianism's debasement of American myth, for the necessity of questing and risktaking is implicit in the millennialistic idea of the American as the New Adam who contains within himself unlimited possibilities for expression. The idea is, in fact, a mythic expression of what Mailer believes must go on in each person's life if he is to create his own identity. Within this context, the essential difference between the totalitarianism embodied by Cummings and Croft and institutional totalitarianism is clear: unlike the institution they at least are capable of courage. And so despite the fact that they would deny it to others, they maintain in their own lives a connection to American myth.

Thus one realizes that, in describing institutional totalitarianism as plague or cancer and in saying that America is schizophrenic, Mailer is being quite literal. In an attempt at anticipating critics who would accuse him of projecting his own obsessions upon the nation, Mailer suggests that while he wishes the problem were merely personal, he is convinced that his frequent references to the sickness of life in America resulting from the repudiation of risk actually represent "insight into the nature of things" (CC 2). For the "essence of biology seems to be challenge and response, risk and survival, war and the lessons of war. It may be biologically true that life cannot have beauty without its companion—danger" (PP 167). One can, of course, accept or reject both Mailer's view of nature and his critique of America, but in any event, one must grant that he intends to describe objective conditions. In fact, Mailer is always insisting that his descriptions of American life have validity precisely because they are rooted in reality. From Mailer's point of view, the power of plague, cancer, and schizophrenia as metaphors for the totalitarianism and cowardly conformity of American life depends upon the contention that they may function in other rhetorical contexts as direct descriptions of the perverse effect that such conditions have on us once they begin to dominate. According to Mailer, totalitarianism and cowardly conformity actually produce cancer. Similarly, a nation that separates action from responsibility and past from present while denying the millennial heritage that has throughout history given it a unique identity, inevitably becomes schizophrenic. Aside from constituting a serious ontological and political statement, such a contention has decided rhetorical advantages. First of all, it strengthens the sense of equation in Mailer's use of illness as metaphor, as, for example, when he writes of the cancerous spread of totalitarian architecture. Secondly, it broadens the associative frame of reference since no careful reader of Mailer can note his application of cancer or schizophrenia to the political sphere without thinking of these conditions in human beings and vice versa. In the final analysis, one is impressed over and over again with the depth of Mailer's conviction that there is most certainly a correspondence between the American body politic and the physical, psychological, and moral well-being of each American citizen.

The existence of this correspondence is one of Mailer's fundamental assumptions, and the aesthetic corollary of this assumption is quite clear: since each American is implicated in the problems that beset America, the details of anyone's life, when rendered with sufficient imagination and craft, can represent the life of the nation. The individual life may be fictional or real, and the setting of the action may even be quite limited, as limited, for example, as the Brooklyn boardinghouse of *Barbary Shore* or the town of Provo, Utah, where Gary Gilmore committed two murders. Furthermore, as Mailer notes in *Cannibals and Christians*, there exists "the probability that society partakes of the plague and its critic partakes, and each wars against the other" (2–3). In fact, virtually all of Mailer's work implies that totalitarian influences in society to a great extent shape both the structure and the content of one's own thoughts and language. Indeed, the fear that one's expressions are not one's own may well constitute the crucial factor in politicizing the romantic imagination, and I strongly suspect that such is the case with Norman Mailer. As Mailer knows, the cost of failing to find one's own voice is repeating the forms of expression which have imposed themselves on one and which may partake of the plague that one is attempting to combat.

In Mailer's work it is characteristically the protagonist's responsibility to discover authentic forms of expression that represent significant opposition to the prevailing tendencies of society. Ironically, it was Mailer's assumption of the protagonist's representativeness through his embodiment of the nation's ills that undoubtedly made it so difficult for him in his first three books to create strong protagonists who would be capable of expressing significant opposition. For the protagonist would have to embody both the plague and a possible solution. He would have to be capable of engaging in a dialectic between apparent contradictions in value, an engagement that would be possible only if he were able to represent all that the society expresses through its institutions and all of the possibilities for expression that those institutions outlaw or deny.

Of course, both the aesthetic and the ethical implications of creating such a protagonist are complicated. As his character's actions range over the field of human possibility, the writer must be able to sustain a clear moral focus while abandoning all traditional moral categories in confronting the conflicts and paradoxes of each dramatic situation. The reader should then be able to evaluate the actions of the dialectical protagonist while nevertheless understanding that there are no *a priori* standards for making judgments and that values are constantly shifting with the ambiguities of the moment. Both writer and reader must therefore be able to accomplish a transvaluation of values such that a particular action in any given situation may not only change in value from being good to being evil but may actually be both good and evil at the same time.

Mailer was able to elaborate this existential ethic in "The White Negro," and as a result, he freed his characters from the vulnerability of their passive relationships to institutional violence.[6] In Mailer's first three books, violent behavior was dramatic and therefore attractive. But in the first two books, it seemed categorically wrong, and in *The Deer Park*, only Mailer's characterization of the proto-hipster Marion Faye suggests that the expression of violence might be necessary to maintain one's personal integrity. In writing "The White Negro," however, Mailer realized that the stance of nonviolence was often no more than an abnegation of personality and that the real question was how the irremediable human capacity for violence would be expressed. He was discovering that the same instinctive energy that might issue in the violence of a character such as Croft could likewise manifest itself in the inspired manic rap of D. J. Jethroe. Indeed, just as any particular action might undergo significant transformations in moral value, so might the instinctive energy that impels violence assume a thousand different forms.

The ability to sustain this dialectic and thereby represent both the plague and a possible solution distinguishes Stephen Rojack, D. J. Jethroe, and the various personae of Mailer himself from the relatively weak protagonists of the first three books. At the beginning of *An American Dream*, Rojack is a self-proclaimed failure who fears for the extinction of his soul as the result of a life in which he has wasted his talent and compromised his ideals for the opportunity of acquiring wealth, prestige, and social power. Rather than remain a victim and acquiesce to the cancer which he believes has literally begun to grow within his body and which he, as well as Mailer, views as a sign of spiritual extinction, he extricates himself from the society that has seduced his soul. As the first step in this process, Rojack murders his wife, Deborah. For marriage to her has been both the center and the circumference of his life of compromise, at once his most expensive prostitution of self and the one compromise that in its scope implies the motivation for all of the others. Rojack's unpunished murder of Deborah has driven critics who read the book as traditional realism to cry foul and fault its lack of verisimilitude. On the other hand, as Robert Merrill notes, more sympathetic critics have either defined the work as a romance, viewed its "extravagant events" as "the literary creations of its narrator-protagonist," or hastened to place the book within the less threatening confines of the "dream-vision" so that the murder is only metaphorical, literary, and not really wrong at all.[7] As I will show, however, the novel insists that the metaphorical significance of the murder depends upon its being interpreted realistically while at the same time suggesting that the act itself is not simply good or evil but both good and evil—undeniably murder and undeniably necessary to the survival of Rojack's soul.

In *Why Are We in Vietnam?*, Mailer's characterization of D. J. likewise balances opposing values. As Robert Solotaroff suggests, D. J. is both a critic and a victim of American society.[8] For his unrelenting disc jockey rant is both a critique and an embodiment of the electric insanity of corporate America: the very diction and syntax that D. J. uses to criticize the corporation have been imposed on him by it, but the brilliance and energy of D. J.'s switched-on mind enable him to communicate an odd sense of the most eccentric individuality emerging out of the domination of the collective.

In *The Armies of the Night*, Mailer uses a comic persona of himself to contain cultural contradictions. The "Mailer" of this book is a character of "monumental disproportions,"[9] by turns courageous or cowardly, egomaniacal or humble, wise or foolish. He is both a participant and an observer whose idiosyncratic point of view becomes the centered consciousness of an ironic third person narration that succeeds in establishing a standpoint of detachment and objectivity.

The most significant and fascinating political implication of Mailer as a dialectical protagonist is undoubtedly his self-professed left conservatism, which advocates a radical social critique and political activism as ways of protecting "the welfare of the nation" (Arm. 185), which, he believes, depends in part upon preserving America's connection to history and myth and reaffirming the value of personal and cultural differences. Mailer's left conservatism also informs the observations of "the reporter" in *Miami and the Siege of Chicago* and Aquarius in *Of a Fire on the Moon* and *St. George and the Godfather*. In each of these books the dialectical protagonist continues to represent the strengths and weaknesses of the American character, but finding a significant form of activist expression or even discovering a way of participating in events of national importance now becomes a crucial problem. Paradoxically, by integrating important elements of the ideologies of both the left and the right, Mailer's protagonists have made it difficult for themselves to identify with either side or to have either side identify with them, despite the fact that they have defined a position that suggests a comprehensive point of view that can transform political polarization into dialectic.

It is, in fact, this standpoint of lonely comprehensiveness that defines the narrative viewpoint of *The Executioner's Song*, a book in which the central theme is estrangement. Indeed, the most disturbing aspect of the book, apart from the brutality and horror of Gary Gilmore's two murders, is its dramatization of the incredible separation between America's western and eastern voices: between the morally chaotic lives of such people as Gilmore, Nicole, and April, who seem stranded in the vast emptiness of the great American West, and the lawyers, judges, and media people, who are connected to the mainstream of American life and who act with a well-defined and at times ruthless sense of purpose dictated by professional commitments and ambitions. At the same time, however, the book is able to suggest that an exhaustive, naturalistic rendering of the details of a representative group of Americans can, without the aid of explicit commentary, imply a radical critique of American society and that such a critique has a sufficiency of its own, as if finally perceiving, imagining, and writing were indeed significant political acts, true expressions of Man Thinking. In this way, the act of imagination itself, the capacity to comprehend multiple and apparently contradictory perspectives, becomes a form of activism. For it is limited imagination—demonstrated in the inability of one segment of society to live inside the point of view of another—that is to a great extent responsible for the contemporary crisis of estrangement in America.

Thus in *The Executioner's Song*, the complexities of a comprehensive point of view, which is capable of both criticism and sympathy, provide a tentative solution to the question of how to participate in the public life of the nation when the very nature of national events would seem to deny personal involvement. The great advantage of such a response is that it identifies the synthetic imagination as the source of the expression of significant political protest. And certainly this is the ultimate implication of Mailer's left conservatism. But it should not be surprising that it would take Mailer so long before he could depend with equanimity upon the resources of the synthetic imagination as a way of responding to both the schizophrenia and the totalitarianism of American life. Perhaps he was able to do so in *The Executioner's Song* partly because he had no other choice. Mailer agreed to write the story of Gary Gilmore after Gilmore's death. As a result, there was no possibility for Mailer to become involved, even indirectly, in the issue of whether or not Gilmore should be executed. Certainly if Mailer had been on the scene, *The Executioner's Song* would have been a very different book, and it is not altogether impossible that the question of how to participate would have again seemed critical as it does in much of Mailer's nonfiction. For there remains in Mailer's work an unresolved conflict of loyalties. On the one hand, the ultimate implications of Mailer's left conservatism, with its emphasis on maintaining a dialectic between the conflicting segments of society, would seem to suggest that he must create a protagonist who can continue to live within a standpoint of lonely comprehensiveness at the center of the society that he opposes. On the other hand, Mailer's deep commitment to the tradition of the romantic hero would apparently demand that he continue to create charismatic characters who are capable of strong action that confirms their alienation from society. Suggestions of this conflict are retrospectively apparent at the very beginning of Mailer's career, even before he conceived of the possibility of creating dialectical protagonists. For Mailer's naturalistic technique in *The Naked and the Dead* succeeds in establishing a standpoint of comprehensiveness that anticipates a commitment to dialectic. By the end of the novel, however, it is clear that the omniscient narrator shares Hearn's need to find a way to act to express opposition to totalitarianism and partakes of Hearn's despair over the apparently limited range of choices so that finally the book identifies itself with the plight of its alienated romantic hero.

In a 1964 *Paris Review* interview with Steven Marcus, Mailer associates the ability to write in the third person with having "a coherent view of life," by which he means a world view that paradoxically has its foundation in a satisfactory expression of the fluid[10] nature of personality. Unless the novelist can make sense of the apparent contradictions of a personality that is changeable, Protean, now and always in motion so that the sense he makes is itself the expression of an identity, then his view of the world does not cohere even if he is able to describe in detail the operation of social and political institutions. In Mailer's first three novels, there is certainly an implicit explanation of the relationship between American social and political institutions and the lives of individual Americans. Each book suggests that there is a conflict between the totalitarian aims of social and political organizations and the desire of each person to pursue his own particular idea of fulfillment. Nevertheless, the books show that ironically most people are participating—whether out of ignorance, fear, or a desire for power—in the very social and political process that will result in the absolute denial of personality. Those few who would protest find it extremely difficult to discover significant means. In fact, they even have difficulty in avoiding outright complicity in the power structure that they oppose. For Mailer, such impotence makes no sense. He refuses to accept it as final, but as long as there is apparently no way to express a solution to the problem, experience remains fragmented. At the same time, in searching for a solution, Mailer came increasingly to see that realistic descriptions of the fragmented surfaces of life may yield only surface reflections and that it may be necessary in the absence of "a coherent view of life" to abandon traditional realism to uncover the truth about ourselves and our society.

Chapter 2

The Naked and the Dead:
Beyond Liberalism;
the Politics of Risk

Despite the seeming assurance of its narrative voice, *The Naked and the Dead* remains primarily a drama of the inevitability of human failure and the incoherence of human experience. Since knowledge in the novel is primarily skeptical, it produces dichotomies rather than a synthesis born of dialectic. To know all is to expose "the shoddy motive" (79, 183) that gives the lie to humane concern and establishes one's identity with the evil that one is so desperately trying to oppose. Knowledge therefore leads one away from a liberal belief in human progress and toward a recognition of human limitations, for one is able to do anything but act both powerfully and humanely. In *The Naked and the Dead*, it is this realization and the resulting pressures of incoherence that compel Mailer's narrator to distrust his own omniscience and drive him toward the standpoint of Robert Hearn, in effect moving the point of view of the book closer to the uncertainties of first person narration and anticipating Mailer's decision to adopt the first person in writing the novels that follow.

In view of the skepticism of *The Naked and the Dead*, it is clear that the shift in the novel's attitude toward Hearn by no means signifies an affirmation of liberalism. It comes, in fact, at the end of a book-length criticism of Hearn's liberalism and coincides with Hearn's own recognition that liberalism is an ineffective means of responding to totalitarianism, though he is forced to utilize those means in the apparent absence of any satisfactory alternative.

From the very beginning of the novel's exposition of Hearn's character, one is impressed both by his limitations and by the inchoate nature of his personality. Hearn is a curious combination of self-awareness and myopic self-righteousness. One therefore expects that his education throughout the course of the novel will develop in him a new attitude that will supersede his liberalism. For Hearn's mind does at least register the idea that his humanism is suspiciously abstract, that emotionally he is "'nothing but a shell'" (79), and that he cherishes a sense of intellectual elitism that is the reverse side of his bourgeois guilt over the fact that his family background and his status as an officer make him a member of a privileged class. Hearn's confrontation with Colonel Conn over the colonel's racist table conversation with Major Dalleson, Major Hobart, and three other officers perfectly illustrates these qualities. Hearn challenges Conn not out of any heartfelt empathy with the plight of minorities but because he is profoundly offended by all that Conn and the other officers represent: an attitude of reactionary anti-intellectualism and crass, hedonistic good fellowship that Hearn associates with his father's generation.

The failure of Hearn's father and other men like him to create significant values and pass them on to the next generation is the source of Hearn's disillusionment with America and his overriding sense of isolation. Indeed, Hearn's belief that other young men of his generation are as isolated as he and share his disillusionment prompts him, upon embarking from San Francisco to fight in the South Pacific, to conceive of his generation as "a bunch of dispossessed . . . from the raucous stricken bosom of America" (353). Because of Mailer's attraction to the idea of the alienated protagonist, the novel itself by no means disavows the self-congratulation that is implicit in Hearn's sense of rejection and betrayal. At the same time, however, the logic of Hearn's characterization demands that he abandon the liberalism that is so intimately connected to his sense of alienation. One realizes, however, that Hearn will certainly resist this change. Despite his ability to perceive some of the limitations of his viewpoint, he does not want to admit the necessity of abandoning the liberalism that constitutes the primary distinction between his position and the reactionary attitudes of many of the men of his father's generation.

The initial exposition of the weaknesses of Hearn's position lends authorial weight to General Cummings' criticism of Hearn's liberalism throughout their conversations, despite the fact that the novel clearly condemns the general's totalitarian philosophy. In fact, during these sessions Cummings is always in control and is easily more impressive than Hearn. In these scenes it is as if Mailer has dedicated himself to mounting as ruthless an attack as he can against the liberalism that he formerly espoused. Consider, for example, Cummings' acute analysis of Hearn's belief in simplistic moral dichotomies: "'Somewhere you picked it up so hard that you can't shake the idea "liberal" means good and "reactionary" means evil. That's your frame of reference. Two words. That's why you don't know a damn thing'" (84). When one combines this statement with Cummings' remark on the validity of the public terms of debate, namely that "'politics have no more relation to history than moral codes have to the needs of any particular man'" (177), one has a pretty good idea of Mailer's own indictment of liberalism: by invoking traditional moral categories that no longer apply and by accepting the public terms of debate as real when in fact they may be nothing more than rhetorical diversions to direct attention away from the true concern, which is most often an amoral attempt either to gain wealth or to seize and consolidate power, the liberal reveals the naive limits of his own imagination. Mailer's comment in his 1954 *Dissent* essay, "David Riesman Reconsidered," characterizes perfectly the liberal failure to perceive that the sources and the nature of real power in America remain hidden: Mailer notes that the "forms of power are taken for the content, and there is no attempt to distinguish

between those who lead and those who are led" (Adv. 197).
Whether this failure is manifested in an inability to see through
the patriotic rationalizations for America's involvement in World
War II (or for that matter Korea or Vietnam) or an incapacity
to understand the inhumanity implicit in the banalities of
bureaucracy, it suggests to Mailer a lack of vision and a serious
underestimation of the essential ruthlessness of power politics.
As Mailer points out, the result is the advocacy of a healthy
moderation and an inexorable tendency toward appeasement as
the fiction of pluralism is accepted as fact. Again, Mailer's
comments on Riesman illustrate his criticism of liberalism in
general: "One feels Riesman's desire to find something justifiable, something *functional*, in all aspects of society. Ultimately, his credo seems to be that what-is must necessarily
contain something good. . . . At last all things are equal, are
justifiable—one is drawn to quietism and acceptance"
(Adv. 202).

General Cummings' explication of his totalitarian philosophy
reveals the credulity of such liberal faith in the benign character
of American social and political institutions. Of course, almost
all of Mailer's major work is devoted to investigating the nature
and purpose of the conspiratorial power structure in America, but
in Cummings' conversations with Hearn, Mailer dramatizes the
psychology of the will to power with a directness that is matched
only by his handling of the climactic confrontation between
Barney Kelly and Stephen Rojack in *An American Dream.*

Cummings' philosophy is based on the assumption that "'man's
deepest urge is omnipotence'" (323). According to Cummings,
the collective expression of the will to power is reaching its
historical culmination in the twentieth century, as reflected in the
rise of Nazism, fascism, and American imperialism supported by
a buildup of overwhelming military might. He therefore believes
that "'this is going to be the reactionary's century,'" and may well
represent the beginning of "'their thousand-year reign'" (85).
The purpose of the war is to facilitate this totalitarian process.
Thus the army is seen by Cummings and, indeed, by the novel

itself "'as a preview of the future'" (324), for the organization of the military fits every person into position along "'a fear ladder'" (176) that makes great numbers of men simultaneously the instruments and the objects of oppressive power. The result is anxiety, which Cummings perceives as "'the natural role of twentieth-century man,'" (177) and a tremendous susceptibility to being galvanized by a single idea: the promise that the compensation for enduring the vicious contradictions of the fear ladder will be transcendence through identification with the myth of national supremacy. As one learns in Cummings' "Time Machine" chapter, he realized several years before America became involved in the war that such an idea was crucial to Hitler's success. Cummings observes that Hitler "has the germ of an idea, and moreover you've got to give him political credit. He plays on the German people with consummate skill. That Siegfried business is fundamental to them" (420). America's millennial heritage and its unwavering certitude in its own primacy as a nation make it particularly susceptible to similar invocations of mythic supremacy. As Cummings says to Hearn,

"There are countries which have latent powers, latent resources, they are full of potential energy, so to speak. And there are great concepts which can unlock that, express it. As kinetic energy a country is organization, co-ordinated effort, your epithet, fascism. . . . Historically the purpose of this war is to translate America's potential into kinetic energy. The concept of fascism, far sounder than communism if you consider it, for it's grounded firmly in men's actual natures, merely started in the wrong country, in a country which did not have enough intrinsic potential power to develop completely. In Germany with that basic frustration of limited physical means there were bound to be excesses. But the dream, the concept, was sound enough. . . . America is going to absorb that dream, it's in the business of doing it now. When you've created power, material, armies, they don't wither of their own accord. Our vacuum as a nation is filled with released power, and I can tell you that we're out of the backwaters of history now." (321)

In an essay on Mailer's politics, Robert Alter argues that "of all the long retrospective portraits in *The Naked and the Dead* only those of Croft, Cummings, and Hearn have real relevance to the political argument of the novel. America is wonderfully present in the detailed characterizations of the other soldiers, from the southern redneck and Mexican-American to Boston Irish and New York Jew, but in all this faithful reproduction of an intimately familiar America it is hard to see where precisely in American life lie the roots of the native fascism which Cummings predicts and Croft embodies."[1] If Alter is looking for other Cummingses or Crofts in the book, he will, of course, not find them. But, as the naturalistic sensibility of the novel suggests, in order for Cummings' prediction to come true, it is not necessary for Americans to be acutely conscious of an allegiance to totalitarianism or for them to embody such an attitude to the extent that a character such as Croft does. They would merely have to allow themselves to be drawn by the considerable attraction of nationalist rhetoric. Moreover, there is certainly ample evidence in both the "Time Machine" chapters and the narrative of the Anopopei Campaign itself that most human beings display an abject ignorance and helplessness in the face of large social and historical forces. As two of Mailer's governing images imply, people can be swept up rather easily into the wave of a vast and impersonal historical force or be molded like argil to assume whatever attitude best fits the regimental needs of a totalitarian state.

Whether or not one accepts Cummings' argument that the ultimate purpose of the war is totalitarian, one point is incontestable: almost all of the enlisted men have no clear idea of why they are fighting, yet their cooperation is never in question. As Jean Radford notes, the novel dramatizes "the total alienation of the enlisted men from the war at any level other than their physical participation."[2] Within this context, Sergeant Martinez's confused acquiescence when Croft tells him to withhold from Hearn information concerning the presence of Japanese in a narrow pass reveals much more than Martinez's own relatively ignorant complicity in Hearn's death. It also illustrates precisely how millions of Americans, despite an unalterable belief in their own powers of self-direction, can yield unquestioningly to the pressure to become involved in a social and historical phenomenon that they do not even dimly understand. Clearly their cooperation in going to war is insured not only by their fear of reprisal, which is, of course, the weapon that Croft uses to drive the platoon to attempt to climb Mount Anaka, but also by their acceptance of the obligation to obey laws and follow orders. It is not insignificant, for example, that Croft's only reservation about telling the lie that leads to Hearn's death derives from his associating the lie with disobeying an order, and it is the deeply ingrained imperative to follow orders that constitutes for Croft the closest thing to an actual moral code.

Whatever objections the men do have about their involvement in army life and the war itself are usually expressed in the form of obscene humor. As Mailer affirms in *The Armies of the Night*, the obscenity of the American soldier does indeed exert a moral and humane force, epitomizing much of what is best about the American democratic spirit, by debunking the kind of inflated military posturing and rhetoric that, when left unchecked, can lead to the worst authoritarian excesses and bureaucratic lies. Thus in *Armies* one learns that obscenity represents the source of much of Mailer's love of a canny, common-sensical, sane, and democratic America.

Certainly Mailer is not mistaken in praising the therapeutic powers of obscenity. In *Why Are We in Vietnam?* it acts as a purgative to the insane militarism of corporate America, and in both *Vietnam* and *Armies* its use establishes an innocent, comic counterpoint to the obscene murderousness of the war itself. But often in *The Naked and the Dead* obscenity gives voice to fatalistic grumbling that comically accepts, even as it protests against, the inevitability of dehumanization. The opening of "The Chow Line," one of Mailer's "Chorus" chapters, provides a perfect example of this defeatist attitude:

> RED: What the fug is that swill?
> COOK: It's owl shit. Wha'd you think it was?
> RED: Okay, I just thought it was somethin' I couldn't eat. (Laughter)
> (86)

In fairness to Red Valsen it is important to state that he is, in fact, the one character who has actually developed into a coherent philosophy the kind of reductive cynicism and tough individualism that Mailer in *Armies* associates with obscene humor. Red does at least realize that the war will be just another way for "the big boys" to "get a little more" (234). But this knowledge does not dissuade him from enlisting. He sees enlistment as a way of avoiding marriage and allowing him to continue to lead a drifter's life that is a debased version of the pioneers' sojourn into the limitless American West. And, at any rate, as illustrated in "The Chow Line" dialogue, there is implicit in Red's cynicism the same self-fulfilling belief in the inevitability of victimization that is typical of the attitudes of the rest of the enlisted men. Red sees the ubiquity of failure and feels the sense of "sad compassion in which one seems to understand everything, all that men want and fail to get" (14).

It is also important to stress that balanced against the troops' obscene questioning of authority is an unquestioning and singularly undemocratic admiration for people with power. This attitude is combined with a deep-seated patriotism that would make it rather easy for a charismatic leader with Cummings' totalitarian designs to gain control. Moreover, the admiration that Toglio and Martinez feel for General Cummings and Goldstein's and Martinez's faith in the myth of America as a land of opportunity exemplify the kind of naive trust that Americans place in their leaders and their country. Goldstein believes "'in being honest and sincere in business; all the really big men got where they are through decency'" (449). And as the narrator asserts with regard to Martinez's absorption of the American dream, "little Mexican boys also breathe the American fables. If they cannot be aviators or financiers or officers they can still be heroes. No need to stumble over pebbles and search the Texas sky. Any man jack can be a hero." Yet as the narrator sardonically adds to conclude Martinez's "Time Machine" chapter, "only that does not make you white Protestant, firm and aloof" (67). Indeed, of all the enlisted men, only Red is actually aware of such limitations and is consistent in his criticism of power, noting, for example, that "'there ain't a good officer in the world. . . . They're just a bunch of aristocrats, *they* think. General Cummings is no better than I am. His shit don't smell like ice cream either'" (128).

It is a rather short step from patriotism to nationalism and but a few short steps further to the racist and ultimately genocidal implications of the assumption of cultural supremacy and the quest for total power. For there is indeed the closest connection between racism and totalitarianism. Such a connection is not far from Cummings' mind when he is praising Hitler and predicting that America is capable of realizing "the dream" of total power, and I would again argue that the novel clearly indicates that Cummings might well be right. For it shows that there exists within American culture a pervasive and virulent racism. Although it is most prominent in the chapter on Gallagher's prewar involvement in a violent and reactionary political organization, racism appears as a motif in almost every one of the "Time Machine" chapters, which depict, as Alter suggests, a cross section of American life. These portraits, together with the characterization of the racist Colonel Conn and the brief but poignant sketch of Lieutenant Wakara, the Japanese-American translator whose family lives in an American relocation camp, provide a firm foundation for Cummings' prediction and indicate that from the beginning of his career Mailer has seen that there is a great potential for violent and ignorant reaction at the heart of American life.

Mailer's naturalistic depiction in *The Naked and the Dead* of the extent to which people actually cooperate in the denial of their own freedom reveals a disturbing connection between human limitations and the growth of totalitarianism. But I am sure that Mailer himself was far more disturbed by his novel's suggestion that, because an increase in freedom brings with it an increase in power, the ability to enlarge one's own freedom might at the same time necessarily foster a desire to deny freedom to others. In the book the characters who exercise the greatest degree of freedom and who are often able as a result of the force of their wills to alter significantly the circumstances that surround them are the totalitarians, Cummings and Croft. As Hearn realizes, the primary difference between Cummings and other intelligent men is that unlike Cummings "they did nothing or the results of their actions were lost to them, and they functioned in the busy complex mangle, the choked vacuum of American life. The General might even have been silly if it were not for the fact that here on this island he controlled everything. It gave a base to whatever he said." Of course, the novel later shows that there are limits to Cummings' control. He has difficulty countermanding the lethargy of the troops, and at the end of the book he is forced to admit that he really cannot forge "the circuits of chance" (85), that, in fact, the battle for Anopopei has been won without him. Nevertheless, Hearn's observations focus on an essential truth: Cummings does possess "an almost unique ability to extend his thoughts into immediate and effective action" (77), an ability derived in great part from his rich Yankee trader father, Cy Cummings, and developed throughout a lifetime of strategic risktaking, with each successful maneuver gaining more power and making it possible for him to take even greater risks of command in the future. Cummings' success in boldly and directly attacking the Toyaku line, despite the fact that he knows he is exposing his right flank to a counterattack, perfectly illustrates his capacity for accomplishing stunning and unorthodox military maneuvers—and for ignoring, with godlike detachment, any incidental casualties that such actions might incur. His decision to send Croft's reconnaissance platoon with Hearn in charge to reconnoiter behind enemy lines in preparation for a daring attack on the Japanese rear also has its strategic inspiration in the attractions of risk, while the general's personal motive is clearly to crush Hearn's rebelliousness, thereby teaching him a lesson about the ruthless and autocratic exercise of power. The decision does, of course, lead to Hearn's death and shows both the limits of Hearn's freedom and power and the extent of Cummings' ability to translate will into potent action. To paraphrase Cummings, at the crucial moment in their personal battle, it is indeed the general rather than Hearn who is "'holding the gun.'" It is Cummings who is in control, and that control is not an "'accident'" but "'a product of everything [he has] achieved'" (84).

Croft's power over the platoon is also a result of all that he has achieved throughout a lifetime of confrontation and risktaking. The source of this ability to take risks is in Croft's frontier heritage: "his ancestors pushed and labored and strained, drove their oxen, sweated their women and moved a thousand miles" in an attempt at fulfilling an urge for westward expansion that would prove insatiable, for it would not be fulfilled by the apparent taming of a continental wilderness. Thus one realizes that Croft's hatred is also intimately related to his ancestry and the settling of America. And although the source of his hatred is ultimately as inexplicable as the origin of evil itself, one can at least try to describe its immediate cause. As the narrator suggests, the closing of the frontier set an absolute and intolerable geographic limit on the expression of Croft's inherited pioneer lust for infinite expansion and drove that passion inward so that "he pushed and labored inside himself and smoldered with an endless hatred"— for his father, for women, for, as Croft imagines it, "EVERYTHING WHICH IS NOT IN MYSELF" (164). Like his pioneer forebears, Croft would conquer America, but when there seemed to be no land left to conquer, he was defeated in the very recognition of his ancestral victory, and the country had its revenge, leaving Croft until the war with an overwhelming desire for omnipotence but with only the will rather than any satisfactory means to express that desire.

With the war, Croft has the means, an all but unconditional license to kill and to risk his own life while patrolling jungle land that is truly a *terra incognita*. Croft knows instinctively, as the overly cautious and therefore doomed Hennessey and Roth do not, that it is only by embracing the existential dread that arises out of confronting the immediate possibility of one's own sense-less annihilation that one can maintain the charmed conscious-ness of invulnerability that in the war of life is absolutely essential to survival. Since the terms of human existence are uncertainty and conflict, there is nothing for one to do but plunge into the uncertainty and engage in conflict in an attempt to move with the rhythms of chance until one may even come to believe, as Croft characteristically does, that one's survival is assured by the forces of destiny. On the other hand, seeking refuge in circumspection involves one in the futility of trying to locate a point of stability that does not exist. Thus it would be difficult to find a sentiment more opposed not only to Croft's principles but to Mailer's too than Roth's idea that "it was better to live in a cellar than to walk a tightrope" (638). In fact, the phrasing of Roth's axiom anticipates the statement of its antithesis in *The Prisoner of Sex* when Mailer as the Prizewinner muses that it is "better to expire as a devil in the fire than an angel in the wings" (16). Croft is a most ruthless embodiment of this idea, and when he regards the self-absorption and care with which Hennessey tends to a minor irritation of the knee, Croft thinks, "that boy is too careful" and then a moment later realizes with precognitive certainty that "'Hennessey's going to get killed today.'" After Hennessey is killed, Croft senses that his own life has been changed dramatically: "Hennessey's death had opened to Croft vistas of such omnipotence that he was afraid to consider it directly. All day the fact hovered about his head, tantalizing him with odd dreams and portents of power" (40). It is as if Croft's instinctive knowledge of the necessity of risktaking and his willingness to take risks have not only given him a way of recognizing and successfully negotiating the dangers and complexities of life as war but have also established a point of view from which he might predict or even shape the outcome in situations in which the end is ostensibly unknown.

The idea that risktaking can give one the magical ability to understand, synchronize with, or even influence the phenomena of a nonrational world recurs in much of Mailer's later work. One thinks of Eitel and Faye's shared belief that their indulgence in "dirty" sex will somehow "change . . . or blow up the world":[3] Rojack's ability, won through risktaking, to hear inner voices that act as guides to behavior in a nonrational world of magical connections; D. J.'s switched-on mind, electrified by the powers of the North, which reveals to him the collective madness of America; on a comic level, Mailer's decision in *The Fight* to walk across a parapet in an attempt to improve Muhammad Ali's chances against George Foreman; and in *Ancient Evenings* the elder Menenhetet's much maligned ritual investigations into the mysteries of all that is strange and forbidden. As these examples suggest, Mailer believes that the intense experience of the risk-taker is revelatory, for it transforms an uncomprehending view of an apparently flat and meaningless surface of life into a charged perception of a reality whose depth and meaning are revealed in signs and portents. If one can correctly interpret the world as an arcane repository of meanings, one has a chance of controlling the future. I will have more to say about these ideas later in this book when I consider Mailer's relationship to transcendentalism and define exactly what he means by "magic." It is sufficient here merely to note that the idea that risktaking can provide one with a foreknowledge of events in a world of synchronous relationships is implicit in the dream of power which tantalizes Croft in the aftermath of Hennessey's death and which is the source of his obsession with climbing Mount Anaka, an act of domination that Croft senses would give him greater power over life and death. For it would allow him to exploit in more complex and dangerous situations the kind of power that he has exercised in the past by covertly killing a striking worker, by predicting Hennessey's death, and by heartlessly toying with a Japanese prisoner before blowing out the man's brains with a single bullet. Climbing the mountain would give Croft such power because, as Mailer suggests throughout his canon, in any act of domination, one takes on the powers of one's vanquished foe, which in this case is nature itself, nature as an indifferent and impersonal force that gratuitously determines who will live and who will die, thus making all that is personal and human seem utterly insignificant.

Of course, having been sent by Cummings to replace Croft as leader of the platoon, Hearn is the only man who can prevent the sergeant from climbing the mountain. The fact that Hearn represents such an obstacle intensifies the power struggle that would have at any rate gone on between him and Croft. In this struggle Hearn is at a decided disadvantage, for his painful grappling with the question of the morality of power fails to provide him with a standpoint from which he can fully comprehend Croft's amoral will to power. As a result, Hearn never imagines the treachery that Croft is capable of and pays for his naiveté with his life. Indeed, despite an exhaustive examination of the problem, Hearn is incapable of conceiving of an ethical standard that would allow him to resolve or at least endure the moral ambiguities that arise from a recognition in himself of a ruthless will to power and the impossibility of determining the exact nature of his motives in any given exercise of power. Once he sees an affinity between himself and both Cummings and Croft, manifested, for example, in the desire for command and the decision to humiliate Croft just as he himself was humiliated by Cummings, Hearn has certainly moved far beyond the assumption of human perfectibility that Mailer associates with liberalism. In fact, Hearn's long-held conviction that there is a "shoddy motive" behind almost all human activities has always been in conflict with the liberalism that he rather abstractly espouses, but the contradiction does not effectively negate his liberalism until he abandons self-righteousness and seriously questions his motives while leading the reconnaissance patrol. This serious questioning reveals to Hearn not only such conflicting personal motives for succeeding with the reconnaissance mission as spiting Cummings and winning the general's approval but also the knowledge that he is just as capable of continuing the patrol and jeopardizing the men's lives to savor the satisfactions of command as he is capable of pressing on to try to help the war end a little sooner.

The recognition of moral ambiguity represents a movement away from liberalism to the kind of "moral radicalism"[4] implicit in Mailer's existential ethic as personified first in the figure of the hipster and later developed both in Mailer's novels from *An American Dream* to *Tough Guys Don't Dance* and in the nonfiction novels and reportage in which various incarnations of Mailer act as the left-conservative protagonist. But Hearn is still incapable of living within such a paradoxical standpoint. Though he has implicitly rejected liberalism, he remains paralyzed by the so-called "shoddy motive." In fact, he is surprisingly like Hawthorne's Goodman Brown in that he is similarly incapable of distinguishing the human potential for evil from the decision actually to perform evil actions. Moreover, Hearn is unable to consider his conflicting motivations and discern what constitutes the fundamental reason for making a particular decision. Finally, when making such a distinction proves impossible, he cannot simply live with the uncertainty and go on, like Stephen Rojack, to magnify his sense of moral complexity by continuing to choose among the ambiguities. Instead Hearn decides to try to recapture the clarity of the liberal categories of good and evil that he has already abandoned and preserve the purity that he has already lost by recognizing his affinity with Cummings and Croft: in what seems to him the absence of any alternative, Hearn returns to the liberalism that he has rejected and chooses to resign his commission, taking spiritual refuge in the reductive paradox that "'it is better to be the hunted than the hunter'" (584). It is a decision which represents an abdication of power because of the fear of corruption and which consigns Hearn to a position of isolation and ineffectuality. In fact, even Hearn admits the limitations of his decision when his and the narrator's voices come together in despairing self-criticism of what they believe is the best available expression of political protest, saying "Hearn and Quixote. Bourgeois liberals." At the same time, Hearn identifies his true political orientation at this point while admitting the inadequacy of his political response by lamenting that it is "drought season for anarchists" (586). Certainly these unfortunate political implications undercut the idea advanced by Ihab Hassan that Hearn as "victim hero" fulfills the role of scapegoat and thereby performs a symbolic act that has some redemptive value,[5] for there is no redemption in a gesture that in its self-destructive expression of the desire for a better world would thereby surrender all power to the totalitarians.

In criticizing Hearn's decision, I am not suggesting that he should have forced the platoon to climb Mount Anaka, and I must strongly disagree with Robert Solotaroff when he writes that the novel is confusing on this point and that, in fact, "Mailer has clearly lost control of the novel's symbolic lines,"[6] particularly with respect to whether or not Hearn should have given the order to climb the mountain. The entire novel supports Hearn's idea that "Croft had the wrong kind of command, a frightening command" (503), and the enforced climbing of Mount Anaka provides the most dramatic example in the book of the ultimate tendency of Croft's oppressive command: in driving the entire platoon up the side of the mountain, Croft reveals that he is willing to subordinate the practical task of reconnaissance to his secret purpose of pursuing a monomaniacal vision of absolute power. In so doing, he is engaged in an act directly analogous to Ahab's decision to abandon the business of whaling in order to pursue Moby Dick. If Hearn were to give the order to climb the mountain, he would not simply be a potential Croft but would in fact become an actual Croft as Ahab. Moreover, in thinking that Croft exercises "the wrong kind of command," Hearn is necessarily suggesting that a right kind of command conceivably exists as a point of comparison. It is just such a command that could have been defined if Hearn had continued as an officer at the head of the platoon and thereby explored existentially the moral ambiguities of the will to power.

What remains problematic about *The Naked and the Dead* is not the symbolic significance of the decision to climb Mount Anaka but the fact that the novel rejects liberalism yet allows its protagonist to choose as his definitive expression of political protest an act that, in terms not only of the political vocabulary of the book but also of the rhetoric of Mailer's entire career, is undoubtedly liberal. Interestingly, Mailer himself suggests the best context for discussing this problem. In "Some Children of the

Goddess," a 1965 *Esquire* essay in which Mailer reviews the work of several of his contemporaries, he discusses writing as risktaking and argues that one may gauge the greatness of a writer by judging how far he has been able to pursue the exigencies of his vision. Mailer conceives of writing as an existential situation in which every choice represents either a greater exploration of the unknown or a flight into relative security. According to Mailer, the writer is always implicitly questioning himself: "'Can I do it,'" he thinks. "'Should I let up here? Should I reconnoiter there? Will dread overwhelm me if I explore too far? or depression deaden me if I do not push on? Can I even do it?'" (CC 107). With Hearn's decision to resign his commission, Mailer "'let up'" and reached the limit of his ability at this very early point in his career to pursue the political implications of his vision.

Of course, Hearn is killed before he is able to resign his commission, but Mailer's brilliant rendering of Ridges and Goldstein's brutally exhausting attempt to carry the mortally wounded Wilson through the jungle and back to shore in order to save him dramatizes the futility of self-sacrifice. Moreover, it is immediately following the failure to save Wilson that Red Valsen finally tries to rebel against Croft as the sergeant mercilessly drives the platoon up the side of Mount Anaka. Valsen backs down, however, knowing that Croft will murder him just as he contrived to have Hearn killed. As the ultimate humiliation, Red actually feels relieved that his abject defeat absolves him from the obligation to rebel, allowing him instead to submit meekly to obeying all future orders. At this point, having dramatized the limitations of liberalism, self-sacrifice, and cynical individualism, Mailer was apparently left with nothing but the resources of naturalism as a means of defeating Cummings and Croft. Thus it is chance that places a hornet's nest in Croft's path and prevents him from climbing the mountain. And it is likewise chance that removes Cummings from Anopopei and puts the inept, bureaucratic Major Dalleson in command as the decisive battle for control of the island is about to be fought. After the island is won, Cummings concludes that his strategy has been irrelevant and that his reports were all in error. In fact, he acknowledges "that anyone could have won this campaign" (716) and that "it would be the hacks who would occupy history's seat after the war, the same blunderers, unco-ordinated, at cross-impulses" (718). Yet, as the brutal executions of the mop-up scene suggest, despite its banal surface, anticipated and epitomized by the image of Colonel Dalleson's Betty Grable map, post–World–War–II American bureaucracy will be capable through the systematic buildup of nuclear weapons of preparing for the most impersonal and savage violence that the world has ever witnessed.

Chapter 3

Barbary Shore:
Bureaucracy and Nightmare

The apocalyptic danger of bureaucratic totalitarianism serves as the disturbing subject of *Barbary Shore*. Mailer's second novel focuses on an America perpetually engaged in building up its military might and expanding its influence while at the same time feeling an ever-increasing economic need to use its destructive power as it competes against an equally bureaucratic and predatory Soviet Union. As virtually every critic who has commented on the book has noted, however, the novel is seriously flawed. In the final analysis the novel's problems are the result of imperfect execution. But it is important to emphasize that to a significant extent these problems derive from a self-imposed structural limitation that makes the book almost incredibly ambitious. If one can imagine Conrad in *Heart of Darkness* trying to suggest the genocidal tendency of colonialism while restricting himself to writing only about those indifferent secretaries who sit placidly in the Company's home office and knit black wool, one has some idea of the task that Mailer set for himself in *Barbary Shore*, where he has certainly strained to the limit his assumption that any American life and any American setting may be representative. For it is through the extremely limited actions and vague purposes of his Brooklyn boardinghouse characters that Mailer attempts to dramatize the idea that the United States and the

Soviet Union are locked into military and economic policies that have brought the world to the brink of holocaust.

The all but inevitable result of placing such a terrible burden of meaning on these characters is a tendency toward political allegory, with Guinevere, for example, standing for a greedy, cheap, promiscuous, and identityless America which has traded its heritage of spiritual questing for expansionism but which is ready at the same time in order to free itself from economic and political uncertainty to embrace even the most demeaning form of right-wing oppression. Moreover, insofar as she is sought after herself by every other major adult character in the book, a situation that represents for the first time in Mailer's work the elusiveness of the apparently accessible sexual object, Guinevere also suggests the debased middle-American consciousness that the conflicting political ideologies of this country would like to seduce and subsequently control.

These allegorical associations work at cross-purposes with Mailer's fascinating attempt in the novel to suggest that if one were able to break through the banal surface of the American scene, one would see a complete inversion of all democratic ideals and perceive at the heart of the national life our own equivalent of Kurtz's horror: a depraved and nightmarish America that is perversely bent on its own destruction. It is precisely this disparity between appearance and reality—between professed American democratic ideals and the historical actuality of the nation—which Mailer believes is productive of schizophrenia and which has drawn him to the conclusion, best expressed by the narrator in "The Man Who Studied Yoga," that "reality is no longer realistic" (Adv. 179). The suggestion of nightmare lurking beneath the surface of the commonplace and of a conspiratorial web of relationships existing among the various elements of the American power structure has become one of Mailer's most compelling themes. In fact, the dramatization of this theme represents one of the most impressive, though still largely unacknowledged, achievements of *An American Dream*, where Rojack's paranoid perception of a world of nonrational associations takes on greater epistemological validity than a common-sense view of a world of cause and effect relationships. *Barbary Shore* certainly suggests the existence of this world, for it does indeed provide chilling intimations of both conspiracy and nightmare. Moreover, the novel does have, as Mailer suggests in *Advertisements for Myself*, "a kind of insane insight into the psychic mysteries of Stalinists, secret policemen, narcissists, children, Lesbians, hysterics, revolutionaries—it has an air which for me is the air of our time, authority and nihilism stalking one another in the orgiastic hollow of this century" (94). But the effect of these insights is muted and the spasmodic brilliance of the novel undercut not only by the limitations of the action and the vacuity of the protagonist but also by the fact that the characters' purposes remain vaguely defined for all too long. But the most serious flaw certainly involves the fact that in the final section the novel's tendency toward lecturing takes over almost completely as the ex-Stalinist McLeod delivers his seemingly interminable sermon on the dangerous internal contradictions of monopoly and state capitalism.

Despite these structural weaknesses, *Barbary Shore* does succeed in projecting a frightening view of a world bent on self-destruction. The novel is also all too accurate not only in its anticipation of McCarthyism and the growth throughout the fifties and sixties of FBI- and CIA-directed domestic surveillance but also in its perception of both the United States and the Soviet Union as expansionist powers deeply committed to arms production as an essential part of their economic programs. The novel's fundamental argument is that, as world markets have become "glutted" with commodities and as developing nations have turned increasingly to some form of state capitalism or nationalization, it has correspondingly become more and more difficult for American monopoly capitalism to invest its profits. As a result, the United States has begun to resort to all but unlimited military production as an economic alternative: "for there was a new consumer and new commodities, and every shell could find as

customer its enemy soldier."¹ At the same time, the state capitalism of the Soviet Union has been unable to raise its people's
standard of living by providing necessary goods and services but
has found itself locked instead into the production of machinery
and tools that will make possible further production. As an
alternative, it has become involved in "'seizing new countries,
stripping them of their wealth, and converting their economy to
war'" (277–78). Thus the novel argues that both superpowers are
producing "'wholly for death'" (279), for they are committed to
economic and military policies that make war not only inevitable
but, once begun, perpetual so that "'the deterioration'" will
continue "'until we are faced with mankind in barbary'" (282).

It is from this exceedingly grim world that Mikey Lovett, the
novel's orphaned, war-scarred, amnesiac protagonist, has with-
drawn in order to write and to try to create a sense of identity.
With only fitful and flickering memories of the past and a wholly
uncharted future and with only the most tenuous connection to
society, Lovett certainly fulfills Mailer's later definition of the
existential hero. Thus one can readily understand why Mailer
would write in *Advertisements for Myself* that *Barbary Shore* was
the "first of the existentialist novels in America" (106). Indeed, it
is as if in his characterization of Lovett, Mailer were trying to
solve the problem of discovering a significant response to totalitarianism by starting at the point of self-creation. Accepting as a
given Hemingway's knowledge that one is necessarily wounded
by experience, Mailer tries in *Barbary Shore* to discover through
his protagonist what identity one might choose to make and what
the nature of one's political commitment might be if one had the
freedom to attempt to recreate oneself virtually out of nothing.
Nevertheless, because of Mailer's extremely dark view of a world
engaged in an ever-deepening crisis, a world that necessarily
impinges upon the solitary questing self, Lovett, as the wounded
New Adam, is faced with a severely limited range of choices. As
the inevitability of his involvement with McLeod suggests, Lovett
cannot choose to be free of politics. Human existence is itself
political, and even Lovett enters into "'social and economic

relations independent'" (162) of his will. Thus he can choose to accept the existing political situation and live in complicity in a world turned "'prison'" (212), hoping to be allowed for a time "'a corner in which to write a book'" (124). Or he can despair of freedom altogether and, like Lannie Madison, a badly disillusioned, indeed mentally disturbed ex-Trotskyite, join forces with Hollingsworth and the bureaucratic totalitarianism of the right. In so doing, he would retaliate against those, like McLeod, who have betrayed the revolutionary dream of the left and at the same time align himself with the totalitarianism that Lannie believes, and the novel fears, is the wave of the future—if there is to be a future at all. Lastly Lovett can take the risk of identifying himself morally and politically with McLeod, who is being interrogated by Hollingsworth for having been a communist and for having stolen from the United States government an unspecified "little object." Such a choice, however, would require Lovett to recommit himself to the cause of revolutionary socialism and mark himself as a target of the right. And he would have to make this choice despite the fact that he has tried to abandon politics altogether as a result of his disillusionment over the oppressive state capitalism of the Soviet Union and over the Stalinist purges, in which McLeod was so deeply involved.

Unfortunately, while Lovett struggles to rouse himself from his narcissistic torpor and choose among these difficult alternatives, he remains, as I have suggested before, a rather nebulous character. As a result, even if one cares very much about the political questions involved, one still does not care as much as one should about how Lovett feels while he contends with the dilemma of commitment. In fact, of all the characters in the book, it is really Leroy Hollingsworth who is the most compelling, for he comes very close to embodying Mailer's theme that America is a schizophrenic nation with a strong underlying attraction to reactionary politics and a deeply ingrained contempt for intellect and culture. As the facts of increased industrialization and the influx of new money have given the lie to the security of the modest midwestern city that Lovett imagines his parents remembering—"an earlier

world, illumined in the transitory splendor of a calendar sunset"
(84)—so, on the other hand, does the figure of Hollingsworth
expose the naiveté of the images that many of us preserve of that
simple and decent small-town America nurtured by its faith in
God, motherhood, and country. Hollingsworth's blond hair and
blue eyes, his neat appearance, and his deferential manners all
suggest the image of the archetypal small-town American boy,
but the image is always slightly skewed by the insinuation of the
sinister: Hollingsworth's "china-blue eyes" hold "a hint of
aggression" (111). His neat appearance is contradicted by the
violent disarray of his room. And his politeness is wooden and
insincere, not a mark of civility but a clumsy cover for the
boorishness that is always threatening to break out in a lascivious
and juvenile leer or the humorless "hir-hir-hir" of "his excessive
laughter" (39, 41).

Thus in his characterization of Hollingsworth, Mailer expresses an idea that he has returned to repeatedly throughout his
career, namely the tremendous capacity for brutal and impersonal violence which lurks within the heart of middle America
and which, Mailer believes, attempted to find its ultimate purgation in the war in Vietnam. For Hollingsworth is a fictive antecedent of both the Goldwater youth of "In the Red Light" and the
insanely callous Grandma with orange hair of *The Armies of the
Night*. He is likewise a near relative of the anonymous neighbor of
Marilyn Monroe's youth who killed her pet dog with a shotgun
blast and so confirmed the fears of her guardians, the Bolenders,
who were "poor, pious, stern, kindly, decent, hard-working, and
absolutely terrified of the lividity of the American air in the street
outside,"[2] terrified of "that violence which lives like an electronic
hum behind the silence of even the sleepiest Sunday afternoon"
(Mar. 27). It is precisely this sense of barely contained violence
that Mailer succeeds in communicating through Hollingsworth.
One thinks, for example, of the scene in which Hollingsworth
stares at Lannie with "a polite look upon his face, an expression of
mild curiosity in his eyes as if he would be the hick who has paid
money and now watches the carnival girls strip their costumes.

This is the magical evil of the big city, but he is wary of being taken in: 'I come to see pussy,' he says to his neighbor, 'and I ain't seen pussy yet.' He will smash the carnival booths if he is cheated" (143). One thinks too of Hollingsworth's furious reaction after being bitten in the hand by Monina, Guinevere's five-year-old daughter: " 'When I see that kid again,' " he says, " 'I'll cut her fucking heart out' " (147). One also senses Hollingsworth's violence in his provincial anti-intellectualism which views education as nothing more than a tool for getting ahead and which scoffs in ignorance and resentment at the world of ideas. As he remarks at one point during his interrogation of McLeod, " 'you can shove theory. . . . Respect your father and mother' " (270).

Hollingsworth's reactionary ignorance is epitomized by the fact that he is willing to act as an instrument of the United States government and investigate McLeod despite the fact that he has no idea what the little object is that McLeod has supposedly stolen and therefore cannot possibly know what the moral and political implications of the theft might be. Indeed, as McLeod notes, perhaps " 'nobody knows' " (192) what the little object is. All that anyone does know is that something important is missing, and it is this sense of uncertainty—which suggests that the disruption of one small part of the system may eventuate in the total loss of social, political, and economic control—that is absolutely intolerable to the bureaucratic powers that be.

Whereas the vagueness of Lovett is crippling to his characterization, the unspecified nature of the little object is the key to its success as a literary device, for in the course of the novel the object takes on a host of provocative meanings. It represents first of all any part of the current capitalistic system, which derives its sustenance from " 'stolen labor from the past' " (191). The object is consequently an accretion of past injustice, " 'an end product . . . delivered into the world trailing corruption and gore, laden with guilt, a petrifaction of all which preceded it' " (192). Thus as an object produced through exploitation, its quality and monetary value determined primarily by the profit motive and the desire to maximize the differences in the standards of living of rich and poor, it also suggests the failure of revolutionary possibilities. Yet once the object is stolen and thereby freed from its relation to the system of capitalistic control, it represents the recreation of revolutionary possibilities, signalling both an affirmation of the romantic dream of freedom and equality that has always been associated with millennial America and a rejection of the dream of wealth and power that has likewise always been connected with the idea of America.

McLeod's theft of the little object was an attempt, along with dedicating himself to revolutionary political theory, to redeem himself for past political betrayals. As Lannie remarks, McLeod had become "'the undertaker of the revolution'" (187), having participated in the Stalinist purges and having subsequently been a cog in the American governmental bureaucracy. As Lovett understands, "the actions of people and not their sentiments make history" (162). McLeod's theft clarifies the implications of this favorite line of Mailer's,[3] which is certainly not a denigration of thought but an insistence on the necessity of maintaining an intimate connection between thought and action that are both imbued with the spirit of risk. For it was the risk involved in taking the object that confirmed McLeod's recommitment to revolutionary ideals. Moreover, since the liberation of revolutionary possibilities that the act represents is opposed to the political self-interests of both the United States and the Soviet Union, stealing the object was "'a moral act'" (227) that has made McLeod an enemy of both powers. And as McLeod knows, the risk of retaliation against him from either side continues to increase as long as he insists on remaining a threat. As a result, he must finally choose: he can either compromise himself once again and turn over the object or venture his life in the attempt to disrupt the bureaucracies that he opposes. His decision to refuse to turn over the object to Hollingsworth encourages Lovett finally to commit himself politically and offer to assume the risk of harboring the object himself in view of the likelihood of McLeod's arrest or death. And so when Hollingsworth kills McLeod,[4] Lovett receives the bequest of the "poor hope" of "the remnants of

[McLeod's] socialist culture" along with the responsibility of the little object, while the world continues to move toward apocalypse. As Lovett observes,

> From out the unyielding contradictions of labor stolen from men, the march to the endless war forces its pace. Perhaps, as the millions will be lost, others will be created, and I shall discover brothers where I thought none existed.
> But for the present the storm approaches its thunderhead, and it is apparent that the boat drifts ever closer to shore. So the blind will lead the blind, and the deaf shout warnings to one another until their voices are lost. (311–12)

The mood of this conclusion is foreboding, indeed. The failure of revolutionary socialism to create freedom and equality in the Soviet Union has all but negated its moral force. Indeed, in the course of the novel, McLeod asserts that revolutionary socialism has no more stature than "a point in the political horizon" (224), and Mailer himself would abandon the ideology altogether shortly after finishing *Barbary Shore.* Clearly the hope that does exist lies in Lovett's commitment to risktaking as a means of combating totalitarianism and expanding the possibilities for expression in America. Unfortunately, Lovett remains little more than a shadowy figure on the periphery of society, for his commitment to risk begins precisely as the book ends. As a result, Mailer is left with the problem of fleshing out his protagonist and dramatizing the implications of risktaking as a significant response to totalitarianism.

Chapter 4

The Deer Park:
The Cost of Cowardice

In his next novel, *The Deer Park*, Mailer again focuses on the absolute necessity of risktaking in an America that has an insatiable desire for novelty, sensation, and romance, an incurable case of juvenility, a profound commitment to conformity and hypocrisy, and a fear of communism raised by political expediency to the level of paranoia. He elaborates this theme through the education of Sergius O'Shaugnessy; the personal, artistic, and political failures of director-writer Charles Francis Eitel; and the hipsterlike attitudes of Marion Faye.

Like Mikey Lovett, Sergius is an orphan who has been scarred by war. In this case, however, the problem is impotence, which was brought on by the fact that he was unable to maintain an amoral detachment that would allow him to view dogfights as "impersonal contests" or contemplate in utter simplicity the symmetry of bomb patterns and the explosive brilliance of "a city in flames" (45, 46). Nor was he able to continue simply to enjoy the decidedly sexual sense of transcendent power and freedom that suggested that he could magically "control the changes of the sky by a sway of [his] body as it was swelled by the power of the plane" (96). For after staring one day at the badly burned arm of a Japanese K.P. who had just injured himself in a kitchen accident, Sergius "suddenly . . . realized that two hours ago [he] had been busy setting fire to a dozen people, or two dozen, or had it

been a hundred?" (46). He knew then that there was a "real world
. . . where orphans burned orphans" (47) and began associating
flesh with the real world of burning bodies so that for him murder
and holocaust were real, while sexuality became a dream that was
lived by people, like the carefree, heartless pilots, whose cool
had never been violated by the image of atrocity.

Thus, after experiencing "a small breakdown" (46), receiving
a medical discharge, and staking himself with fourteen thousand
dollars won in a poker game in Tokyo, Sergius sets out from the
Far East for the American West with the need for physical and
spiritual regeneration and the romantic desire to become a writer.
He arrives in the Southern California town of Desert D'Or, built
on the site of Desert Door, a gold mining settlement which
prospectors had hoped to turn into their own version of El Dorado
but which has long since vanished without a trace. For in Desert
D'Or, a resort frequented by a host of elegant and inelegant
transients—movie people, politicians, gamblers, businessmen,
sportsmen, tourists, jetsetters, hangers–on, mobsters, call girls,
and pimps—all is new and rootless. As Sergius realizes, in
Desert D'Or "everything is in the present tense": not only the
buildings, which are all of post–World–War–II construction, but
the consciousness of the people, who remain ensconced, like
some contemporary species of cave dweller, in bars and casinos,
living as if the world were a perpetual party, oblivious to the
passage of time, indeed never even knowing if it is day or night.
Desert D'Or is therefore a manifestation of an America that
perpetually denies history and so can never grow up. In this
regard, Sergius observes that in the resort "one hardly came
across a building which was not green, yellow, rose, orange, or
pink" (2), a perception that anticipates Mailer's description of
Los Angeles in "Superman Comes to the Supermarket" as the
"city which is the capital of suburbia with its milky pinks, its
washed-out oranges, its tainted lime-yellows of pastel on one
pretty little architectural monstrosity after another, the colors not
intense enough, the styles never pure, and never sufficiently
impure to collide on the eye . . . a city without iron, eschewing

wood, a kingdom of stucco, the playground for mass men" (PP 32–33). Both observations serve as prolepses to a question that an Australian journalist would ask of Mailer as they are on a plane en route to San Francisco, where Mailer will cover the 1964 Republican Convention: "'Why is it,'" he asked, "'that all the new stuff you build here, including the interior furnishings of this airplane, looks like a child's plastic nursery?'" In "In the Red Light," Mailer acknowledges the incisiveness of the question and ruminates on the possible causes of this patent, chronic, yet largely unadmitted case of America's arrested development, thinking "and that is what it was. The inside of our airplane was like a child's nursery, a dayroom in the children's ward, and if I had been Quentin Compson, I might have answered, 'Because we want to go back, because the nerves grew in all the wrong ways. Because we developed habits which are suffocating us to death. I tell you, man, we do it because we're sick, we're a sick nation, we're sick to the edge of vomit and so we build our lives with materials which smell like vomit, polyethylene and bakelite and fiberglas and styrene'" (CC 8). This fixation on juvenility certainly pervades the entire culture, but for Mailer, architectural manifestations of it are most prevalent in the West. In *The Executioner's Song*, Mailer again describes this phenomenon, using language that combines the observations found in *The Deer Park*, "Superman Comes to the Supermarket," and "In the Red Light." From Orem to Provo, Utah, "there were shopping malls and quick-eat palaces, used-car dealers, chain clothing stores and gas stops, appliance stores and highway signs and fruit stands. There were banks and real estate firms in one-story office compounds and rows of condominiums with sawed-off mansard roofs. There hardly seemed a building that was not painted in a nursery color: pastel yellow, pastel orange, pastel tan, pastel blue. Only a few faded two-story houses looked as if they had been built even thirty years ago. . . . those looked as old as frontier saloons."[1]

The evocation of the idea of the old frontier saloons suggests the norm that Mailer is using when he implies through such motifs as "pastel" and "nursery" that the American romantic spirit is sick and debased. For the old saloons recall the dusty frontier towns of the Wild West and the figure of the pioneer, whom Mailer sees as an authentic embodiment of the idea of the romantic quester, a true incarnation of the mythic desire to make one's life eternally new through heroic action. In contrast, a culture of "mass men" given over to filling the American landscape with images of juvenility is guilty of substituting the trash of novelty for mythic recreation and confusing regression with romantic transcendence.

As Mailer realizes, the essence of these polar expressions of the American romantic spirit is captured in Hollywood films and apotheosized in the mystique of the movie star. In "Superman Comes to the Supermarket," Mailer notes that America was

the country in which the dynamic myth of the Renaissance—that every man was potentially extraordinary—knew its most passionate persistence. Simply, America was the land where people still believed in heroes: George Washington; Billy the Kid; Lincoln, Jefferson; Mark Twain, Jack London, Hemingway; Joe Louis, Dempsey, Gentleman Jim; America believed in athletes, rumrunners, aviators; even lovers, by the time Valentino died. It was a country which had grown by the leap of one hero past another. . . . And when the West was filled, the expansion turned inward, became part of an agitated, overexcited, superheated dream life. The film studios threw up their searchlights as the frontier was finally sealed, and the romantic possibilities of the old conquest of land turned into a vertical myth, trapped within the skull, of a new kind of heroic life, each choosing his own archetype of a neo-renaissance man, be it Barrymore, Cagney, Flynn, Bogart, Brando or Sinatra, but it was almost as if there were no peace unless one could fight well, kill well (if always with honor), love well and love many, be cool, be daring, be dashing, be wild, be wily, be resourceful, be a brave gun. (PP 39)

If the closing of the West forever consigned the American frontier to the realm of the romantic imagination, still the movies stimulated that imagination through countless Saturday afternoons given to elaborating the psychology of the cliff-hanger and magnifying the charisma of Hollywood stars so that successive generations of Americans were able to continue to identify, for example, with the legends of the pioneer and the fast gun. In fact, the movies even helped to create contemporary, urban counterparts of these heroes in the form of such figures as the private eye and the streetwise rebel so that films kept alive, however transformed, the myth of the American as the new man or, in Mailer's words, the "neo-renaissance man," who is "extraordinary" insofar as he is the equal of any situation, living the ideal of the hero by acting courageously in the face of the unknown and maintaining his own integrity despite the persistent pressure of compromise. Yet if the motion picture industry has been capable of stirring this culture's unquenchable desire for romance, even to the extent of exacerbating the frustration if the romance could not be acted out in real life, it has been even more proficient at pandering to and indeed further debasing the mentality of the lowest common denominator of Americans, that manifestation of leveled democratic man that is sentimental yet boorishly violent, novelty-ridden yet reactionary, its deepest conviction a fierce patriotism ubiquitously voiced for the sole rhetorical purpose of terminating debate.

In *The Deer Park*, movie mogul Herman Teppis and his son-in-law, producer Collie Munshin, exploit this mentality for all it is worth. As Teppis's assistant at Supreme Pictures, a position that calls for the combined talents of a manipulator, a flunky, and a pimp, Munshin epitomizes in slick Hollywood love-ya-baby style the commercial bureaucratic mind. No doubt, as Eitel notes, Munshin will one day run not only the studio but the world as well. With the warmth and comic appeal of an incurable con artist, he goes from luncheon date to luncheon date indefatigably stealing ideas and kneading them into the pulp from which cinematic blockbusters are made. What's more he is equally adept at offering in the course of a minute at least a dozen rationalizations that make a total sell-out of one's art seem like a monumental act of honor and integrity that a grateful public will inevitably reward with profit and acclaim. As the dictatorial head of Supreme Pictures, Herman Teppis specializes in giving the

American public what it wants. Sensing an undercurrent of confusion in the culture—resulting, one imagines, from some fugitive hints of questioning and protest making their way from the avant-garde to the American mainstream—Teppis is ready to exploit the situation: " 'People are confused today,' " he notes. " "So what do they want? They want a picture that confuses them. Wait till they get really confused. Then they'll want a picture that sets them straight' " (72). To be set straight means, of course, to have reinforced in one's heart and mind through the power of motion pictures and the fabled lives of the movie stars themselves belief in the preeminent and permanent value of motherhood and religion. To accomplish this noble task and roll up the profits as well, Teppis not only produces movies but tries to arrange marriages that will appeal to the American public's " 'big red heart' " (265). Thus at two private but secretly taped meetings, which provide one with a good working definition of moral hypocrisy, Teppis talks separately with popular actor Teddy Pope and sex bomb Lulu Meyers to convince them to marry and thereby become, in Teppis's words, " 'the Number One royal couple of America, and America is the world' " (274). Nevertheless, despite all of the appropriate hosannas to God, family life, and motherhood; the shedding of tears; and assurances of popularity and financial security, Teppis fails to make the match, not because Teddy insists that he is a homosexual but because Lulu has just secretly married the relatively minor star, Tony Tanner. Of course, the demands of the studio are not to be denied: after a timely bit of oiling—courtesy of Collie Munshin—Teppis merely shifts gears to accommodate the new situation and directs the studio's formidable resources for propaganda toward making Lulu and Tony " 'the Number One married lovers of America' " (273). As a finishing touch, Mailer punctuates the hypocrisy of this episode by revealing how a hard working studio president simultaneously relieves his anxiety and vents his hatred for women. And so the scene concludes after Teppis summons, through Munshin, a newly hired stock girl whose naive ambitions prompt her, as the narrator puts it, "to serve at the thumb of power" (284) and satisfy Teppis's secret penchant for fellatio.

The moral contradictions that Mailer dramatizes in this scene and the movie industry's ability to express both authentic and debased forms of romantic aspiration are epitomized by the female sex symbol of motion pictures, represented in *The Deer Park* by Lulu Meyers and quintessentially in Mailer's as well as America's imagination by Marilyn Monroe. For the Hollywood images of Lulu and Marilyn embrace the same sexual tension, a tension that, as I have noted, is also implicit in the character of Guinevere in *Barbary Shore*. As Mailer has written of Marilyn, her image does, indeed, suggest that she was easily accessible, that she was, in fact, "sweet, democratic provender for all" (Mar. 16). Yet at the same time, she was ever elusive, always beyond reach—the sexual treasure of every man and no one at all. And certainly these contradictions aptly describe the effect of Lulu's sexual persona as well. Thus one realizes that, in appearing to say "yes" while ultimately meaning "no," the images of Marilyn and Lulu point to a schizophrenic moral, which teaches that in America "sex is sin and yet sex is paradise" (Adv. 343).

But Mailer believes that if one could somehow defy this logic and make love to a woman whose paradigmatic image expresses both the sexual contradictions and the romantic ambiguities of an entire culture, the reward would be great. It would be as if one had gained carnal knowledge of an entire nation. In *The Deer Park*, Sergius fulfills this fantasy by making love with the coquettish Lulu, whom he has previously seen only in Korea, where she did her patriotic duty and, "like some fairy princess of sex," blessed the poor American troops with her "tiny favors, a whiff of her perfume, a lift she lost from her heel, a sequin from her evening gown" (35). Their first time alone together the prospect of sex with Lulu cures Sergius of impotence. And after being forced for hours to play seemingly endless variations on the story of old King Tantalus, Sergius is finally "led to discover the mysterious brain of a movie star" (95)—that brain that has an intimate intuitive understanding of how to heal and how to exacerbate the division within America's sexual imagination while knowing instinctively too that a sex symbol can embody the romantic possibilities of transcendence only as long as she can satisfy the public's desire to experience the ephemeral sensation of worshiping yet another pretty face.

One realizes from the implications of this scene that Sergius's brief and rocky relationship with Lulu is, nevertheless, crucial not only to the restoration of his physical and spiritual health but also to his initiation into the complexities, indeed for both Sergius and Mailer, the mystery of America—an initiation that is a prerequisite to his beginning the difficult task of becoming a writer. Moreover, it is the prevailing concern of Sergius's education that gives unity to the novel, providing a thematic connection between the sections that focus on Sergius and Lulu and the chapters devoted to Eitel's artistic and political compromises and the failure of his relationship with Elena.

Interestingly, Sergius relates Eitel's story for the most part from the standpoint of an absentee narrator who uses his novelistic imagination, like the later Mailer, to discover the truth when facts are unavailable or inconclusive. This story is implicitly the narrative of Sergius's own education, and it emphasizes again and again, through Eitel's struggles and ultimately his negative example, the absolute importance of having the moral courage to take risks if one is to retain one's personal, artistic, and political integrity, which the world and one's own self-betraying meanness are always eager to compromise.

When one first meets him, Eitel has just decided, after considerable vacillation, to defy the McCarthylike Congressional Committee on Subversive Activities. He refuses to identify so-called communist sympathizers despite the fact that he is no longer even involved in leftist politics, as he was years ago when married to his activist first wife, and is actually now indifferent to former acquaintances who are targets of the witch hunt. He takes this risk, which results in his immediate blacklisting and banishment into what Herman Teppis delicately calls the "'pigpen'"

(63), "'to give'" himself "'another chance'" (44) as a man and an artist. For with the exception of a few serious films that he wrote and directed at the beginning of his career, films that were influential artistic successes but financial failures, Eitel's moviemaking has up to this point paralleled the history of Hollywood schlock, making money for the studio and satisfying popular audiences composed, according to Eitel, of "'sentimental necrophiles'" (33). But finally, after quitting the set of a monstrosity of a musical, entitled *Clouds Ahoy*, and feeling emotionally, sexually, and artistically spent, he is able for once to choose uncertainty over continuing as a studio hack.

Having made this choice, Eitel has the opportunity to take an even greater risk, the risk of loving Collie Munshin's mistress, Elena Esposito, who is clearly Mailer's most compelling purely fictional female character, surpassed only by his later depictions of Marilyn Monroe, Nicole Baker, and Bessie Gilmore. Elena is a much abused, insecure young woman whose courage, dignity, and real capacity for love are invisible to the shallow manipulators and pleasure seekers of Desert D'Or. Because they are incapable of even imagining the existence of the depth of humanity that Elena is capable of if only she can receive something like real love in return, they see her basically as an unsophisticated, indeed ignorant, failed dancer who is no more than a half-step removed from being a whore. Collie Munshin, for instance, in offering Elena to Eitel, can only mouth a hypocritical parody of understanding, insisting in language derived from the jargon of psychotherapy that, despite her promiscuity, Elena is really seeking "'a decent healthy mature relationship'" (58). Elena's promiscuity is, of course, a search for love and attention, but Munshin is merely paying lip service to an ideal which has no real meaning to him and which he has never in reality sought or seen exemplified in the community of Desert D'Or.

Real love is what Eitel has the chance of finding with Elena. But to do so, he must be able to overcome the terrible snobbery that aligns him with the frauds and cheats of Desert D'Or. He must refuse to scrutinize Elena's flaws and reject the desire to make her conform to his own elitist image of a classy woman. For such snobbery is really an attempt to turn a love affair with a complex human being from an existential situation in which the "end is unknown" into a monument to one's own prejudices. Instead of opting for the security of control, Eitel must continually fight his fear by taking the risk of accepting Elena as she is. Such a choice would not only represent a commitment to love, it would also constitute a significant political act. It would show that humanity is more important than false ideals and therefore implicitly protest against the totalitarian and self-aggrandizing actions of the Subversive Committee as it destroys careers and even lives while pursuing the professed purpose of stopping the spread of communism. Moreover, exercising courage in his relationship with Elena would create in Eitel the moral courage to continue to defy the Committee and finally write and direct his projected film masterpiece. Thus one observes again that in Mailer's work courage is always the primary virtue. In *The Deer Park* courage is what makes love possible, while love in turn provides a foundation for authentic political and artistic expression, the kind of expression that Mailer would later refer to as existential.

One realizes then that Eitel's love affair opens up, however briefly, the possibility that he can develop into a dialectical character, a character who wages a daily battle to overcome his own failings such as cowardice, materialism, and debased romanticism to act courageously and who by virtue of such struggles comes to dramatize both the source of many of America's problems and a possible solution. But it is only at the very beginning of the affair that Eitel shows any promise of rising to this stature. Indeed, he betrays almost from the very start the extent to which the worldly values of Desert D'Or have become his own. Eitel's own theory of personality, related by Sergius, best explains the problem:

The core of Eitel's theory was that people had a buried nature—"the noble savage" he called it—which was changed and whipped and trained by everything in life until it was almost dead. Yet if people were lucky and if they were brave, sometimes they would find a mate with the same buried nature and that could make them happy and strong. At least relatively so. There were so many things in the way, and if everybody had a buried nature, well everybody also had a snob, and the snob was usually stronger. The snob could be a tyrant to buried nature. (121–22)

For several idyllic weeks Eitel is able to live in the knowledge of Elena's love and prepare himself to take the artistic gamble of beginning his screenplay about "a modern saint" (126) who, in Miss Lonelyhearts fashion, is destroyed by his empathy with the suffering that he once exploited for fame and profit by supplying glib advice. But eventually the "tyrant" of snobbery returns "to torture" Eitel with Elena's "little faults, her ignorance, her inability to be anything but his mate" (122). As Eitel's love weakens, so does his artistic integrity, and the direction of his work betrays this weakness, inevitably turning "into something shoddy or something contrived, into something dull, something false" (168).

With an uncanny sense of timing, Collie Munshin arrives on the scene at the precise moment when Eitel's lust for commercial success is really beginning to heat up. Almost immediately the story is compromised, transformed into a meretricious potboiler with a priest for a hero and "an upbeat ending," in Munshin's words, "'something with angels' voices in the background. Only not full of shit'" (180).

Eitel's failure to resist the temptation to sell out and falsify his story marks the end of his chance of being a real artist. Marion Faye, the bisexual pimp, who once respected Eitel, makes this point in a cruelly honest but fitting judgment on Eitel's career and life. Above all, Faye values courage and maintaining the integrity of his own nihilistic philosophy while despising compassion and sentimentality. He therefore shows no sympathy in explaining why he now hates Eitel, telling him simply and forcefully, "'you might have been an artist, and you spit on it'" (184).

Of course, once Eitel's artistic integrity is lost, his political capitulation is a foregone conclusion, determined by the symbiotic relationship existing between the studio and the Subversive Committee: negotiations with the ubiquitous Munshin and Congressman Crane, a member of the Committee, ease Eitel's move from the blacklist back into bona fide membership in the Hollywood establishment; public testimony and a published confession confirm the return of the shriven Prodigal Son of movieland to the family fold; and the gossip columnists work a magical transformation of Eitel's image from pinko traitor to "the hero of a sermon" (308).

In the meantime, with cold calculation and cruel detachment, maintained paradoxically by the realization that the failure of the relationship is his fault and that "he must hurt [Elena] as little as possible," Eitel has been alternating acts of alienation with words of reassurance and love to bring about all but imperceptibly the end of the affair. Indeed, in the terms in which Eitel himself conceives of the process, he has been reeling in Elena as if she were a "big fish on slender tackle" and as if "he must slowly exhaust her love, depress her hope, and make the end as painless as the blow of the club on the fatigued fishbrain" (203). This process is counterpointed by Eitel's infidelity to Elena and by his proposal of a marriage to be followed quickly by a divorce. The proposal is obviously a pale caricature of real commitment. Indeed, it is motivated by Eitel's perception of his own cowardice and his feeling that somehow marriage will give Elena respectability while comforting her with the knowledge that someone once cared enough about her to give her his name. When Elena reveals her own inner strength and dignity by refusing the offer, choosing instead the uncertainty of life without him, Eitel realizes what the essential difference is between himself and Elena and, in so doing, formulates what is finally the moral vision of the novel itself:

The essence of spirit . . . was to choose the thing which did not better one's position but made it more perilous. That was why the world he knew was poor, for it insisted morality and caution were identical. He was so completely of that world and she was not. . . .

Young as she was, he had heard experience in her voice which was beyond his own experience, and so if he stayed with her, he would be obliged to travel in *her* directions, and he had been fleeing that for all of his life. (257)

When the affair finally collapses, Eitel is left to ponder his own compromises, while Elena chooses to live with Marion Faye, desperately envisioning for herself a life of prostitution. Faye, however, proves to be more interested in using Elena for testing the limits of his ability to live out his nihilistic philosophy. As many critics have noted, Faye's nihilism anticipates Mailer's philosophy of Hip. Both reject all socially imposed attitudes and values—in Faye's words, "'the whole world is bullshit'" (17). And in the search for an authentic self, both approve of violence as a sign of rebellion and a way of liberating primitive energies and thereby accelerating personal growth. Moreover, the fact that Faye's primary values are courage and integrity also aligns him with the hipster. Nevertheless, there are significant differences. Faye's remark that "'it's easy to kill a man. Easier to do that than chase after a roach and squash it'" (16) illustrates that for him violence is not so much a necessary concomitant to humanity's rejection of the distorted values and unwanted restrictions of civilization as it is an expression of disdain for humanity itself. According to Faye, one achieves authenticity by satisfying two requirements: first one must liberate one's instinctual drives to copulate and to kill; then one must adopt an attitude of absolute indifference while engaging in sex or performing acts of violence. Unlike the hipster, Faye is not interested in finding immediate orgasmic gratification but in exercising a ruthless will to power manifested in achieving absolute control over his emotions. He is therefore dedicated paradoxically to a rationalist emancipation of instinct for the purpose of achieving power.[2] The result is not the freedom of Hip but a kind of self-inflicted, Croftlike totalitarianism through which one dominates oneself to gain greater control over others.

Yet, as Robert Merrill notes, Faye "is by nature sensitive, even tender."[3] In forcing himself to be cruel, in denying all emotion, and in choosing to believe that "'there is no pleasure greater than that obtained from a conquered repugnance'" (146), Faye is actually torturing himself. And what is even more disturbing, in trying to fulfill the self-imposed obligation to push himself to immoralist extremes, he is forcing himself to commit the crime of violating the human heart. In fact, it is just such a false imperative that suggests the idea that he must persuade the weak and vulnerable Elena to commit suicide. When Elena finally cannot bring herself to end her life and Faye is unable to persist in trying to convince her, he knows his own limits and realizes that he has "his drop of mercy after all" (341). A few days later, when Elena is preparing to leave, he even offers her the kindness of buying her plane ticket. But, despite this gesture, Faye is in the end still committed to his nihilistic philosophy and to self-testing, as evidenced by his attempt, while driving Elena to the airport, to pass a car on a curve, despite the fact that he knows another vehicle is coming. The ensuing accident puts both Faye and Elena in the hospital, and Faye is eventually sent to jail for carrying an unlicensed gun in the glove compartment of his car, a fate that he is able to accept by viewing it as part of his ongoing "education" in how "to make it" (342) to immoralist extremes.

As for Elena, at this point she is in misery, emotionally spent and utterly alone. Thus when Eitel, who has been summoned by Sergius, arrives at the hospital, Elena begs him to marry her. This act of desperation, however, after previous gallant refusals of Eitel's offers, in no way suggests a loss of dignity. Instead it implies that Elena has reached the point in her life when she must simply clutch at whatever hope she can, however poor. From Eitel's point of view, his acceptance of Elena's plea, while feeling "cold as a stone," certainly does not carry with it any depth of commitment. Indeed, he is still thinking in terms of divorcing Elena if she can find someone else. But Eitel's decision to marry Elena does represent a small act of courage after so much cowardice. For he arrives at what is undoubtedly the central moral perception of Mailer's entire canon: "there was that law of life so cruel and so just which demanded that one must grow or else pay more for remaining the same" (346). And so he realizes that "if he did not marry her he could never forget that he had once made her happy and now she had nothing but her hospital bed," realizing too that "they were mates, the wound of one's flesh soothed by the wound of the other, and that was better than nothing" (346–47).

Of course, the narrative premise of *The Deer Park* is that Eitel's perceptions belong to Sergius as well. And Sergius is able to derive from the failed Eitel's knowledge of life a code of living that provides the key to the survival of his integrity as a human being and an artist. Certainly there is no better way to express that code than to say that Sergius must continue to take the risk of thrusting himself into situations in which the "end is unknown," for there is, indeed, a "law of life" that demands "that one must grow or else pay more for remaining the same." In the final analysis then it is Sergius who must "gamble" his "way to the heart of the mystery against all the power of good manners, good morals, the fear of germs, and the sense of sin" (374).

Robert Merrill has complained about the vagueness of this passage, noting that one does not know what Sergius is "looking for," adding that "even as the novel ends, he cannot really tell us." Indeed, writes Merrill, if Sergius "has arrived at the heart of the mystery, he doesn't reveal its secret to the reader."[4] Undoubtedly, Mailer has not dramatized Sergius's arrival at "the heart of the mystery." But one does know the purpose of the quest. For the novel does make clear—as does the American romantic tradition, of which the book is a part—that "the mystery" is life envisioned from the standpoint of the romantic imagination, life as ever-expanding possibility. In fact, Mailer's image of "the heart of the mystery" suggests his integration of romantic vision with the existential ethic of growth through risk-taking. For it is romantic aspiration, given existential form through a commitment to risk, that creates the possibility for human growth. And so one certainly does know what it means for Sergius to be, like Mailer, an existential artist working within the American romantic tradition: it is his vocation not only to announce the truth of the romantic vision of life but also to explore through the risks of his art the limitless possibilities of expression. In this way he himself brings the vision into being, revealing the intersection of vision and actuality in the language of art while extending for all of us the possibilities of experience. At the same time, he must rebel against any social or political structure that would impose a limit on expression, and so he must indeed "'blow against the walls of every power that exists, the small trumpet of [his] defiance'" (374). In particular, Sergius must rebel against America as the totalitarian betrayer of its own embodiment of romantic vision. For one realizes both that America is the image of "the mystery" and that this image has engendered its own denial. In other words, America is both the land of millennium and the land where anti-subversion committees are convened to protect millennial America's self-proclaimed greatness by extinguishing the freedom of dissent which can make it great and which is but one manifestation of how America has served as an image of ever-expanding possibilities.

Having made these points, one must finally say that the real problem with the conclusion of *The Deer Park* is not the vagueness of "the mystery" but the vagueness of Sergius himself. In fact, Mailer's characterization of Sergius is the source of most of what is problematic about the novel itself. The characterization represents yet another example of Mailer's struggle to create a protagonist who is capable of expressing a significant response to totalitarianism. Although the novel's prevailing thematic interest in Sergius's education is clear and although few readers could fail to grasp the contrast between the failure of courage and integrity in Eitel and his generation and the rebirth of these virtues in Sergius as the romantic artist of a new generation, these concerns are less compelling than they should be because Sergius is insufficiently realized as a character. Most important, Mailer does not dramatize sufficiently the newly educated Sergius, the Sergius who approximates the maturity of the narrator of the novel, who, as the hipsterlike artist, offers a more provocative "rhetoric of engagement" than either Robert Hearn or Mikey

Lovett. One is therefore forced to infer the requisite experience from the substance and style of the narrative voice rather than accept the voice as an expression of dramatized experiences. Thus in the final analysis, Sergius is thematically central without being dramatically interesting.

To solve the problem of characterization that plagues the conclusion of *The Deer Park*, Mailer would have needed at the very least the Sergius of "The Time of Her Time." Rather than the bare outline of Hip narrative that one gets at the end of *The Deer Park*, one would then have the dramatic details of a Sergius in full Hip career as a sexual adventurer defying "the power of good manners, good morals, the fear of germs, and the sense of sin" and gambling his sense of manhood while in pursuit of the ever elusive apocalyptic orgasm. Then one would know full well what Sergius and Mailer mean by the notion, crucial to Hip consciousness, that "'Sex [is] Time, and Time . . . the connection of new circuits'" (375). One would know that both Sergius and Mailer define time in terms of the intensity of one's experience and that both view the quality of the sexual act as the paradigmatic indicator of one's capacity for intense experience. In saying then that "Time [is] the connection of new circuits," Sergius and Mailer are really stating in Hip terms the wisdom of the risktaker, who knows that having intense experience, as, for example, during good sex, makes one capable of even more intense experience in the future.

Of course, "The Time of Her Time," in which Mailer integrates these ideas into the structure of a narrative, was not published until 1959, four years after *The Deer Park* and two years after the first appearance of "The White Negro," Mailer's seminal essay in which he first formulates his philosophy of Hip. And, as I will show, this new Hip consciousness was crucial in liberating Mailer's imagination so that he could begin creating characters who are more dynamic, more resourceful, and, indeed, in some cases, more violent than the protagonists of the first three books. It is these later characters who are able finally to represent within themselves the dialectic of millennial America—a dialectic between the cancerous growth of totalitarianism and moral cowardice, which results in a denial of history, and the abiding possibility of achieving a mythic sense of freedom through risktaking, which could allow one to experience in one's own life the discovery of a New World of limitless expression.

Chapter 5

"The White Negro": Seminal Mailer

The seminal importance of "The White Negro" in Norman Mailer's canon raises several crucial questions concerning the nature of both Mailer's imagination and his work that critics have never satisfactorily answered. First of all, why should the writing of an essay have had such a profound effect on the career of a writer who has always considered himself to be preeminently a novelist? In this regard, how precisely did the figure of the hipster and his violent, nihilistic philosophy generate for Mailer possibilities for characterization and narrative action that were not previously available to him? As I have argued, totalitarianism was the source of Mailer's early aesthetic problems, and it has served throughout his career as the cultural and political object of his theme of rebellion. How then did the philosophy of Hip liberate Mailer's imagination so that he could solve his early aesthetic problems and give significant form to his rebellion against totalitarianism? And finally, since violence is central to the nature of both the totalitarian threat to Mailer's art and his response to that threat, what for Mailer is the precise relationship among violence, freedom, and creativity, and what are the ethical implications of that relationship?

To begin with, one must say that Mailer is the kind of writer whom critics with rather limited notions of genre find difficult to understand. Not only is he at home in such literary twilight zones as the nonfiction novel, the novel biography, and the imaginary memoir, but he produces novels that derive much of their force

69

and direction from theological, philosophical, and political ideas. The critical response to Mailer's attraction to nonfiction and his commitment to ideas has been predictable. Motivated perhaps by the desire to protect the purity of narrative fiction against the intrusion of ideas, not to mention ideology, many critics have eagerly relegated novelist Mailer to the rank of journalist or essayist, as if they were giving him a literary demotion. Of course, by such a standard, Melville, Dostoevsky, Mann, and Lawrence might likewise be demoted. Quite clearly, in some very great writers the novelistic imagination may be impelled rather than impeded by ideas.

In American literature ideas have extraordinary prominence. This book has taken as its constant frame of reference the prevailing theme of millennialism in the history of American ideas and has implied that throughout American literature the novelistic, as well as the poetic, imagination has been inspired by the idea of the American as Adam in a New World of limitless possibilities. And such is certainly the case with the imagination of Norman Mailer. However idiosyncratic in detail, his work has always stood at the center of the American literary tradition, for it has shared the same millennialistic assumptions about America that have helped shape virtually all great American literature. Indeed, to reveal what truly animates Mailer's work, one must go even further and state that it is characteristically involved in an implicit defense of the American myth itself. As I indicated in chapter 1, totalitarianism is, at its most intimidating, not evil but amoral. It does not typically reenact the myth of the Fall through a new corruption of innocence but instead denies the validity of the myth altogether—eliminating meaning as dialectical relatedness while extinguishing personality and asserting the inconsequence of life. The terms of the Adamic myth, however, provide the key to its preservation, for the Adamic figure is by definition prior to society. Although, as Melville dramatizes in *Typee*, such a state of prelapsarian innocence has, likewise by definition, no historical validity, as a romantic conception it nevertheless has the greatest imaginative value: it establishes that the imagination can create for itself an Archimedean point from which it can initiate rebellion. In other words, it reveals the romantic possibilities inherent in alienation as an existential approximation of the Adamic condition, allowing the modern romantic hero a point in space so that, standing in imagination apart from society, he can slough off "the old skin" and experience rebirth.[1]

It is only within this mythic context that one can understand why "The White Negro" represents a turning point in Norman Mailer's career. Mailer's early protagonists are alienated but empty, the force of their protest a romantic derivation from the American literary tradition. To free his work from its derivativeness and give his characters the force of individuality, Mailer first had to make the tradition his own. He did this by recreating in his own terms the generative myth of American culture. For "The White Negro" is essentially an act of myth-making presented in the form of an essay; it is a work of fiction that has as its hero a prototypical character, manifestly Adamic and manifestly the model for both Stephen Rojack and D. J. Jethroe.

The extent to which critics have not recognized the mythic quality of "The White Negro" provides an accurate measure of their failure to apprehend the prevailing spirit of American literature itself. Speculating, for example, on how many hipsters were walking the streets of Greenwich Village in 1957 or wondering whether there were ever really any hipsters at all, at least as Mailer describes them, misses the point about as much as the recent search of several misguided fundamentalists for the wood that composed Noah's Ark. In either case, one should not be concerned with an excavation of history but with a contemplation of mythic materials. In other words, though Mailer as author is allowed the luxury of believing in the historical hipster, perhaps as a necessity of composition, the literary critic should be largely unconcerned and care about the hipster as White Negro only insofar as he serves as the raw material of myth, thereby providing at last the means for Mailer to formulate a significant response to the threat of totalitarianism.

"The White Negro" constitutes this response. And it chooses

for its point of departure the relationship between death and meaning, as exposed in most intimidating psychological and moral detail by the totalitarian interpretation of life. As Mailer notes,

Probably, we will never be able to determine the psychic havoc of the concentration camps and the atom bomb upon the unconscious mind of almost everyone alive in these years. For the first time in civilized history, perhaps for the first time in all of history, we have been forced to live with the suppressed knowledge that the smallest facets of our personality or the most minor projection of our ideas, or indeed the absence of ideas and the absence of personality could mean equally well that we might still be doomed to die as a cipher in some vast statistical operation in which our teeth would be counted, and our hair would be saved, but our death itself would be unknown, unhonored, and unremarked, a death which could not follow with dignity as a possible consequence to serious actions we had chosen, but rather a death by *deus ex machina* in a gas chamber or a radioactive city. (Adv. 338)

In this opening passage of "The White Negro," Mailer lays bare the fundamental message of totalitarianism as communicated through the instrument of holocaust. Quite simply, it is that human beings do not matter, for what is annihilable is assumed to be necessarily inconsequential. Two prior conclusions are implicit in this message: (1) human beings are nothing more than biochemical machines; (2) the forms of organic material are phenomenologically diverse but essentially equivalent. They are nonmoral counters that derive their significance only from their utility. The assumption of racial or national supremacy in no way belies these conclusions, for it is, for example, the Aryan race or the German nation, abstracted from its relation to any individual Aryan or German, that is assumed to be significant and enduring, and each person has value only insofar as he contributes to perpetuating the collective ideal of the Third Reich.

Thus from the totalitarian point of view, if one were able to complete an inventory of the human biochemical makeup and note the phenomena attending the various atomic or subatomic combinations, one would reach the epistemological limits of psychology and exhaust all that could be said about the human machine. Furthermore, in assuming an equivalence of forms, totalitarian thought goes beyond substituting for the concept of identity a biochemical summing of parts and obliterates all intrinsic distinctions of value. Given this logic, in the final analysis a living and breathing human being shares with a pile of radioactive ash, a bar of soap, or a lamp shade composed of human remains the same absence of value. And so one realizes that totalitarianism is actually a political application of the most reductive conclusions of nihilism. Once such a view gains ascendancy, morality is rendered irrelevant, while the only principle left to direct social and political behavior is the monomaniacal imperative to satisfy a despotic will to power, which attempts to establish historical legitimacy and a popular basis of support through claims of racial or national supremacy.

Certainly Mailer is right in insisting that it is not only people who have lived through internment in concentration camps or survived the bombing of Hiroshima or Nagasaki who are marked by the horror of World War II's mass exterminations. We are now all psychological victims of holocaust. As the threat of an impersonal death by atomic annihilation looms over the entire world, we have each been compelled to absorb the nihilistic message of totalitarianism, which asserts that human life is inconsequential and that death is extinction. Like Bellow's Sammler, we must all crawl out of the grave dug by history and struggle to find a way in which we can yet believe in the significance and dignity of our own lives.

In affirming this imperative, Mailer attempts to resurrect meaning through a method that is provocative both in the boldness of its approach and in its subtle philosophical syncretism. For he attempts to rediscover meaning precisely at the point at which one might assume it to have been lost: he responds to the ever-present threat of collective, impersonal annihilation and the totalitarian assumption that death is extinction with the belief, unsupported by any orthodox religious foundation, that death must become the source of meaning for modern men and women. At the same time he combines the apparent incompatibles of existential ethics, a nihilistic rejection of the demands of civilization, and a transcendentalist faith in the life of the spirit in order to find a way to recreate the possibility of rebellion on the political left, which had been paralyzed partly by an ironic intersection of liberal and totalitarian viewpoints and partly by a simple lack of courage.

Mailer assumes correctly that most liberal humanists believe in the existence of nothing beyond what they may infer from sensory data while evaluating this information with a thoroughgoing skepticism derived as much from personal and political betrayal as from the relativistic conclusions of twentieth-century science. Indeed, there would seem to be no other tenable epistemology available, and with the assumption that atheism is prerequisite to intellectual legitimacy, one would seem to have little choice but to forge a philosophy from the conclusions of positivism, Freudian psychology, or Sartrean existentialism.

For the atheistic humanist, all but hopelessly skeptical about the ethical foundations of civilization—seeing through the mask of religious ideas, cultural ideals, and art to the amoral instincts of copulation and killing—the holocaust of World War II provided an undeniable confirmation, a kind of historical précis and proof, of the truths that he feared the most, namely the tenuous continuity of civilization and the enduring depravity of human beings. For it is the shock of these truths that can transform humanistic concern for the well-being of others into self-interested nihilism. Moreover, as Mailer notes, "since he conceives of death as emptiness," the atheist "can, no matter how weary or despairing, wish for nothing but more life," for "his pride" depends on renouncing the "romantic longing for death" that would self-deceptively turn "weakness and spiritual fatigue" (Adv. 342) into a beautiful personal tragedy and so substitute narcissism for the search for meaning. Thus once he abandons his humanism, the only real choice for the atheist is to continue to live at any cost and so draw the fine distinction between the value of an all-encompassing self-interest and a romantic and morbid narcissism.

As Mailer knows, the result of such skepticism and despair, driven by the instinct to survive, is all too often the politics of conformity, politics actively advanced by the right and silently supported by the forlorn left, precisely the politics which dominated the American scene throughout the 1950s and which has reemerged disturbingly with an even more widespread complicity of the left in the values of the so-called Me Generation of the 1970s and early 1980s. The logic behind such conformity is clear: since civilization is deemed to have value only insofar as it insures one's own survival, one is willing to accept the prevailing social order as long as it does not interfere with the cultivation of one's own garden, a decidedly insular interpretation of "life, liberty, and the pursuit of happiness." Thus one would oppose, for example, the apocalyptic threat of Nazism but accept in silence the less immediately threatening forms of native totalitarianism, such as McCarthyism or the growth of the secret, conspiratorial power of the CIA. In the end, like Charles Francis Eitel of *The Deer Park*, one publicly applauds the appearance of freedom that is really the right to remain politically unthreatening, while one justifies cowardice with a cynical and elitist insistence on the importance of continuing one's own work.

In response to such intellectual and political conformity, Mailer offers in "The White Negro" the example of "the American existentialist—the hipster, the man who knows that if our collective condition is to live with instant death by atomic war, relatively quick death by the State as *l'univers concentrationnaire*, or with a slow death by conformity with every creative and rebellious instinct stifled (at what damage to the mind and the heart and the liver and the nerves no research foundation for cancer will discover in a hurry) . . . then the only life-giving answer is to accept the terms of death, to live with death as immediate danger, to divorce oneself from society, to exist without roots, to set out on that uncharted journey into the rebellious imperatives of the self" (Adv. 339).

With this announcement Mailer creates his Adamic figure and distinguishes him from the erstwhile humanist who lives in a relation of bad faith with civilization, clinging to it as a safeguard against human depravity but defending it only when his own life is threatened. What Mailer might later call a left-conservative alternative to such isolationism would be to push skepticism to the limits of self-consciousness and so become "skeptical about skepticism."[2] Such an attitude would recognize the inherent self-destructiveness of single-minded skepticism, concluding with Thomas Mann that cultural ideals and art, "the lies of life," are "indispensible" to survival and that one must live those lies for love of the truth "in bitter irony and anguished pessimism."[3] In so doing, one would transform bad faith into ironic virtue and recreate social concern upon a new foundation.

The Mailer of *The Armies of the Night* could embrace such a view enthusiastically and delight in its strategy of renewing humanistic faith through a subtle, paradoxical doubling of doubt. But at the time of the composition of "The White Negro," Mailer's romanticism was at its peak, unabashed and unrestrained, and so he had to struggle to render convincing quite a different paradox. Thus in "The White Negro," he continues to challenge, as he had in his earlier work, the optimistic bias of conventional liberalism, arguing that the murderousness of society reflects the capacity for murder within each of us. At the same time, however, Mailer is compelled by his romantic faith in the limitless expressive possibilities of the free and isolate self to insist that it is the institution of society that activates the potential for inhumane violence that exists within us all. Accordingly, it is society as a "collective creation," a Frankenstein monster of history lost to individual control, which is unjust and which presents a "crippled and perverted . . . image of man" (Adv. 338) even as it continues to cripple and pervert him, inciting greed and ruthlessness with the prospect of securing a disproportionate share of wealth and political power.

Thus in "The White Negro," Mailer rejoins the familiar debate between romanticism and classicism over the relationship between the self and society, countermanding the modern humanist's ethical critique of social organization: rather than protecting humanity against self-destructive urges, society perverts those urges and renders them inhumane and destructive. What is required is therefore not an ironic recommitment to sublimation and social cooperation to perpetuate for the sake of human survival a society in which one no longer believes but a romantic rejection of society and a liberation of instinct in order to regain for oneself an identity of Adamic innocence, correspondent to Whitman's "Me myself," that was all but irremediably lost to history. Moreover, if it is ultimately society that is evil, then acceptance of the values of society is anathema as total conformity becomes equivalent to the death of innocence. Indeed, Mailer argues that it is only by accepting alienation as a given, only by living outside the values of a corrupt society and thereby becoming a psychological outlaw, that one has the chance of discovering within oneself that particle of innocent being that may be left unperverted and so preserve the hope that one may yet recover one's individuality. And it is precisely this imperative to reclaim the self that constitutes the romantic program and purpose of the philosophy of Hip. As Mailer notes,

whether the life is criminal or not, the decision is to encourage the psychopath in oneself, to explore that domain of experience where security is boredom and therefore sickness, and one exists in the present, in that enormous present which is without past or future, memory or planned intention, the life where a man must go until he is beat, where he must gamble with his energies through all those small or large crises of courage and unforeseen situations which beset his day, where he must be with it or doomed not to swing. The unstated essence of Hip, its psychopathic brilliance, quivers with the knowledge that new kinds of victories increase one's power for new kinds of perception; and defeats, the wrong kind of defeats, attack the body and imprison one's energy until one is jailed in the prison air of other people's habits, other people's defeats, boredom, quiet desperation, and muted icy self-destroying rage. (Adv. 339)

Once again Mailer identifies courage as the primary virtue, a preeminence underscored in the case of the hipster since his status as outsider liberates him from the security of convention and routine and transforms his life into a series of existential situations in which the "end is unknown" and danger is ever present. For Mailer, the historic model for the hipster is the Negro since he has been forced by the legacy of slavery and the persistence of racial hatred and discrimination to live "on the margin between totalitarianism and democracy for two centuries" (Adv. 340), a description that remains substantially true today, despite the advances won by the civil rights movement, especially for blacks who have not been assimilated culturally and economically into white, middle-class America.

Mailer's use of the Negro, however, as a historic source for his myth of rebellion remains problematic. For it involves him in creating an image of the Negro as a latter-day noble savage who is able to survive despite discrimination not only by developing a healthy paranoia that can alert him instantly to the presence of danger but by "following the need of his body" and living for a virtuosic indulgence in sensual pleasure. Clearly, Mailer intends only high praise while wishing to provide an antecedent for his hipster-hero, who also cultivates a self-protecting paranoia and gives full range "to his rage and the infinite variations of joy, lust, langour, growl, cramp, pinch, scream and despair of his orgasm" (Adv. 341). But Mailer's depiction of the Negro can easily be interpreted as an approximation of the racist stereotype of the black as an irresponsible, pleasure-seeking, sexual athlete who wears his subjection lightly. At the same time it perpetuates a social fiction, which has appeared in both left romantic and aristocratic conservative versions and which insists respectively that primitivist virtue or an exploitable immorality flourishes in racial minorities in particular and the lower class in general.

Actually Mailer uses the social fiction of the Negro as primitive merely to illustrate his own myth of primitivism, which has its symbolic source in the Adamic tradition of American literature and its psychological basis in a Reichian critique of the pessimistic and ascetic conclusions of *Civilization and Its Discontents*. Moreover, Mailer is attempting to press the integrity of an idea that must be considered separately from the primitivist social fiction with which it has been associated. He is arguing that if one is forced to remain outside bourgeois society, then by virtue of that exclusion, one may be freed at least in part from the bondage of sublimation and hypocritical middle-class morality. In short, Mailer is insisting that there is indeed a psychological and moral advantage to remaining outside society and that the situation of the Negro is emblematic of the condition of all outsiders—even Hip dropouts from America's middle class. According to Mailer it was jazz that further heightened the sense of alienation in the white urban avant-garde who "had absorbed the lessons of disillusionment and disgust of the twenties, the depression, and the war" and accepted the "categorical imperative," which Mailer associates primarily with Hemingway, "that what made [one] feel good became therefore The Good." Thus in "such places as Greenwich Village a ménage-à-trois was completed—the bohemian and the juvenile delinquent came face-to-face with the Negro, and the hipster [as white Negro] was a fact in American life" (Adv. 340).

Clearly, Mailer's strategy is to turn loss into gain and despair into hope as the windfall of alienation creates the freedom to live dangerously in the knowledge that it is only through risktaking that psychological and moral growth is ever possible. This strategy is best illustrated by Mailer's description of the hipster's attitude toward death. Condemned by his consciousness of holocaust to live with an absurd sense of the constant threat of death, the hipster as existentialist avoids being limited to the vulnerability of the atheist's desire for more life, choosing instead to engage death by embracing a faith born of despair. As Mailer notes, "the real argument which the mystic must always advance is the very intensity of his private vision." If his visionary experience gives him intimations of possibilities for relationship that move beyond the physical and the subjective and into the mystical and the mysterious—intimations of Buber's I and Thou—he will certainly pause before speaking about his experience. But he knows that it cannot be dismissed by rationalist incomprehension or be explained away by a thousand "skeptical reductions." Neither will he be silenced by the hypothesis of "oceanic feelings,"

Freud's rather facile explanation of the mystic's sense of the unity of all creation as being a remnant of the infantile confusion of subject and object. For his "inner experience of the possibilities within death" has become "his logic" (Adv. 342).

In "The White Negro" precisely what Mailer means by "the possibilities within death" remains implicit, but in subsequent writings he has clarified and developed these early suggestions into an elaborate view of death, which one might describe as eschatological existentialism. Mailer's introduction to "The Eleventh Presidential Paper—Death" provides perhaps the best explanation of this view, for he argues there that "existentialism is rootless unless one dares the hypothesis that death is an existential continuation of life, that the soul may either pass through migrations, or cease to exist in the continuum of nature." In this way, "authenticity and commitment return to the center of ethics, for man then faces no peril so huge as alienation from his own soul, a death which is other than death, a disappearance into nothingness rather than into Eternity" (PP 214).

Mailer uses the word "soul" conventionally here with the significant exception that he does not mean that which is immortal in humanity but that which can be immortal. According to Mailer, one lives through death only if one has had the courage to live his life as a war in which he is always conscious in the "enormous present" of how every action makes him a little better or a little worse as a human being, for every action increases or decreases his possibilities of expression. Once he adopts this view, "authenticity and commitment return to the center of ethics" because life is again seen as being consequential as one assumes responsibility for one's actions. A sense of meaning likewise returns to life since death is no longer understood as the termination of all relationships. Instead it becomes the ultimate existential experience.

The existential ethic that Mailer espouses has another significant implication. In allowing one to exist in that "enormous present which is without past or future, memory or planned intention," it substitutes personal for historical time and so

defeats the most subtle and insidious effect of totalitarianism—
the determination of the very nature and rhythms of one's experience. As Mailer indicates in "Hip, Hell, and the Navigator," a
1958 interview with Richard G. Stern that serves as a kind of
informal appendix to "The White Negro," as one's awareness
intensifies, one's sense of time alters. Each moment fills, becoming more resonant and complex. Correspondingly, one's experience of time slows down. Such an alteration in one's sense of time
is a key element of the Hip quest for freedom. It means that one is
now able to control the rhythms of one's own experience and live
out of what is really a transcendentalist sense that one can
recreate one's own identity out of the eternity of the present
moment and so escape temporarily from the limits of history.
From this subjective standpoint, the future exists only as vision, a
romantic vision of ever-expanding possibilities merging with
one's experience of freedom in the present. At the same time,
while a sense of moral responsibility, reflected by a belief in "the
possibilities within death," persists, thereby maintaining an existential connection to history, the past itself is perceived only in
terms of a psychological and moral inheritance that must be
rejected. As Mailer notes,

Generally we are obliged to act with a nervous system which has been
formed from infancy, and which carries in the style of its circuits the
very contradictions of our parents and our early milieu. Therefore, we
are obliged, most of us, to meet the tempo of the present and the future
with reflexes and rhythms which come from the past. It is not only the
"dead weight of the institutions of the past" but indeed the inefficient
and often antiquated nervous circuits of the past which strangle our
potentiality for responding to new possibilities which might be exciting
for our individual growth. (Adv. 345)

But as "a philosophical psychopath" (Adv. 343) who rebel-
liously pursues the desire for immediate gratification while maintaining at the same time the detachment necessary to understand
why he acts as he does, the hipster attempts to liberate himself
from the burden of the past by passing through prohibitions,
meeting them at the very point "of their creation":

and so the psychopath exploring backward along the road of the homosexual, the orgiast, the drug-addict, the rapist, the robber and the murderer seeks to find those violent parallels to the violent and often hopeless contradictions he knew as an infant and as a child. For if he has the courage to meet the parallel situation at the moment when he is ready, then he has a chance to act as he has never acted before, and in satisfying the frustration—if he can succeed—he may then pass by symbolic substitute through the locks of incest. In thus giving expression to the buried infant in himself, he can lessen the tension of those infantile desires and so free himself to remake a bit of his nervous system. (Adv. 346)

The hipster's program of liberation raises, of course, the controversial question of the ethical implications of the theme of violence that is so prominent in much of Mailer's work. Indeed, its prominence has served for years a a pretext for some of the most vehement *ad hominem* attacks on Mailer himself. The most vulgar and the most common of these attacks assume, either unreflectively or cynically, that a simple, one-to-one relationship exists between life and art. The purpose is typically to do a hatchet job on Mailer, so, with an ill-disguised sense of moral superiority, such incidents as Mailer's stabbing of his second wife, Adele Morales, or his support of murderer-writer Jack Henry Abbott are combined with references to the theme of violence as it appears in Mailer's work to substantiate the preconception that Norman Mailer is a brutish, reckless, and immoral man who writes brutish, reckless, and immoral books.

Mailer has, of course, left himself amazingly vulnerable to such underhanded intellectual violence. He has chosen throughout much of his career to lead a public life that has been consistently sensationalistic, sometimes with disastrous results, and his combative personality and immense ego have exacerbated literary jealousies. In short, Mailer has made enemies while helping them to create a caricature of himself in the public mind. In making such a point, however, one is likewise indicating that Mailer's harshest critics are seldom disinterested. And certainly Mailer's personal flaws in no way extenuate intellectually dishonest criticism or diminish the disservice done to readers by critics who insist that a writer's life may be used as a ready weapon to attack his work. Moreover, an artist's life is never a perfect reflection of his work, and only a highly gifted and exhaustive critical biographer is ever able to express with reasonable approximation the actual relationship between an artist's life and work, combining psychological and critical analysis to arrive, by an integration of daring and restraint, at a truth that seeks to be both comprehensive and tentative.

The purposes of critical biography lie well outside the range of this book, which attempts as much as possible to elucidate and evaluate Mailer's work without being distracted by his imposing personality. And when one takes such an approach to Mailer's view of violence, attempting to understand it as it is embodied in his work, one realizes that, like virtually every other aspect of his writing, it is far more complicated than most critics have yet acknowledged. As I indicated in chapter 1, initially Mailer had a rather conventional view of the morality of violence. Though he felt its emotional and aesthetic attraction, he saw it as necessarily inhumane, associating it with totalitarianism as personified in such characters as Cummings, Croft, and Hollingsworth. But then he began to develop in *The Deer Park* and in several of his 1956 *Village Voice* pieces a belief that the totalitarian denial of personality forced one into the position of either passively accepting or absolutely rejecting conventional sexual and moral standards that helped to perpetuate a right-wing political establishment. In other words, he saw American life in the mid-1950s as a war between totalitarian repression and romantic aspiration and believed that liberation from repression necessarily involved one in compensatory violence sanctioned by the ethics of a just war.

The problem with this view is that Mailer begins ironically to sound all too much like G. Gordon Liddy, an ideological opposite, who continues to argue on talk shows and the college lecture circuit that the United States government—by which he means the extreme right wing of the Republican Party—is engaged in a de facto war against communism, which justifies not only political dirty tricks in general and the Watergate burglary in particular but every imaginable criminal act, including kidnapping and assassination. Of course, Mailer separates himself completely from the likes of Liddy not only by affirming radically different political goals but also by maintaining, at least from the mid-1950s to the writing of *The Armies of the Night*, an absolute faith, however naive, in the creative potential of the free, unrepressed, primitive self, a faith that is given definitive expression in a central passage of "The White Negro":

the nihilism of Hip proposes as its final tendency that every social restraint and category be removed, and the affirmation implicit in the proposal is that man would then prove to be more creative than murderous and so not destroy himself. Which is exactly what separates Hip from the authoritarian philosophies which now appeal to the conservative and liberal temper—what haunts the middle of the twentieth century is that faith in man has been lost, and the appeal of authority has been that it would restrain us from ourselves. Hip, which would return us to ourselves, at no matter what price in individual violence, is the affirmation of the barbarian, for it requires a primitive passion about human nature to believe that individual acts of violence are always to be preferred to the collective violence of the State; it takes literal faith in the creative possibilities of the human being to envisage acts of violence as the catharsis which prepares growth. (Adv. 355)

Of course, with his penchant for paradox and his love of extremes, Mailer gets himself into trouble by admitting the risk involved in such romantic faith: hoodlum hipsters might seek to "purge" their violence by beating in "the brains of a candy-store keeper" (Adv. 347). Individual violence might merge with collective violence, with hipsters turned "storm troopers" following "the first truly magnetic leader whose view of mass murder is phrased in a language which reaches their emotions." Clearly, however much Mailer values a free and untrammeled self, in such cases what feels good would not turn out to the "The Good" but evil incarnated in a Mansonlike orgy of blood. But for Mailer, at the time of writing "The White Negro," there seemed no real alternative to maintaining the romantic faith that, once outside society, the hipster would realize "that his condition [was] no more than an exaggeration of the human condition, and that if he would be free, then everyone must be free" (Adv. 355), precisely the truth that Cummings and Croft, operating within the confines of the American military, were not willing to admit. And so unlike the nihilism of the purely self-interested humanist manqué or the monomaniacal totalitarian, the hipster's nihilism is, according to Mailer, creative as well as socially and politically liberating as the quest for "the apocalyptic orgasm" (Adv. 347) draws the hipster as sexual revolutionary to embrace the principles of political democracy.

In addition to his democratic potential, the hipster maintains as central to his vision of existence a religious belief that likewise redeems him from the tendency toward either narcissistic self-interest or nihilistic self-destruction. According to Mailer, the hipster believes in the existence of God, but it is not a conventional faith in an all-powerful creator who exists eternally, apart from his creation, in a state of inscrutable perfection. Instead the hipster believes that the imperfections of existence itself—most significantly the conflicts of human experience—belie the possibility of a perfect creator. For the hipster, God is conceivable only as a reflection of reality, existing "as a warring element in a divided universe" (Adv. 380). In other words, God is immanent, existing within nature and humanity in a state of becoming. Accordingly, God is not only limited in knowledge and power but involved in promoting a vision of reality that may not succeed, for the outcome of the conflict of existence, epitomized by the conflict between good and evil, is still unknown. Thus the hipster believes that the purposes of God and man are interdependent and that in each moment one's actions affect not only one's own moral condition but the moral economy of the universe as well.

This unorthodox theology, no doubt baffling to some readers and critics, has survived Mailer's preoccupation with Hip, assuming a place of central importance in his work but especially in *An American Dream* and *Of a Fire on the Moon*. As Mailer has exhaustively elaborated this theology, along with a host of other metaphysical ideas, it may well have seemed to this puzzled audience to become only more eccentric and arcane. But Mailer's ideas are actually not as odd as they may at first seem. Or perhaps one should state that if they are indeed odd, they are not at all alone in the history of ideas but have rather formidable support. The idea of an immanent God who exists in a state of becoming is implicit in Jung's insistence that there is no empirical difference between symbolic representations of the archetypes of the self and the God-image and in his central concept of individuation, which suggests that human and divine development is integrated in a process that can be interpreted either psychologically or metaphysically. The existence of an immanent God is likewise implicit in Buber's conception of the I-and-Thou relationship. And when one understands that Jung and Buber are both essentially transcendentalist thinkers, using respectively the languages of psychology and theology to describe the existence of an immanent spiritual reality, one has accomplished the kind of distillation of ideas necessary to discover the essential philosophical relationship between them and Mailer while identifying a significant part of Mailer's own intellectual orientation as well. For when one sees through the surface eccentricity of Mailer's theological ideas, one unmistakably perceives that their existentialism is modified to a considerable degree by transcendentalist attitudes and values, epitomized by the belief that man is God become conscious of himself and that through the exercise of individual will the self is able to merge with the immanent will of nature "until the world becomes at last only a realized will,—the double of the man."[4]

Critics have for the most part failed to emphasize the connection between Mailer and transcendentalism despite the fact that there are a multitude of connections that have been obvious for years and that help clarify much that seems obscure or eccentric in his thinking. Perhaps critics have been put off the track by the naturalism of *The Naked and the Dead* or the socialist politics and existential psychology of *Barbary Shore*. Certainly Mailer's subsequent preoccupation with existentialism has helped to direct critical attention away from his transcendentalist cast of mind. Furthermore, there are significant differences between Mailer and the transcendentalists. Despite Emerson's insistence on the power of individual will and his contention that one must be an "active soul," for without action "thought can never ripen into truth,"[5] there remains as fundamental to transcendentalism the assumption that nature is the source of action: nature engenders truth; man observes and asks questions, which the design of nature itself can answer. But as Laura Adams notes, there is nothing passive about Mailer's psychology.[6] His observation that the language of Hip describes man "as a vector in a network of forces" (Adv. 349) also suggests his conception of the paradigmatic risktaking personality. Moreover, unlike the pure transcendentalist, Mailer does not believe that evil is a privation of good. Instead it exists as an active and necessary dialectical principle equal in power to good. Indeed, for Mailer it is impossible to conceive of moral and psychological qualities without also imagining their opposites. For him such qualities exist necessarily in conflict and compensation in a constant state of "Heraclitean flux,"[7] a condition that reflects the state of external reality as well. Thus if Mailer's God is an anthropomorphic expression of the immanence of romantic vision, that is, the existence of a universe of ever-expanding possibilities, then his Devil is the personification of an immanent counteractive tendency toward appropriation that results in universal contraction and decreation. Rather like a black hole, Mailer's Devil is the ontological counterpart of both the totalitarian will to power and nihilistic self-destruction.

For Mailer, human complicity in decreation constitutes both a cowardly defeat and a demonic betrayal of divine potential. But, however detestable, such a defeat is at least moral and, therefore, preferable to the experience of absurd impotence. And so Mailer would argue that in any case his dread-inducing theology presents a view that is elevating and ennobling, giving purpose and dignity to life, for if God "is trying to impose upon the universe His conception of being against other conceptions of being very much opposed to His," then perhaps "we are in a sense the seed, the seed-carriers, the voyagers, the explorers, the embodiment of that embattled vision; maybe we are engaged in a heroic activity, and not a mean one" (Adv. 380–81). Along with the existential ethic implicit in this theology comes a new estimation of the value of guilt, which becomes an emotional indicator of morally significant acts and dictates to the risktaker an inversion of traditional moral imperatives: one performs a forbidden act despite feeling guilt-ridden. Indeed, the experience of guilt serves only to increase the existential ante as one breaks through the inherited prohibition.

Such ideas, largely reflections of Mailer's existentialism, are of course foreign to transcendentalist thought. Having admitted these differences, however, one must emphasize that the beliefs, attitudes, and values that Mailer shares with transcendentalists are numerous and significant and that they often complement his existentialism. Like the transcendentalists, Mailer believes that matter is infused with spiritual significance—to such an extent that he often reveals himself to be an out–and–out animist. Not only does he invariably view almost every aspect of the real world in terms of what he believes are its inherent moral or spiritual qualities, as reflected most dramatically in what for many is his perverse obsession with the spiritual properties and revelatory potential of human waste, but he has attributed to nature a highly active, self-directing life of its own. For example, he believes that various foods may be indigestible because they actually contain moral qualities that one is not yet brave enough to appropriate; that spermatozoa are capable of passion and will; that guilt may be present in one's enzymes; and that any aspect of nature may itself become the habitation of a transmigrating soul.

For Mailer then nature is portentous, epiphanic, and densely populated with armies of spiritual forces. What Mailer calls "magic" is essentially the intervention of these forces into one's own life, and their manifestation, as exemplified in private prophetic voices or synchronistic phenomena, marks the intersection of transcendental reality with the world of sense experience. Mailer's belief in magic likewise represents one of the many points at which his transcendentalism and existentialism meet.

And once one gains an adequate sense of how transcendentalist attitudes are as basic to Mailer's point of view as his existentialism, realizing that they often fuse to help give meaning and depth to life, one also perceives that Mailer's involvement in the irrational and supersensible has a serious philosophical and moral purpose. Moreover, his sometimes bewildering ecclecticism in no way belies the coherence of his attitudes and values. For example, there is no philosophical disparity implicit in Mailer's decision to write a series of reflections on Buber's mystical *Tales of the Hasidim* and his enthusiasm in *The Fight* for Bantu philosophy. In each case, he is affirming a transcendentalist ontology and an existential ethic: magic does indeed exist, and risktaking is life-sustaining and necessary to moral growth. Thus in one of his commentaries on Buber, he notes that the story "The Test," which depicts a synchronous relationship between a man's cynical lack of faith and the death of his son, suggests "an underworld of real events whose connection is never absurd" (PP 153). To comprehend such a world and survive in it, one must abandon the apparent sanity of reductive reasoning and live with a primitive sense of awe before the irrational, thereby risking charges of superstition or paranoia. In this regard, the source of Mailer's attraction to Bantu philosophy is evident, for it conceives of humans as forces rather than beings, a totemic conception—close to Mailer's idea of the vectorlike hipster—suggesting that "a man was not only what he contained, not only his desires, his memory, and his personality, but also the forces that came to inhabit him at any moment from all things living and dead. So a man was not only himself, but the karma of all the generations past that still lived in him. . . . He would take his balance, his quivering place, in a field of all the forces of the living and the dead."[8]

The point of interpreting Mailer's views within a context of transcendentalist and existentialist relationships is not so much to try to tame his wild ideas as it is to elucidate them and reveal their essential consistency, emerging, characteristically for Mailer, out of an interpenetration of philosophies. Furthermore, it is worthwhile to note that most of the attitudes and ideas that critics have so often identified with Mailer's existentialism have a transcendentalist aspect as well. Along with his view that matter manifests spirit, that man is God become conscious of himself, and that the purpose of existence is the evolution of consciousness, one thinks especially of Mailer's epistemological preference for intuition, emotion, instinct, and imagination over reductive reasoning; his substitution of myth and biography for history; his identification of the center of personality as a kind of innocent, Adamic "Me myself," which can be discovered only by rejecting the values of a conformist society in favor of self-reliance; his distinction between organic individualizing development and inorganic replicating growth; his insistence, in architectural critiques and discussions of morphology and style, that form must follow function; and his conception of the writer as a disturbing, experimenting prophet-seer whose vocation is to write literature that saves lives. Though in Mailer's work each of these attitudes and ideas contains an undeniable existentialist component, each is unmistakably transcendentalist in orientation as well.

As I have indicated, when these ideas began to become a force in Mailer's work, developing out of his philosophy of Hip as expressed quintessentially in "The White Negro" and the Richard G. Stern interview, new possibilities for characterization and narrative action became available to Mailer. He became capable of creating, what I have termed, dialectical characters who dramatize the full range of oppositions that Mailer believes are inherent in humanity and nature. Thus instead of being limited to depicting apparently noble self-sacrifice or only fugitive hints of rebellion and political commitment or education through negative example, as in the respective narratives of Robert Hearn, Mikey Lovett, and Sergius O'Shaugnessy, and instead of abandoning epic possibilities for the anti-heroic, Bellovian compromises and resignations of a character such as Sam Slovoda, Mailer now had conceived of a way of dramatizing strength along with weakness and victory as well as defeat. Like the hipster, Mailer's protagonists would still be victims of the totalitarianism of American life, embodying within themselves "the extreme contradictions of the society which formed" them. But now they would also have a complete program of liberation along with a heroic mission that elevated them to the level of divine agents in the conflict between God and the Devil. Indeed, now they could attempt to remake their nervous systems and reclaim a mythic sense of Adamic innocence by violently breaking through internalized prohibitions and acting out their instinctual desires. In so doing, they would attempt to reject society completely and opt for the freedom of alienation. Of course, they might still fail in the end to find new freedom and creativity through the purgation of violence. As Mailer suggests with regard to the hipster, total rejection of society may exist more as a romantic goal than as an achievable reality, and "there are clusters and nests and ambushes of violence in [the hipster's] own necessities and in the imperatives and retaliations of the men and women among whom he lives his life, so that even as he drains his hatred in one act or another, so the conditions of his life create it anew in him until the drama of his movements bears a sardonic resemblance to the frog who climbed a few feet in the well only to drop back again" (Adv. 347). Nevertheless, despite the uncertainty of success, the philosophy of Hip would still provide Mailer's protagonists with an existential strategy and transcendentalist goals directed beyond the self so that a powerful response to totalitarianism would finally be possible—a response that would be both politically and spiritually significant as well as heroic in its ultimate purpose.

Chapter 6

An American Dream:
Dread, Magic, God, and the Devil

The impact of the philosophy of Hip on Mailer's fiction is evident in his characterization of Stephen Rojack, the protagonist of *An American Dream*, Mailer's fourth novel. Like the hipster, Rojack embraces a philosophy of life that develops out of a haunting, undeniable "private vision" of "the possibilities within death," a vision that originates from an existential wartime confrontation with four German soldiers: during the war in the midst of a battle Rojack experiences a moment of grace, that is, a moment in which he is blessed with an instinctive, paradoxical knowledge that if one is to survive in a world of uncertainty and conflict, one must be willing to risk all. One must be willing to die. Empowered through this willingness by a sense of invulnerability, reminiscent of Croft's feeling of omnipotence following Hennessey's death, Rojack charges up a hill under a portentous full moon. He charges, armed with carbine and grenades, into "the aisle of safety" that is magically opening for him amid a ceaseless barrage of machine gun fire and kills "four men, four very separate Germans."[1] In that moment of revelation, that "enormous present," Rojack sees identity take flesh as the buried meaning of each German's life embodies itself in his features, and each is defined in death to the extent that he has defined himself in life. The fourth German, however, carries the crux of Rojack's experience:

I wanted to charge as if that were our contract, and held, for I could not face his eyes, they now contained all of it, the two grenades, the blood on my thigh, the fat faggot, the ghost with the pistol, the hunchback, the blood, those bloody screams that never sounded, it was all in his eyes, he had eyes I was to see once later on an autopsy table in a small town in Missouri, eyes belonging to a redneck farmer from a deep road in the Ozarks, eyes of blue, so perfectly blue and mad they go all the way in deep into celestial vaults of sky, eyes which go all the way back to God is the way I think I heard it said once in the South, and I faltered before that stare, clear as ice in the moonlight, and hung on one knee. (5)

Rojack's confrontation with the fourth German dramatizes Mailer's idea of an existential religious experience, which is definitively a vision of death that totally transforms one's view of life. And it is entirely consistent with the existential ethic that governs the bestowal of grace in Mailer's morally exacting universe that as Rojack allows fear to take hold of him, grace withdraws, and he is left, vulnerable and exhausted of courage, to face the dying German's all-encompassing stare. The source of this paralyzing fear is Rojack's perception of the existential truth, contained within the German's eyes, that death is "a creation more dangerous than life." In other words, Rojack perceives that death is not "zero," not "everyone's emptiness" (7). It is not the extinction of experience but the apotheosis of human possibility and the authentic, apocalyptic expression of the meaning of one's life: at the point of death, with the vision that one has gained in life, one looks "down the abyss" (2) and sees opening before him every possibility. In that moment one realizes "that death is an existential continuation of life, that the soul may either pass through migrations, or cease to exist in the continuum of nature." One also realizes that it is preeminently through such existential confrontations that the truth about oneself and one's relationships is revealed, and so one denies the primacy of reason, abandoning the illusory sense of order, security, and control that are the psychological palliatives of a rational world view, and affirms instead the epistemological significance of the irrational. It is precisely these realizations that lead Rojack to maintain that the conduct of one's life does finally matter, that indeed human

beings are ethical agents whose choices affect the moral balance
of an embattled universe, and that "magic, dread, and the
perception of death [are] the roots of motivation" (8).

These beliefs serve as the source of conflict in the novel since
they necessarily place Rojack in opposition to the totalitarianism
of American society, which insists that life is without moral
consequence. This assumption posits a world without moral responsibility, a finite, material world in which the greatest ends
are wealth and power, and all manner of exploitation is admissi-
ble in order to secure them. Though such a world may be ultimately absurd, one need never face its absurdity as long as one is
able to remain absorbed in pursuing one's material goals. On the
other hand, if one believes, as Rojack does, that death is "a
creation more dangerous than life," dangerous not only because it
is a plunge into the unknown but also because the quality of one's
death is defined by the quality of one's existential choices, then
life has moral significance. Life is meaningful and consequential,
and one is accountable for all of one's ideas and actions.

Rojack's problem, however, is that he has tried to ignore the
implications of his belief in the moral consequence of life in order
to pursue the rewards of wealth and power. His opposition to
society has, therefore, moved within, and he lives in perpetual
conflict with himself. As a result of this schizophrenic separation
between belief and action, Rojack suffers from an acute sense of
dread, an existential condition of awful, even abject, fear. Such a
condition is in Mailer's view a necessary concomitant to the belief
that one is a moral agent in the war between God and the Devil.
But this sense of dread becomes most acute when one opts as a
result of moral cowardice to try to withdraw from the battle or
when one suspects, as Rojack does, that one's soul may be dying
as a result of a life of moral compromise. Indeed, Rojack knows as
a result of his confrontation with the four Germans that if his soul
does survive, it will have to pass through existential reckonings
that will exact full and unthinkable payment for all that wasted
life. The precise nature of these reckonings is suggested by the
images of the Germans, who at the moment of death become

karmic incarnations of the essential moral significance of their lives—flesh and blood ikons of the idea that character is fate. Rojack also knows that his "perception of death" has left him unfit to pursue the American dream of wealth and power, for only those who truly believe that life is inconsequential can remain unconscious of the spiritual consequences of such a life: they live as if they were already "zero" and had no souls to lose. Perhaps if one is exceptionally strong and ambitious, one can be like the power broker Barney Kelly and make the Faustian pact of pledging one's soul to the Devil's camp. But if one is like Stephen Rojack, one is left split and dying:

I could have had a career in politics if only I had been able to think that death was zero. . . . But I knew it was not. I remained an actor. My personality was built upon a void. Thus I quit my place in politics almost as quickly as I gained it. . . . I wanted to depart from politics before I was separated from myself forever by the distance between my public appearance which had become vital on television, indeed nearly robust, and my secret frightened romance with the phases of the moon. (7)

Rojack does leave politics, but the split in his personality does not heal. He does not let it. The demon behind the dream of wealth and power still inhabits him, and he perpetuates the split in other forms. Over a period of years Stephen Rojack, Phi Beta Kappa, winner of the Distinguished Service Cross, and congressman, gradually becomes Stephen Rojack, author, professor, TV talk-show host, and husband of Deborah Caughlin Mangaravidi Kelly. The roles change, but the problem remains the same. Whoever he may really be beneath the accretion of social roles, that person has never been given a chance to live. Thus the Rojack that one sees at the beginning of *An American Dream* is spiritually exhausted, obsessively engaged in an intimate, paranoid communion with the moon as both siren and oracle, an ambiguous guide to action in a world of irrational relations. Indeed, having experienced the loss of all that was best in him, Rojack feels the first stirrings in himself of that inner repugnant rebellion, that cultural symptom of spiritual extinction, that disease which "is other than disease" (PP 271): he feels in himself the growth of cancer.

More than anything else it has been marriage with Deborah Kelly that has brought Rojack to such a wretched defeat. To begin with, Rojack married Deborah to achieve social and political success. Indeed, it is not too much to say that, in marrying Deborah, "the Devil's daughter" (204), Rojack married American society and all of its enticements. The paranoia that may be Rojack's best protection against the repressive and murderous designs of the conspiratorial organization of American social, economic, political, and military power likewise finds expression in his marriage. Since Deborah is "an artist in that great dialectic of uncertainty where lies lead to truth, and truth begets the shimmering of lies" and since, in trying to get at the heart of the mystery, Rojack can never know if his "instruments of detection" are "either wholly inaccurate or unverifiably acute," the truth about his marriage remains inscrutable. It is simply impossible for him to know the exact nature of any man's relationship with Deborah. Is "Old Buddy" a friend, a foe—cuckolding him in the wink of an eye—or is he both friend and foe? With Deborah, as with the American social and political structure at large, "all" is "possible" (10).

Rojack's relationship is certainly nothing less than the war of his life, and as he admits, it has been "a losing war." For the past five years he has been "trying to evacuate" his "expeditionary army, that force of hopes, all-out need, plain virile desire and commitment" that he has "spent on her." But for Deborah, the "Great Bitch," "unconditional surrender" is the "only raw meat" (9). Clearly Deborah is emasculating Rojack by devouring him, doing her best to destroy any sense of virility he might have retained from knowing that he and no one else had succeeded in marrying her. She is even capable of turning his experience with the four Germans into something ludicrous and profane:

"God, you're a whimperer," said Deborah. "Sometimes I lie here and wonder how you ever became a hero. You're such a bloody whimperer. I suppose the Germans were whimpering even worse than you. It must have been quite a sight. You whimpering and they whimpering, and you going pop pop pop with your little gun." (23)

Despite a long history of such cruelty and hatred, Rojack cannot simply leave Deborah, for he is trapped by a polarity of destructive emotions. Living with Deborah, Rojack is murderous; trying to separate from her, he is suicidal. He can extricate himself from this trap only by fully engaging in the war with Deborah and winning it. In other words, in order to save himself, he must kill Deborah. In killing her, he severs his most significant relationship with the society that has seduced his soul. He renounces all of the compromising roles that for so many years have been counterfeiting his identity, and he gives himself a chance to find out what that real identity is. Such an action, however, requires the utmost courage since it contains all possible danger. First of all, though Rojack hates Deborah, he still is agonized by "the remains of [his] love for her" (15). Moreover, she represents to him "the armature of [his] ego" (17). He has been afraid that if he left her, he would collapse. So although his motive in killing Deborah is to save himself, he knows that the act might prove instead to be self-destructive. In addition to these psychological difficulties, there is also the ethical problem. To reconcile the ethics of the killing, Rojack must be able to accomplish a transvaluation of values. He must be able to understand that his action is not simply wrong but both right and wrong. For he must be able to live with the fact that he is a murderer while at the same time understanding that he is his soul's liberator. To achieve that liberation, he has killed an equal. Deborah is certainly just as capable of murdering Rojack as he is of murdering her. In the final analysis their relationship has indeed been a war, and it has been moving inexorably toward some violent conclusion. Of course, such a paradoxical explanation of motivation and morality, grounded in the existential ethics of Hip philosophy, means nothing to society. From the standpoint of the law Rojack would simply be a murderer. Thus, in killing Deborah, he must be prepared to risk retribution. Furthermore, he knows that even if he did succeed in eluding the law, he would have really only begun the process of extricating himself from debilitating social relationships. Though killing Deborah represents Rojack's greatest renunciation of compromise, it likewise establishes a moral obligation for him to make the renunciation complete, requiring him to do battle with society on every level of his relationship with it and emerge victorious. Such a confrontation would force society to drop its mask and reveal itself as the demon that it really is, a demon personified by the man Rojack fears most: Barney Kelly.

Despite all of these dangers, Rojack acts. And as he feels his arm tightening about Deborah's neck, he has a vision of the new life that is waiting for him on the other side of an opening door, a door that is opening onto her death: "heaven was there, some quiver of jeweled cities shining in the glow of a tropical dusk. . . . and *crack* I choked her harder, and *crack* I choked her again, and *crack* I gave her payment—never halt now—and *crack* the door flew open and the wire tore in her throat, and I was through the door, hatred passing from me in wave after wave, illness as well, rot and pestilence, nausea, a bleak string of salts" (31).

As I mentioned in chapter 1, quite a few critics have strenuously objected to Rojack's unpunished murder of Deborah, some combining this objection with criticism of the novel's craft. From this point of view the novel is easy to dismiss: Deborah's murder is simply a foul act; Rojack's success in escaping prosecution is a reflection of Mailer's approval of domestic violence; and the unusual events that crowd the novel are indications that Mailer is constitutionally incapable of sustaining verisimilitude. For example, Elizabeth Hardwick calls *An American Dream* "a very dirty book—dirty and extremely ugly."[2] For her it is finally nothing more than a failed piece of pornography. Philip Rahv notes disapprovingly that the description of the murder "is full of positive imagery" and objects sardonically that it seems to effect "a true renewal" in Rojack. Rahv then insists at some expense to logic that it is "curious" "not only that this murder goes unpunished (Crime without Punishment) but that it is also without any kind of consequence, either external or internal."³ Of course, one of the novel's most important themes is that life has moral consequence. Moreover, the murder itself not only produces the "true renewal," which Rahv disparages, it also places Rojack in open opposition to American society and necessitates the series of confrontations that compose the bulk of the narrative action. Rahv fails to acknowledge these effects because he is seeking in the absence of legal prosecution some other form of retribution. For Rahv to be satisfied, one suspects that Rojack would have to blind himself like Oedipus or suffer perhaps a Promethean punishment at the hands of the gods. Actually the novel does dramatize a form of divine retribution, for in committing murder, Rojack has "attracted the attention of the gods" (204), exposing himself to an invasion of magical forces that is finally overwhelming.

In mentioning magic, however, one is at the same time suggesting a significant part of Rahv's problem with *An American Dream*: he could not reconcile the novel's treatment of magic with its insistence, grounded in a consistent use of the realistic mode, that the moral implications of Deborah's murder must be confronted directly. As Rahv notes, the book "is written in the realistic convention and without a trace of irony."⁴ What then to make of a vindication of murder combined with a dramatized belief in magic? Rahv's solution is to separate the moral and aesthetic questions and condemn the novel on both accounts. Thus from Rahv's conventional moral standpoint, the book is simply Mailer's attempt, as a would-be swinger, to pander to "the fickle moods of a certain sector of American society, by no means the least affluent, which in every sphere but the political has collapsed into total permissiveness."⁵ Technically, the novel is an unsuccessful attempt at achieving verisimilitude, the enterprise horribly undermined by Mailer's uncontrollable eccentricity.

It is easy to understand why the rather simplistic moralism and narrow-minded aesthetics of such reviewers would make them easy targets of more sympathetic critics of *An American Dream*. But despite their lack of sympathy and sophistication, Hardwick's and Rahv's reviews have the undeniable advantage of confronting the controversial question of the novel's morality and of suggesting, however unsympathetically, that its intentions are primarily mimetic. On the other hand, many of the more favorable critics of the book felt that in order to defend it, they would have to defuse the question of the morality of the murder by arguing that the standards of realism were anachronistic and irrelevant to the novel's imaginative concerns. The use of such a diversionary line of defense reveals that these critics are likewise incapable of reconciling the elements of magic and morality. Indeed, one suspects that they are just as unaccepting of Mailer's morality and just as skeptical about his ontology as Hardwick and Rahv.

In "The Interpretation of Dreams," an essay viewed by many pro-Mailer critics as the ultimate vindication of *An American Dream*, moving it forever outside the range of the slings and arrows of vulgar neoclassicists, Leo Bersani argues that Rojack's involvement with magic is a private obsessive pathological fantasy, that the novel is actually "a continuous attack against magic," but that its "strategy of resistance is, inevitably, literary," for "the power of *An American Dream* is in its demonstration of verbal tactics which finally make . . . the psychological question irrelevant."[6] Now all of this is undoubtedly ingenious, but it is essentially wrongheaded, sounding nothing at all like a description of a work by Norman Mailer, whom Diana Trilling describes perceptively, though with some exaggeration, as "an anti-artist, deeply distrustful of art if only because it puts a shield between the perception and the act. His writer's role, as he conceives it, is much more messianic than creative." Trilling rightly insists that Mailer's "moral imagination is the imagination not of art but of theology, theology in action."[7] It is therefore particularly inadmissible when discussing Mailer's work to beg moral questions as Bersani does quite obviously when he suggests that Rojack's murder of Deborah should be understood as merely providing a "literary-novelistic"[8] occasion for Rojack to display his imagination. Furthermore, Bersani badly misinterprets the novel's view of magic. The book is always insisting that magic has an autonomous, external existence and that Rojack's belief in it is therefore not a pathological fantasy. Accordingly, Rojack's use of the word "madness" to describe his involvement in magic merely indicates the possible effect of daring to attract "the attention of the gods," while his desire at the end of the novel to be free of magic represents a failure of courage, an inability to sustain any longer his acute consciousness of the complexities of an irrational world. In the final analysis, Rojack is not fleeing demonic fantasy; instead he is proving himself incapable of enduring an intensified reality.

Bersani's argument that the novel is essentially a virtuosic display of the protagonist's powers of fantasy and imagination rather than a faithful narrative of actual events represents only one of the tactics that critics have used to deny the novel's unique attempt to create a new, paradoxical literary mode: the mimetic representation of a perceptible magical reality. In fact, virtually every sympathetic critic of the book has specifically placed the novel outside the realistic mode, treating it as some species of allegory or romance. Laura Adams states that the "metaphoric level which Mailer develops in this novel runs parallel to the literal level as in a medieval dream-vision." And she evades the question of the novel's morality when she adds that "ironically, many early reviewers took" the book "quite literally and found the violence and uncommon sexual acts particularly offensive, whereas these acts express Mailer's existential ethics on a metaphorical level."[9] In addition, in his frequently quoted critique of the novel, John W. Aldridge argues that the book

was a burlesque treatment of the obscene version of the American Dream that possesses the unconscious mind of America at the present time, and what appeared to be, and patently were, excesses and absurdities were also an integral part of the humorous intent, and perfectly in keeping not only with the psychotic quality of the dream but with the tradition to which the book seemed most clearly to belong, the tradition of the prose romance, in which fantasy and fact, witchcraft and melodrama, myth, allegory, and realism combine to produce what Richard Chase has called "a profound poetry of disorder." The book's antecedents were not the novels of Henry James or Jane Austen but the romances of Cooper, Melville, and Hawthorne, and one of Mailer's contributions was to rehabilitate the form of the romance and adapt it to the literary needs of the immediate present. The book, in short, was an examination not of human and social surfaces but of our fantasy life, a vastly hallucinated yet deeply real account of the American dream become in our day the American nightmare.[10]

The difficulty of taking issue with such interpretations of *An American Dream* lies in the fact that these criticisms obviously reflect more sophisticated readings of the book than do the reviews of either Hardwick or Rahv. Aldridge, for example, would be substantially right in his interpretation of the novel if it were not for the fact that he fails, along with his colleagues, to comprehend a fundamental point, namely the literalness of Mailer's imagination. Indeed, it is perhaps this quality of mind that leads Diana Trilling into the hyperbole of describing Mailer as "an anti-artist." Clearly, in the case of *An American Dream* the essential point to be made is this: for Mailer, Rojack in the act of killing Deborah is not Christian slaying Apollyon. He is first and foremost a man who is murdering his wife precisely because she is literally threatening his soul's survival. Whatever symbolic qualities Deborah suggests, including her identification as "The Great Bitch," are not predetermined but arise out of her characterization and her relationship with Rojack, a relationship that, as I have noted, constitutes Rojack's greatest compromise. She is at bottom a realistic character, far more suggestive of Margot Macomber, her fictive antecedent, than any fairy tale dragon. Furthermore, Mailer is being just as literal in his dramatization throughout the novel of the manifestations of magic. Mailer does not, like Hawthorne, believe that the actual is antipathetic to the imagination and that the artist must, therefore, create a land of romance, "a neutral territory, somewhere between the real world and fairy-land, where the Actual and the Imaginary may meet, and each imbue itself with the nature of the other."[11] Instead he includes in his view of the actual all that Hawthorne believed could exist only in the "neutral territory" of romance. For Mailer, even the apartments, hotels, night clubs, and police stations of New York City can compose such a territory. As Richard Poirier notes, Mailer "wants to show that the world of the demonic, the supernatural, the mad is not simply the reverse side of the world that sets the normal standards by which these other conditions are defined as abnormal. Instead he wants to suggest that these worlds are simultaneous, coextensive."[12] Yet even Poirier persists in describing *An American Dream* inappropriately, noting that "this is our history as Hawthorne might have written it: just as private and nearly as melodramatic and allegorical."[13]

In addition to Poirier, Robert J. Begiebing is the only favorable critic of *An American Dream* who applies to it the term "allegory" while still revealing in the course of his discussion a significant understanding of Mailer's imagination and world view. Begiebing defines allegory ontologically, as well as generically, and on this basis distinguishes rational allegory from true allegory. According to Begiebing, rational allegory establishes a set of one-to-one correspondences between the phenomenal world and the spiritual world. In this way it "separates from the mode its ancient function of representing a spiritual world through the details of the phenomenal world." True allegory, on the other hand, "reunites the spiritual and phenomenal worlds. Such allegories portray mankind's direct encounter with spiritual powers and with an inner, visionary world largely through the details of the phenomenal world."[14]

One might criticize Begiebing's definition by noting that, in attempting to present a more complex and sophisticated definition of allegory, he expands the mode to include any activity of the symbolic imagination so that virtually every imaginative writer, with the possible exception of such dogged realists as William Dean Howells and Anthony Trollope, becomes an allegorist. But as applied to Mailer's work, Begiebing's conception of true allegory is valuable insofar as it emphasizes Mailer's view that the phenomenal and the spiritual are one. In the practice of criticism, however, Begiebing's approach leads him to separate sense and idea whereas Mailer is always insisting on the actuality, on the literalness, on paradoxically the physicalness of the spirit. This insistence accounts, for example, for Mailer's use of pseudo-scientific language in *Why Are We in Vietnam?* to express what he believes is the fact of telekinesis. He is ultimately as insistent on sense as the positivists of modern technology. In the final analysis, Begiebing's approach leads one away from Mailer's attempt to portray the reality of magic to a Jungian discussion of Mailer as "an archetypal allegorist." Thus Rojack becomes the hero of a "mythical Night Sea Journey to rebirth," confronting in the course of his serial ordeal Deborah as "Devouring Dragon" and "Terrible Mother," Ruta as "another aspect of Deborah," Cherry as "Heavenly Bride," and Kelly as "the Anti-Soul."[15] In other words, *An American Dream* is once again reduced to a series of dream images; Rojack's involvement with magic is therefore necessarily interpreted once more as psychological projections (in this case, projections of the collective unconscious); and the murder of Deborah is described in language appropriate to Dorothy's slaying of the Wicked Witch of the West. It is ironic too, given the strong didactic and moralistic component of allegory, that so many of the critics who describe *An American Dream* allegorically should indulge in moral evasion. For such critics the presence of allegorical elements seems unaccountably to defuse moral issues. Thus Begiebing argues that "once we see Deborah as a mythological figure in a visionary world, we will not be marooned on the literal issue of Mailer's sexist portrayal of women, as Kate Millett and Elizabeth Hardwick are. One could make a case against Mailer's sexism, but surely the least effective way of doing so would be to base it on a translation of mythic figures and allegorical agents into merely literal characters."[16]

Though one must always be highly suspicious of writers' commentaries on their own work, in this case Mailer himself does indeed suggest the most accurate and fruitful approach to *An American Dream*. In a 1975 *Partisan Review* interview with Laura

Adams, Mailer responds to Adams' insistence that "the kinds of experiences Rojack has, the vision of shooting arrows into Cherry's womb while she's singing in the night club, for example, seem . . . to exist in a dream allegory but not at the literal level":

> I would disagree. I'd had the experience of being in night clubs and thinking evil thoughts and really barbing them like darts and sending them to people and seeing them react. At the time I didn't know whether I was profoundly drunk or, you know, was I all alone in the world? But I had to recognize that there was a psychic reality to it. It wasn't just a fantasy. . . . my point is that there wasn't a single phenomenon in that book that I considered dreamlike or fanciful or fantastical. To me, it was a realistic book, but a realistic book at that place where extraordinary things are happening. I believe the experience of extraordinary people in extraordinary situations is not like our ordinary experience at all.[17]

Begiebing calls Mailer's description of *An American Dream* confusing,[18] but it really is not. It is perfectly consistent with the paradoxical nature of Mailer's art and thought with which his readers are, or should be, familiar. Mailer is indeed trying to extend the limits of realism by representing extraordinary situations and characters in mimetic detail. And in depicting a magical world in which human beings act as divine agents, he is trying to produce for his readers the kind of experience that a fundamentalist has in reading the Bible. And so, like Begiebing's true allegorist, Mailer is creating art that is "constantly moving toward religion and philosophy,"[19] but the consciousness informing that religion and that philosophy is literal, primitive, and fundamentalist rather than allegorical. For the phenomenal and the spiritual truly are one in Mailer as are the didactic and the dramatic.

This synthetic vision of reality and art is evident throughout *An American Dream*, providing the novel with the unity that some critics have found lacking by removing the boundaries between sense and idea as well as action and apologue. For the novel never suggests that there is an ontological distinction between Rojack's experience of magic and his involvement in the rational quotidian world of liberal politics, except that his experience of magic is far more intense. Magic is therefore if anything a more significant reality, with the novel suggesting not that magic is a profound truth because Rojack experiences it intensely but that he experiences magic intensely because it is a profound truth. At the same time, one of the novel's most important didactic messages—the idea that murder is justifiable as an act of spiritual self-defense and liberation—is fully dramatized not only in the characterization of Deborah as Rojack's existential equal who is perfectly capable of murdering him but in Rojack's murder of Deborah and in his experiences immediately following the killing.

In the aftermath of the murder Rojack feels a "most honorable fatigue"; his "flesh" seems "new" (32). He is once again in "a state of grace" in which he is in touch with his instincts and his senses are acutely alive. Baffled by the ambiguities of his own moral state—"'Am I now good? Am I evil forever?'" (38)—he realizes now as he has in the past through his marriage with Deborah that "goodness" is "imprisoned by evil" and "'that evil'" does have "'power'" (36), realizations that provide respectively a perfect description of Rojack's relation to American society and a rationale for the murder itself. Thus Rojack knows that he must sustain the logic of liberation through what is conventionally called evil. In other words he must continue to try to free himself from spiritually debilitating relationships by living as a psychic outlaw, acting with the purity of a hipster saint and the ruthlessness of the greatest sinner. Convinced that "Deborah would be there to meet [him] in the hour of [his] death" (40), Rojack rejects the conventionally honorable but square option of turning himself over to the police, a choice that would repudiate the existential justification for the murder and perpetuate his spiritual predicament while adding the indignity of physical imprisonment. Instead he chooses to try to evade legal prosecution and continue to seek a new life for himself outside the bounds of American society.

Having made this decision, Rojack feels that "some force" is drawing him out of the room. The murder has released in him the accumulated tension of the years. "Something fierce for pleasure

[is] loose" (40, 41), and he knows that he must have Ruta, the German maid. Though Rojack's two sexual encounters with Ruta may seem merely to constitute a psychopathic plunge into evil, they actually represent both a freeing of energy and the first of a series of intimate and necessary encounters with the conspiratorial power structure (though Rojack does not yet know it, Ruta is Barney Kelly's mistress, posing as a maid to keep watch on Deborah's activities). In addition, Ruta serves Rojack as a source of information that may help him to solve the riddle that was Deborah's life, a solution that would free him from at least one mystery and accomplish the psychological disposal of Deborah's body, a problem that he likewise confronts by way of a cannibalistic fantasy. Most important, both his sexual encounters with Ruta and his fantasy of eating Deborah's corpse as a purgation of the poisons of his past sustain the logic of liberation that informed the murder. To "remake a bit of his nervous system" and thereby create for himself a new identity, Rojack must continue to pass through prohibitions. At the same time, to prepare himself for his series of confrontations with the police, the Mob, jazz singer Shago Martin, and Barney Kelly, he needs to gain power by availing himself of "a host of the Devil's best gifts" (44). Here Mailer dramatizes an idea that he has discussed at length in his nonfiction, namely that waste is the product of the body's existential rejection of all that is either too poisonous or too good for it to use and digest. According to Mailer, all that is lost to life becomes the Devil's gain. Moreover, as I have noted in my discussion of Croft's desire to climb Mt. Anaka, Mailer also believes that one takes on the powers of anything that one is able to dominate. Thus when Rojack has anal intercourse with Ruta, he is able to take from her "mendacity, guile, a fine-edged cupidity for the stroke which steals, the wit to trick authority" (44–45). But coming "to the Devil a fraction too late," just a moment after he might have received a windfall from some long withheld store of infernal grace, he is left instead with a "vision . . . of a huge city in the desert," its "colors" revealing "the unreal pastel of a plastic . . . the main street . . . flaming with light at five A.M." (46); it is a

vision of Las Vegas, the center of the spiritless corruption of American totalitarianism, the antithesis of that promised land "of jeweled cities shining in the glow of a tropical dusk" that Rojack envisioned when he murdered Deborah. Nevertheless, despite the bad orgasm, Rojack has gotten from Ruta what he needs. By the time he wholeheartedly embraces risk and pushes Deborah's corpse out the window of her tenth-floor apartment, he is ready to begin his long, grueling series of confrontations with the powers of American society.

Rojack's first encounter is of course with the police, and it draws greatly on his emotions. Although everything that he does in the aftermath of Deborah's death is for the purpose of freeing himself from compromising social roles, he is forced to begin this process by telling lie after lie and by counterfeiting emotions. The whole process is indeed a "rape of [his] private existence" (60), and the problem is exacerbated by the totalitarian nature of the environments where he must now defend himself. Both the morgue and the police station are stripped of nuance, stripped of mood, the police station in particular designed to wear men down through long hours of ceaseless inquisition. Moreover, the police themselves are hunters, O'Brien and Leznicki breathing violence and Roberts carrying within himself a woman's intuition of Rojack's guilt. As a result of these circumstances Rojack retreats to the very edge of his cowardice and is brought to the point of surrender, holding off at first only because he is too weak "to throw [his] voice across the room" (87) and confess to temporary insanity. But by the time the police release him, either because of the fortuitous circumstance of Mob Boss Eddie Ganucci's arrest or, as Ruta later suggests, because of paranoia over Deborah's amateur involvement in spying, Rojack has a new reason to want to survive: he has the chance of loving Cherry Melanie, the night club singer, whom he has met that evening for the first time.

Cherry fulfills Mailer's (and Rojack's) image of the Blonde. She is Grace Kelly, Marilyn Monroe, and another "dozen lovely blondes." Indeed, she is "a nest of separate personalities," containing within herself much of the curious mix of American images of female sexuality. She can be either ethereal or sensual, inaccessible or promiscuous, in one second "the television wife of a professional football star," in the next "nightclub hard," while in the very next shift of mood she reveals the "clean tough decent" look of "the little boy next door" (96, 97). With her, Rojack has the sensation that life can be something special, that life holds expanding possibilities. But he also senses that Cherry has a past as complicated as his own, a past that would speak "of small Southern towns and the back seats of cars, of expensive hotel suites and years of listening to good jazz, of simple honest muscle in her heart and the taste of good wines, jukeboxes and crap tables, stubborn will, something compromised, inert, and full of gas, something powerful and dull as her friends" (109). In order for them to build a relationship, Rojack and Cherry must first journey together through each other's past. Indeed, it is precisely because each has been so ravaged by the past that when they meet at Cherry's apartment and make love for the first time, their embrace is initially nothing less than a desperate locking together of wills. Thus on their second meeting at Cherry's apartment each has a story to tell. Rojack acknowledges what Cherry already knew: he has indeed killed his wife. On the other hand, Cherry relates the rest of a difficult past already suggested by the tale of her sister's suicide. It is a past that includes her brother and sister's incestuous relationship, sexual liaisons with Barney Kelly and jazz singer Shago Martin, and two abortions as a result. Because of these great difficulties, Rojack's and Cherry's love is held in a delicate, tentative balance. When Shago intrudes upon Rojack and Cherry during their second intimate meeting and a fight inevitably breaks out between the two men, this balance is temporarily destroyed. For the violent confrontation forces Rojack to try to free Cherry from the hold of her past by literally beating it into submission.

Before leaving Cherry's apartment with the defeated Shago's totemic umbrella in hand to keep his appointment with Barney Kelly—an appointment that will bring him face to face with the demonic social power that he has been struggling to reject—

Rojack feels that he and Cherry have at least partially closed the breach in their love. Each realizes that their best hope for the future lies in the relationship and that the future of the relationship depends on their courage. On the way to Kelly's, however, Rojack suspects that he has not yet confronted the full implications of Shago's beating or completely proven his courage and thereby shown himself to be worthy of love. For upon leaving Cherry, Rojack is immediately plagued by guilt. "Some sense of the sinister" (202) oppresses him, and he fears that it may not be safe for Cherry to be alone. Nevertheless, his overriding fear of Kelly impels him toward their meeting.

The conflict between returning to Cherry and confronting Barney Kelly again plunges Rojack into magic and becomes the ultimate test of Rojack's willingness to risk everything for love. In fact, the conflict forms for Rojack a crucial part of a series of wildly irrational existential battles with voices that manifest the intervention of the gods in Rojack's life. His ability to discern the truth amid this babble of divinely inspired directives magically determines whether or not he can keep the love of Cherry and build a new life with her based on the courage to remain free of spiritual compromise. The first voice that Rojack hears tells him to go to Harlem for the evening as a way of risking retaliation for Shago's beating. In this way he would resolve the incident with Shago, heal all wounds through courage, and win the right to build a future with Cherry. Immediately, however, the alternative offers itself:

"Go to Kelly," said a voice now in my mind, and it was a voice near to indistinguishable from the other voice. Which was true? When voices came, how did you make the separation? "That which you fear most is what you must do," said my mind. "Trust the authority of your senses." But I had taken too long to decide: I had no senses. I was now nothing but fear. (203)

The novel here is intentionally recalling Kierkegaard's insistence on the impossibility of assigning ethical values to private inspiration. One recalls too Mailer's commentary on Buber's tale,

"The Teaching of the Soul," in which he states that learning "from an inner voice the first time it speaks to us is a small bold existential act, for it depends upon following one's instinct which must derive, in no matter how distorted a fashion, from God, whereas institutional knowledge is appropriated by the Devil. The soul speaks once and chooses not to repeat itself, because to repeat a message is to give the Devil in one's psyche a chance to prepare a trap" (PP 194). In this case the voice insisting that Rojack go to Harlem does repeat, but it is Rojack's failure to act immediately that renders the situation demonically repetitive. Already Rojack is revealing the limits of his capacity to live with a consciousness of magic. He would put a "'curse on the logic of the saints'" (203). But when Rojack fails to choose, he experiences a loss. And as he ascends the elevator at the Waldorf moments before his meeting with Barney Kelly, Rojack knows the nature of that loss: "some certainty of love was passing away, some knowledge it was the reward for which to live—that voice which I could no longer deny spoke through the medium of the umbrella. 'Go to Harlem,' said the voice, 'if you love Cherry, go to Harlem—there is time.' Then I knew how afraid I was of Harlem, and argued with that voice, saying, 'Let me love her some way not altogether deranged and doomed. It makes no sense to go to Harlem. Let me love her and be sensible as well'" (208).

In Mailer's work romantic possibilities and the unambiguous light of sanity and common sense seldom or never meet. However irrational it may seem, the future of Rojack's love clearly depends on his going to Harlem. Indeed, the novel suggests that if Rojack had gone to Harlem, both Cherry and Shago might not have died. On the other hand, Rojack himself might have been murdered. Before the dizzying complexity of all these irrational possibilities, one fact stands clear: at this point Rojack has been forced to contend with all too many possibilities so that it has become all but impossible for him to know precisely the real meaning or effect of anything that he does. His life has now become an unremitting series of existential situations characterized by uncertainty and dread, the price, Mailer suggests, not only of murder but of choosing to confront the totalitarianism of American social and political power. Thus once Rojack arrives at Kelly's, the complexities only deepen as he finally begins to learn the secrets of Deborah's life and gains an intimate understanding of the psychology of power.

Kelly tells Rojack his life story, revealing that, unlike Mailer's typical amoral totalitarian, Kelly believes, with Rojack, that God and the Devil are embattled and that human beings act as agents in the struggle. In fact, he suggests that he has gained wealth and power by making a Faustian pact with the Devil. As Kelly notes, "'there's nothing but magic at the top'" (246). Kelly tells this story primarily to reveal to Rojack his incestuous relationship with Deborah and by implication admit that Deirdre is his, rather than Rojack's, daughter. Kelly desires this revelation because he feels morally implicated in Rojack's murder of Deborah. As he says to Rojack immediately before telling his life story, "'I'm just as guilty, after all. . . . I was a brute to her. She visited that brutishness back on you. So it comes to the same thing in the end, doesn't it?'" (232). But Kelly by no means seeks any conventional expiation of his sin. Instead he wants to confirm Rojack as his spiritual double. In other words he wants to be able to stand together publicly with Rojack as though all were well, while privately they will have engaged in an orgiastic, anal *ménage à trois* with Ruta as a way of symbolically "gorging on [Deborah's] corpse" (254), this obliterating both the memory and the guilt of the incestuous relationship. By multiplying depravity, by giving himself over to further acts of debauchery on the very same bed where he had committed incest, Kelly would try to reduce the enormity of his brutality with Deborah. Thus Kelly confronts Rojack with the greatest of all temptations, the greatest of all compromises, inviting him into the very heart of the conspiracy he has been struggling to reject, drawing him on to continue to affirm the false American dream of wealth and power that presents lies as truth and substitutes appearance for reality. If Rojack does not accede, Kelly intends to destroy him.

It is at this point too that Rojack again experiences a desire to be free of magic. He sees a paranoiac image of Shago making love with Cherry, an image immediately followed by a vision of murder: "was a man being murdered in Harlem at this instant—the picture in my mind was broken with shock—did I feel a broken–off bat go beating on a brain, was a man expiring, some cry (should it have been mine?) going out into an alley of the night, carrying across the miles to the thirty stories of this room—was a murderer running and caught in the patrols of the gods?" And Rojack once more knows the limits of his courage, feeling the need "to escape from that intelligence which let me know of murders in one direction and conceive of visits to Cherry from the other. I wanted to be free of magic, the tongue of the Devil, the dread of the Lord, I wanted to be some sort of rational man again, nailed tight to details, promiscuous, reasonable, blind to the reach of the seas" (255). But after bypassing Kelly's murmured offer to "'get shitty,'" Rojack steels himself to submit to one more test. A voice says, "'Walk the parapet or Cherry is dead'" (254, 255), and Rojack agrees to make this last attempt to prove his courage and avoid the fatal consequences of his failure to go to Harlem.

Once on the balcony, Rojack learns that Kelly has never felt the imperative to walk the parapet. Having broken the prohibition against incest and having made his pact with evil, Kelly has placed himself beyond the need to prove his courage, though it has been at the expense of his soul and his daughter's life. On the other hand, Deborah was victimized and trapped by the incest. As a result, she had to walk the parapet to try to liberate herself from the power that incest had over her. Rojack now must walk it not only to prove his courage and save Cherry but also to exorcise the memory of Deborah and defeat Kelly and the society that he represents. But the overriding irrationality of all these magical implications finally overwhelms Rojack. After he has traversed the parapet one full time, Kelly attempts to push him off, using Shago's umbrella. Rojack seizes it, however, and drops Kelly with a single blow of the handle. While fleeing the apartment,

Rojack realizes that he has forgotten the command of "the most quiet of the voices" to walk the parapet again. As the voice speaks a second time, Rojack reaches the breaking point and rejects the call of magic, saying "'Damn you . . . I've lain with madness long enough'" (259, 260).

With both Cherry and Shago beaten to death—testifying to the truth of his paranoid imagination—Rojack travels alone to Las Vegas to complete his series of confrontations with American society and meets no resistance. The trip to Las Vegas is actually the first part of a journey to "a jungle somewhere in Guatemala," after which he will move "on to Yucatán" (269). Clearly, like Huck Finn's territory, these places exist somewhere outside the drama of the book, appearing in the epilogue as focuses of romantic aspiration and escape. Indeed, lighting out for Guatemala and Yucatán represents Rojack's desire to be released from drama. Having achieved a personal victory over Deborah, the police, Barney Kelly, and by implication the totalitarianism of a conspiratorial American society and having freed himself from its hold on him, Rojack has certainly outdistanced Mailer's earlier protagonists in the significance of his rebellion. As a result, he may well deserve a simple life without social conflict. In fact, he may have no alternative. Despite his desire to be free of magic, he undoubtedly retains his religious vision of existence, his knowledge that death is "a creation more dangerous than life." Because of this vision and because of the battles that he has fought, there is simply no place left for Rojack in American society. Within society, there is for him only the dream of wealth and power that he has already rejected, a dream that one can pursue either amorally like Eddie Ganucci, who believes that death is "zero," or demonically like Barney Kelly, who has made his pact with the Devil. The idea of remaining in but not of society and continuing to confront it on one's own terms is not a possibility that the book presents. And even if it were, Rojack seems to be incapable of further confrontations by the end of the novel, having reached the limits of his courage and having lost Cherry as a result. Thus the significance of Rojack's victory is reduced by the

significance of his defeat. He has indeed won his spiritual freedom, but the society that he has rejected remains substantially
the same—like Kelly, stunned but quickly back in operation. At
the same time, the new life that Rojack has won must remain a life
of isolation, for he has lost everything but his knowledge of the
"intensity of his private vision."

Chapter 7

Why Are We in Vietnam?:
The Madness of America

Not surprisingly, with the completion of *An American Dream*, Mailer's view of America grows darker. This deepening pessimism is particularly evident if one considers Mailer's contrasting attitudes toward American millennialism as presented in his first two pieces on presidential conventions. For all of its criticism of the rootlessness of "mass man" as the decultured by-product of the marriage between electronic communications and advertising and for all of its denigration of the supermarket ambience of Los Angeles, "Superman Comes to the Supermarket," Mailer's account of the 1960 Democratic Convention, proceeds nevertheless from an impulse that is undeniably optimistic. It is in fact a romantic call for America to fulfill its millennial ideals through a renewal of faith in the myth of the hero. The piece insists that such faith could give rise to an existential politics that would replace the stultifying security of the political clichés that typified the Eisenhower fifties with a courageous activism that could test the limits of personal freedom and expose the oppressive governmental policies that lay concealed beneath the conventional, soporific rhetoric of party politicians.

In the introduction to his reprinting of "Superman Comes to the Supermarket" as "The Third Presidential Paper—The Existential Hero," Mailer argues that "conventional politics has had so little to do with the real subterranean life of America that" no one

116

knows "much about the real—which is to say the potential—historic nature of America. That lies buried under apathy, platitudes, Rightist encomiums for the FBI, programmatic welfare from the liberal Center, and furious pips of protest from the Peace Movement's Left." As an example of an existential political act that reveals the "historic nature of America" as a nation committed in the face of any opposition to living the myth that it is indeed the land of freedom and equality, Mailer cites "the drive by Southern Negroes, led by Martin Luther King, to end segregation in restaurants in Birmingham." As a further illustration of how a commitment to the American myth can be renewed by testing the limits of political freedom, Mailer adds that "if a public speaker in a small Midwestern town were to say, 'J. Edgar Hoover has done more to harm the freedoms of America than Joseph Stalin,' the act would be existential. Depending on the occasion and the town, he would be manhandled physically or secretly applauded. But he would create a new reality which would displace the old psychological reality that such a remark could not be made" (PP 26). Mailer's faith that such actions might awaken in Americans a kindred commitment to mythic possibilities is rooted in his contention that a millennial idealism has survived in this country despite all attempts to extinguish it. A frequently quoted passage from "Superman Comes to the Supermarket" underscores this faith: Mailer insists that over the years the "myth, that each of us was born to be free, to wander, to have adventure and to grow on the waves of the violent, the perfumed, and the unexpected, had a force which could not be tamed no matter how the nation's regulators—politicians, medicos, policemen, professors, priests, rabbis, ministers, *ideologues*, psychoanalysts, builders, executives and endless communicators—would brick–in the modern life with hygiene upon sanity, and middle–brow homily over platitude; the myth would not die. . . . it was as if the message in the labyrinth of the genes would insist that violence was locked with creativity, and adventure was the secret of love" (PP 39–40).

For Mailer it is this potential energy, the energy of the mythic new man, that constitutes what is best about America. And if it is true that "the life of politics and the life of the myth [have] diverged too far," then according to Mailer what the nation needs is appropriately one extraordinary man, one authentic new man, who can bring romantic aspiration into reality, drawing to the surface of practical politics the country's "ferocious, lonely and romantic desires, that concentration of ecstasy and violence which is the dream life of the nation" (PP 38, 41). Indeed, America needs "a hero central to his time, a man whose personality might suggest contradictions and mysteries which could reach into the alienated circuits of the underground, because only a hero can capture the secret imagination of a people, and so be good for the vitality of his nation" (PP 41–42). Mailer hoped that John F. Kennedy, whom he calls "The Hipster as Presidential Candidate" (PP 44), would prove to be such a hero. And so, setting aside a score of misgivings about Kennedy's conventional politics, Mailer wrote "Superman Comes to the Supermarket" for the expressed purpose of enhancing Kennedy's chances of being elected President, hoping that charisma might substitute for substance and that substantial political change might result from a renaissance of heroic possibilities.

Four years later, however, Mailer's optimism is gone. Such national disasters as the Bay of Pigs, Kennedy's assassination, and the escalation of the war in Vietnam, along with Mailer's own increasing conviction, dramatized in *An American Dream*, that political power in America is conspiratorial and malevolent, all combine to draw his attention to the darker aspects of America's millennial heritage. "In the Red Light: A History of the Republican Convention in 1964" chronicles this change in perspective. In this piece Mailer wonders if as a legacy of the Puritan vision, which sought to establish a theocracy of the elect, America is "extraordinary or accursed, a junkyard where even the minnows [give] caviar in the filthy pond in the fierce American night" (CC 8). The epigraph from *The Day of the Locust* sets the tone of the piece: the nation is going mad. But now according to Mailer the insane are in disguise. They are not the obvious social misfits of West's novel who have "come to California to die." Instead they are people who appear in every way to be the most deeply conservative. And they have traveled west in search of a more stimulating sensation than one can get from moving close to the whisper of death. They have moved to the Sunbelt for the promise of fast, new money and the opportunity to establish a regional political base for a pure right-wing ideology. For them in 1964, as for Nathaniel West's misfits, a "super 'Dr. Know-All Pierce-All' had made the necessary promise of miracles and they were marching behind his banner in a great united front of screwballs and screwboxes to purify the land. No longer bored, they sang and danced joyously in the red light of the flames" (CC 6). Or so they might, fears Mailer, if their "super 'Dr. Know-All Pierce-All,'" alias "Sheriff B. Morris Goldwater, the Silver Gun of the West" (CC 12), succeeded in becoming President.

For Mailer, Goldwater's candidacy was dangerous precisely because of its idealism and the purity and simplicity of its nationalism, which "brought you back to the bright minted certitudes of early patriotism when you knew the U.S. was the best country on earth and there was no other" (CC 24). On the one hand, such an ideology appealed to young men and women capable of the righteous zeal that maintains that faith in God and country is the highest form of knowledge. As Mailer notes, "taken altogether, boys and girls, they were like the graduating class of a high school in Nebraska. The valedictorian would write his speech on the following theme: Why is the United States the Greatest Nation on Earth?" (CC 9–10). On the other hand, it attracted the support of new money from Sunbelt oil and aeronautics companies backed by huge defense contracts and spurred by the idea that a military–industrial coalition might be able to buy back the lost America of Goldwater's "bright minted certitudes," shifting the balance of power in America from the northeastern establishment to the transcendental capitalism of the Southwest. Interestingly, in order to expose the subversive nature of both this source of capital and Goldwater's so-called conservatism, which would pit Main Street against Wall Street, Mailer turns to

Edmund Burke, who warns in his *Reflections on the Revolution in France* that

in this state of . . . warfare between the noble ancient landed interest and the new monied interest, the . . . monied interest is in its nature more ready for any adventure; and its possessors more disposed to new enterprises of any kind. Being of recent acquisition, it falls in more naturally with any novelties. It is therefore the kind of wealth which will be resorted to by all who wish for change. (CC 10)

Quotations from Burke's *Reflections* appear repeatedly throughout Mailer's piece, establishing a true conservative standard to juxtapose against Goldwater's right-wing fanaticism while suggesting an ironic correlation between the political goals of Goldwater Republicans and supporters of the French Revolution. Though they are ideological opposites, both advocate apocalyptic changes in the body politic, endangering the welfare of the nation for the sake of realizing their political ideals. In this way Mailer correctly identifies the Goldwater Republicans as right-wing revolutionaries, and he admonishes them, in Burke's words, that "they should not think it amongst their rights to cut off the entail, or commit waste on the inheritance, by destroying at their pleasure the whole original fabric of their society; hazarding to leave to those who come after them a ruin instead of a habitation" (CC 37).

Thus in "In the Red Light" one sees the beginnings of Mailer's left conservatism, which places him at the same time to the left and the right of almost everyone in the country. For Mailer, if Goldwater's complacent rhetoric of the practicality of "low-yield atomic weapons" (CC 38) raised the proximate threat of nuclear war and if his opposition to the Civil Rights Bill gave every indication of hastening the immolation of American cities while both stands exposed his conservatism as sham and reaction, Lyndon Johnson's candidacy promised only to lead the nation imperceptively "down a liberal superhighway into the deepest swamp of them all" (CC 43) so that the country might slip into war without even knowing it. Moreover, with Johnson in power the press would merely continue to perform its essential function. It would continue "to tinker with the machine, to adjust, to prepare a seat for new valves and values, to lubricate, to excuse, to justify, to serve in the maintenance of the Establishment" (CC 27), activities that dramatize for Mailer the essence of practical liberal politics.

In Mailer's view the country was at this point divided into "Cannibals" and "Christians." As he notes in the introduction to his miscellany of the same name, there were the Cannibals, who wished to "save the world by killing off what [was] second-rate." They could "think of Jesus as Love, and get an erection from the thought of whippings, blood, burning crosses, burning bodies, and screams in mass graves." On the other hand, there were the Christians, who believed that "man is good if given a chance" and that "science is the salvation of ill." Indeed, they were "utterly opposed to the destruction of human life" but had succeeded nevertheless "in starting all the wars of our own time" (CC 4). Given these oppositions, Mailer concludes both here and in "In the Red Light" that the "country was in disease. It had been in disease for a long time. There was nothing in our growth which was organic" (CC 42). Moreover, presiding over the sickness and incipient violence is "the new chic of the mindless," which echoes throughout "In the Red Light" in the leitmotif of the Goldwater delegates' chant of *Viva-Ole*—annotated appropriately by Mailer as the cannibalistic cry "Live-Yay," "Eager to slay" (CC 28, 42). Indeed, it is precisely the sense of exuberant, gratuitous, and ignorant amorality suggested in the delegates' mindless cheer that leads Mailer to an explicit repudiation of his earlier hope for a rebirth of the myth of the hero. For he notes that

the American mind had gone from Hawthorne and Emerson to the Frug, the Bounce, and Walking the Dog, from *The Flowering of New England* to the cerebrality of professional football in which a quarterback must have not only heart, courage, strength and grace but a mind like an I.B.M. computer. It marks the turn we have taken from the Renaissance. There too was the ideal of a hero with heart, courage, strength, and grace, but he was expected to possess the mind of a passionate artist. Now the best heroes were—in the sense of the Renaissance—mindless: Y. A. Title, John Glenn, Tracy, Smiling Jack; the passionate artists were out on the hot rods, the twist band was whipping the lovers, patriotism was a football game, a fascism would come in (if it came) on Live-Yay! Let's live-yay! The hype had made fifty million musical-comedy minds; now the hype could do anything; it could set high-school students to roar *Viva-Ole*, and they would roar it while victims of a new totalitarianism would be whisked away to a new kind of camp—hey, honey, do you twist, they would yell into the buses. (CC 28–29)

In response then to America's spiritual disease and mindlessness, Mailer finds himself hoping momentarily for the purgation and definition that might come from a Goldwater presidency. For if Goldwater were "elected, America would stand revealed, its latent treacheries would pop forth like boils," while with "Johnson elected, the drift would go on" (CC 44). Of course, Mailer immediately retracts his ironic support. He recalls Goldwater's red-baiting cowardice and the man's self-righteous delight over the prospect of destroying "a foe one-hundredth our size" (CC 45), whether it be North Vietnam or Cuba. But Mailer's momentary support of Goldwater is revealing, for it is precisely this attitude of cynical left radicalism, impelled by a conviction of America's madness and disease, that informs *Why Are We in Vietnam?* And it is Mailer's attraction to the idea of intensifying conflict and risking further social and political polarization for the chance of curing the nation's ills that temporarily defers his transformation into an ambivalent and somewhat aloof left conservative, skeptical of violence and revolution. Thus "In the Red Light" not only gives one an insight into the politics of *Why Are We in Vietnam?*, in which Mailer pushes his radical left advocacy of violence to its limits, it also reveals that his shift from the radical leftist of *Vietnam* to the left conservative of *The Armies of the Night* was not as abrupt as it might seem.

Of course, *Why Are We in Vietnam?* gives little indication itself that a less violent Mailer is about to reveal himself. Of all Mailer's novels *Vietnam* is the least restrained, the most violent. It is an experiment in excess, an attempt to imitate in prose the roaring madness of America as expressed through that embodiment of hip and corporate consciousness—the disc jockey's nonstop electronic rap. And so through language that is a free and manic association of puns, obscenities, hip slang, jive-talking rhyme, technologese, and mutated psychological jargon, Mailer creates D. J. Jethroe, a self-proclaimed genius, "Disc Jockey to the world," and "Grand Synthesizer of the Modern Void."[1]

D. J. presents himself as a hip Voice of America, spreading the word about "how to live in this Electrox Edison world," where "the way you make it is on the distractions" (6, 8). Yet as the novel repeatedly insists, one must always be skeptical about voices of authority, including D. J. himself, for we are all constantly bombarded by messages in which truth and falsehood are complexly mixed or in which lies present themselves as truth. What is more, our powers of perception and interpretation are continuously conditioned by these mentally debilitating messages so that communication becomes necessarily an ambiguous affair. As D. J. suggests, society acts as a kind of succubus upon the unconscious of Americans so that "you never know what vision has been humping you through the night" (208). As a result, one is invited to conclude that just as "there is probably no such thing as a totally false perception" (8), there is also probably no perception that is wholly true. In D. J.'s case, ambiguity resounds with every word that he speaks. For the reader is cautioned repeatedly that there is no security whatsoever in D. J.'s voice. Though the evidence strongly suggests that D. J. is a white, eighteen-year-old boy mentally projecting the story while attending a dinner at his parents' Dallas mansion, a number of other explanations of his identity are offered, most notably the possibility that D. J. is actually a crippled black from Harlem imitating a white Dallas adolescent. As D. J. remarks, "the fact of the matter is that you're up tight with a mystery, me, and this mystery can't be solved because I'm the center of it and I don't comprehend, not necessarily, I could be traducing myself" (23).

Furthermore, there is the additional complication that D. J.'s hip tirade against technological America is the product of a consciousness profoundly influenced by technology. Thus the very act of satire becomes oppressive, indeed maddening, since there seems to be no way, at least within society, to create a satirical vocabulary free of the dehumanizing influences that one wishes to criticize. As a result, one can achieve originality only through wit, through a startling and often humorous combination of essentially intimidating linguistic materials. Similarly, in the absence of innocence and authenticity, one attempts to create a compelling facsimile of the truth not through a direct report of the facts but rather through a clever manipulation of the language of lies.

Yet in insisting that the novel is obsessed with ambiguity, one is likewise suggesting that it is centrally concerned with recovering a portion of the truth. The very title *Why Are We in Vietnam?* implies that the book will provide an explanation for America's involvement in the war. It does so in part by revealing the insane will to power and lust for violence that lie concealed behind the smiling image of the friendly American offering good will and industrial progress both to fellow Americans and to the developing nations of the world. Despite being bombarded by ambiguity himself and despite the fact that his identity remains uncertain, D. J. acts as the inspired seer who makes such a revelation possible. For D. J. is blessed or cursed with double vision, which allows him to see the demonic intention behind the banal political grin. As D. J. puts it, he "suffers from one great American virtue, or maybe it's a disease or ocular dysfunction—D. J. sees through shit" (49).

Throughout the novel, shit serves, along with electricity, as a metaphor for cultural waste so that finally two images prevail— the world as dung heap and the world as a perverse Global Village in which the mind of every human being has become a receptacle for all the psychological waste of the planet. Thus it is altogether apropriate that D. J.'s imagination is obsessed with scatology. As he self-consciously notes, imitating the language of a psycholiterary handbook, "D. J. is marooned on the balmy tropical isle of

Anal Referent Metaphor" (150). The price that D. J. pays for this self-consciousness and for his ability to see "through shit" is alienation and dread. He sees, for example, the duplicity of his own father, Rusty. As an executive at Central Consolidated Combined Chemical and Plastic (4C and P) in charge of "Four C-ing the cancer market" (30) by manufacturing a cigarette filter that absorbs carcinogens while nevertheless causing cancer of the lip, Rusty is "the cream of corporation corporateness" (29). He normally resembles "a high-breed crossing between Dwight D. Eisenhower and Henry Cabot Lodge" (31), with eyes that are "sort of dead ass and dull with a friendly twinkle—typical American eyes" (36). But when D. J. is inspired to see "through to the stinking roots of things" (34–35), as when he is high on pot, he is able to perceive the threatening but vacuous personality that lies beyond the amiable corporate facade. Looking into his father's eyes, D. J. is consumed with dread

because they remind him of his favorite theory which is that America is run by a mysterious hidden mastermind, a secret creature who's got a plastic asshole installed in his brain whereby he can shit out all his corporate management of thoughts. I mean that's what you get when you look into Rusty's eyes. You get voids, man, and gleams of yellow fire—the woods is burning somewhere in his gray matter—and then there's marble aisles, better believe it, fifty thousand fucking miles of marble floor down those eyes, and you got to walk over that to get to The Man. (36)

D. J. first learned of Rusty's character and thereby got a glimpse into his own possible future at age thirteen when he and his father were playing football on the back lawn of their "Dallas ass mansion" (39). D. J. was roundly trouncing his father when he made the mistake of feeling sorry for him. He let Rusty tackle him and was promptly rewarded with a bite "in the ass, right through his pants, that's how insane he was with frustration, that's how much red blood was in *his* neck, and man, he hung on" (40). After the game D. J. tried to avenge himself by hitting Rusty over the head with a pick-axe handle—to no effect. From that day on, D. J. knew that Rusty was "the most competitive prick there is,"

(38) concluding too "that Rusty bit his ass so bad because he was too chicken to bite [his wife] Hallelujah's beautiful butt—she'd have made him pay a half million dollars for each separate hole in her marble palace" (41). The anecdote is broadly comic and rich in thematic suggestiveness. It encapsulates the theme of father hatred and mother love that runs throughout the novel and suggests the macho motivation for the Alaskan bear hunting trip, which took place two years before the opening of the novel and which serves as the narrative focus of the book. Interestingly, in view of Mailer's own macho image, the anecdote burlesques the equation of machismo with authentic manhood, implying that exaggerated male bravado may well be impelled by sexual inadequacy and that it takes cowardly delight in feeding off of the weak while never really testing itself against the strong. Furthermore, as the Alaskan hunting trip fully dramatizes, the problem of this false masculine ideal and father hatred are inseparable. And since its implications are cultural and political as well as psychological, extending to the character of America as fatherland, it provides the thematic context for the novel's explanation of America's involvement in Vietnam.

Rusty's purpose in going on the hunt is, of course, to reaffirm his masculinity and corporate status by nabbing a bear for a trophy and impressing the boys back at 4C and P. Accompanying Rusty on the trip are D. J.; D. J.'s best friend and alter ego, Tex Hyde; and two corporate flunkies, Medium Asshole Pete and Medium Asshole Bill, who "laugh each of them separately and respectively like Henry Fonda and Jimmy Stewart" (50). The leader of the expedition to the "Brooks Range, north of Arctic Circle, Alaska" is "Mr. Luke Fellinka, head guide and hunter extraordinaire for the Moe Henry and Obungekat Safari Group" (38). D. J. originally notes that Luke is both admired and feared by corporate types because he is a real man. But one soon discovers that "Big Luke, despite the big man death-guts charisma, may have had his day" (60). Not only would he just as soon accept his fee without risking a true confrontation with the grizzly, but, as one later learns, he is willing to subvert the equity of the hunt by tracking the game by helicopter to insure satisfied customers. One also learns from Luke's assistant, Ollie, that technology has already defiled the Alaskan wilderness. As Ollie expresses it, "Brooks Range no wilderness now. Airplane go over the head, animal no wild no more, now crazy" (65). As a result of such factors as Luke's moral compromise, the invasion of technology, and even Ollie's parodic diction, together with the comic attitude of the novel itself, the authenticity of the initiation rite that marks the beginning of the hunt is undercut. Though Luke does give D. J. and Tex each a cup of blood to drink, drawn from a wolf that Tex has just killed, and though the act intentionally recalls Sam Fathers' ritual initiation of Isaac McCaslin into manhood, the allusion serves only to emphasize the relative pointlessness of Luke's gesture, for there is no true community of hunters that the boys can enter, and the communal values of patience and humility have no place in an "Electrox Edison world" in which the wilderness has retreated thousands of miles beyond Uncle Ike's Delta, all the way up north past the Arctic Circle. Though drinking the wolf blood does at least communicate to D. J. one truth of the hunt, making him "up tight with the essential animal insanity of things" (70), neither he nor Tex is Luke's apprentice, nor does Luke act as a surrogate father. Instead Luke is simply one more fallen hero without a heritage to pass on. Thus one realizes that the true values the boys do learn must be essentially private rather than communal, and though D. J. and Tex can form a bond of blood with each other, they can establish no true relationship with the generation represented by Rusty, Luke, and the minions of Corporation Land.

The false masculine ideal and moral bankruptcy of this generation are reflected in the fact that Rusty and his corporate colleagues resort to technological overkill to reinforce their sense of male potency. The necessity for overkill urges itself because the men are insecure about their hunting expertise and courage. But since they see technology as an extension of male power, they need not acknowledge that it is a cowardly substitute for the inherent strength that they lack. At the same time overkill provides what is for them the double advantage of eliminating risk while promising the pleasure of slaughter. As Rusty admits, "I like the feeling that if I miss a vital area I can still count on the big impact knocking them down, killing them by the total impact, shock!" (85).

This attitude is implicit in M. A. Pete's choice of weapon. Hardly a purist about questions of equity, Pete "wants a grenade and bullet all in one sweet cartridge package—he wants a bomb which will drop a grizzly if it hits him in the toe" (81). So he brings along an "African rhinoceros-hippo-elephant-soften-the-bullet-for-the-lion double-barreled .600-.577 custom, only-one-of-its-kind-ever-built Jeffrey Nitro Express carrying a 900-grain bullet for Shot # 1, a 750-grain for Shot # 2, and a recoil guaranteed to knock a grand piano on its ass" (82). When Pete uses this exotic weapon on a caribou, mortally wounding the animal, Luke insists on tracking and killing it to put an end to its suffering. But the integrity of Luke's action is immediately compromised by his decision to call out the helicopter, thereby saving time and giving himself and his clients a cheap technological thrill. As D. J. notes, Luke "was an American, what the fuck, he had spent his life living up tight with wilderness and that had eaten at him, wilderness was tasty but boredom was his corruption, he had wanted a jolt, so sees it D. J., Big Luke now got his kicks with the helicopter. . . . so the rest of the hunt, all next seven days he gave what was secretly wanted, which was helicopter heaven" (98–99).

The use of the helicopter turns the hunt into the moral equivalent of an unjust war, for which Vietnam was the obscene contemporary example. The hunt is unjust and meretricious because there are no true tests and no true rewards. For D. J., however, there is a moral price to pay. Already conscious by virtue of his blood initiation of the presence of raw nature, aware, that is, of "the essential animal insanity of things," he is able to establish an empathy with his first kill, a mountain goat that he bags with pointless ease, and understand the degree of his own compromise. Thus "the pain of [the goat's] exploding heart shot like an arrow into D. J.'s heart, and the animals had gotten him, they were talking all around him now, communicating the unspoken unseen unmeasurable electromagnetism and wave of all the psychic circuits of all the wild of Alaska, and he was only part of them, and part he was of gasoline of Texas, the asshole sulfur smell of money-oil clinging to the helicopter" (99–100). Later that night, lying safe in bed, D. J. is struck "with a second blow on his heart from the exploding heart of the goat" (101–102). Drawn outside, he gets "one breath of the sense of that *force* up in the North, of land North North above him and [dives] back to the bed, his sixteen-year-old heart racing through the first spooks of an encounter with Herr Dread" (102).

D. J.'s moral predicament is typical of the situations in which Mailer's existential heroes find themselves. For them, the choice is always stark and the standard unbending. Acting in the presence of such absolutes as God and the Devil or untamed nature, they can either experience the dread of testing their courage, risking their sense of self and opening themselves up to the invasion of divine forces in the struggle to achieve greater personal freedom and power, or they can shrink from the challenge and embrace cowardice and compromise, trying perhaps, as the corporate hunters do, to mask the failure by identifying their own prowess with institutional power. Of course, under the aegis of the compliant Luke, the hunting expedition offers only dark comedy rather than any heroic possibilities. As D. J. notes in a quintessentially Maileresque generic distinction, "comedy is the study of the unsound actions of the cowardly under stress, just as tragedy is equal study time of the brave under heroic but enigmatic, reverberating, resonant conditions of loss" (81). Certainly the effect of this comedy of cowardice on "America's last unspoiled wilderness" (113) is anything but funny. Technology has upset the balance of nature in the Brooks Range, driving the grizzlies mad. The response of "Big Luke General Fellinka" to this situation is worthy of the Joint Chiefs of Staff. To counter the tech-induced madness of the grizzly, Luke will simply apply more technological force. He decides that he and the rest of the party "must be in position to bomb and superblast any grizzer who attacks. Therefore they will all make it together—five clients, five guides" (116).

With the decision to go collective, all possibility of authentic testing is gone. The only brave alternative is clearly to leave the group. In that way one might attempt to restore the equity of the hunt through a true confrontation between man and beast. Of course, Rusty could hardly care less about justice and fair play, but he does care passionately about bringing back a trophy. In a chapter devoted to a stream of consciousness venting of Rusty's right-wing paranoia about women's liberation, minority civil rights, miscegenation, the youth rebellion, European anti-Americanism, U.S. industrial incompetence, the threat of communism, white athletic inferiority, Jewish liberal political power, and the substitution of the use of hallucinogenic drugs for religious belief, Rusty concludes that all these threats to God's Country, America, can be overcome if only he is good enough. Thus one realizes that in Mailer's world the right as well as the left may see itself as God's agent in the battle against evil, thereby establishing an opposition between judgments of what is God's will and what is the Devil's desire. As Rusty imagines it, "he, Rusty, is fucked unless he gets that bear, for if he don't, white men are fucked more and they can take no more. Rusty's secret is that he sees himself as one of the pillars of the firmament, yeah, man—he reads the world's doom in his own fuckup. If he is less great than God intended him to be, then America is in trouble" (111). As far as Rusty is concerned, the cowardice of overkill is perfectly acceptable. He kills his bear, and he can claim it as his own, notwithstanding the excessive firepower. But getting lost in the crowd is intolerable. So once the men begin hunting as a group and firing in unison, Rusty becomes concerned. And when Luke awards M. A. Pete the bear that Rusty thought he had actually shot himself, he fears that his cherished trophy is in jeopardy. As a result, he decides to bolt the group, taking along his elated son, D. J., to stalk bear on their own.

In this moment of united purpose and heroic potential, with

Rusty and D. J. "off on a free, father and son" (124), a rush of filial love briefly replaces father hatred. But the sense of an exhilarating emotional buildup is immediately aborted as D. J. abruptly shifts the focus of the novel ahead two years to the dinner at the Dallas mansion, whereupon he informs the reader that "between D. J. and Rusty it is all torn, all ties of properly sublimated parental-filial libido have been X-ed out man . . . torn by the inexorable hunt logic of the Brooks Range" (126). At the outset, however, of their independent trek through the wilderness both D. J. and Rusty do enjoy the full existential benefits of plunging into a risktaking situation. Rusty begins to liberate himself from the waste of Corporation Land, "shedding those corporation layers, all that paper ass desk shit and glut" (127–28). And as their senses come alive, he and D. J. are able to tune in to the nuances of the wild, "listening to the *mood*" and experiencing the sensation that they would be able "to *smell* that bear" (128). Father and son even begin to chat intimately. Indeed, in one of the novel's most explicit references to the United States as a predatory nation, Rusty confides to his son his disgust over the fact that the eagle serves as the country's emblem. Says Rusty, with unintentional irony, "I think it's a secret crime that America, which is the greatest nation ever lived, better read a lot of history to see how shit-and-sure a proposition that is, is nonetheless represented, indeed even symbolized by an eagle, the most miserable of the scavengers, worse than a crow" (132–33).

Despite such confidences, D. J.'s hatred of his father remains close to consciousness. His fear of an imminent bear attack touches off a traumatic childhood memory of his father beating him, indeed wanting to kill him, perhaps for screaming and thereby interrupting Rusty and Hallelujah in the midst of making love. Thus, smelling death while on the trail of the bear, "D. J. for first time in his life is hip to the hole of his center which is slippery desire to turn his gun and blast a shot into Rusty's fat fuck face, thump in his skull, whawng! and whoong! with the dead-ass butt of his Remington 721" (136–37). This acknowledgment reinforces the sense of foreboding created by D. J.'s Dallas dinner party announcement that the father-son relationship has been destroyed. One realizes once again that competition between D. J. and Rusty is highly charged and sexual. Furthermore, each has actually felt the desire to kill the other. So it should not be surprising that Rusty would ultimately be incapable of fully cooperating as part of a father-son hunting team just as he was unable to tolerate remaining a member of Luke's group expedition. For Rusty subscribes completely to "the inexorable hunt logic of the Brooks Range," which dictates that shooting a bear and claiming a trophy as one's own must override all other considerations. Thus as father and son pursue the hunt together, the stage is clearly set for a betrayal.

The gravity of such a betrayal is increased by the fact that the actual confrontation with the bear is clearly D. J.'s first true test of manhood. The dauntless ferocity of the bear's attack amplifies the lesson that D. J. learned from drinking the wolf's blood, for he now knows "that if the center of things is insane, it is insane with force" (143). The moral relationship that this lesson establishes between the blood ritual and D. J.'s confrontation with the bear further emphasizes that he is engaged in an existential encounter that will define, at least initially, his identity as a man. Impelled in part by the thought of Tex's derision if he chose not to pursue the wounded, tech-crazed bear, D. J. gathers his courage and leads his father down the slope through the treacherous brush in an effort to flush and finish off the beast. The enterprise recalls Francis Macomber's coming of age on a buffalo hunt, dramatizing the same mortal danger of flushing a fatally wounded wild animal and suggesting the intimate knowledge of nature that the true hunter derives from such a confrontation. It is precisely this knowledge, along with the values of the true hunter, that D. J. is attempting to discover and embrace. And it is the sacredness of this knowledge and these values, together with the sacredness of the father-son relationship, that Rusty violates when he chooses the moment of D. J.'s most intimate communion with the dying bear to shoot and thereby claim his cherished trophy. In that moment "griz went up to death in one last paroxysm, legs thrashing, brain exploding from new galvanizings and overloadings of massive damage report, and one last final heuuuuuu, all forgiveness gone."[2]

For D. J. all forgiveness of his father is likewise gone. Arriving at camp, after not speaking to Rusty on the entire way back, D. J., in one final test of his father's integrity, announces that the nine-hundred-pound bear belongs to Rusty. Thus when Rusty betrays him through silent acceptance of the unearned prize, it is truly the "final end of love of one son for one father" (147). This scene of betrayal represents one of Mailer's most disturbing dramatizations of the problem of the father, a problem that has been a central theme of Mailer's from the very beginning of his career, reflecting an abiding concern with a deep, unresolved conflict in America's cultural identity growing out of a historic national identification with the millennial myth of the American as the New Adam. For it requires but the most subtle shift in perspective to see the American Adam not as a mythic figure of innocence freed from the limits of history to pursue the romantic dream of ever-expanding possibilities but as an orphan, bereft of antecedents, adrift in a hostile or, at least, brutally impersonal world. In this way one turns from Emerson's self-reliant "new individual" who "can owe his fathers nothing"[3] as well as from Whitman's solitary yet all-encompassing "Me myself" to the isolated vulnerability of the orphaned Ishmael and Huck Finn. One likewise turns to the tragic inevitability of the plight of Donatello and Billy Budd, whose innocence is sacrificed to the ethical and political exigencies of history.

The ambiguity in the status of the Adamic figure has been intensified by the fact that the myth of the New Adam has now become part of America's heritage. For example, in the case of Mailer's work the self-conscious appropriation of elements of American millennialism actually represents a paradoxical attempt to establish a connection to America's heritage while at the same time explicitly affirming the primacy of the self. Thus even at the height of Mailer's romanticism, a period extending from

"The White Negro" to *Why Are We in Vietnam?*, his anti-historical attitude is highly qualified. During this period, Mailer would view totalitarianism's collectivist opposition to history as malignant since it denies the self while leaving one marooned "in an endless hallway of the present" (PP 186). On the other hand, he would support the Hip rejection of history, believing that it promotes organic growth and fulfills the self by substituting millennial myth for history. In this way Hip would allow one to live in an "enormous present" of increased existential freedom and power while still maintaining a connection to a nourishing national heritage.

Such at any rate is the theory as Mailer expresses it in "The White Negro" and many of the pieces collected in *The Presidential Papers*. Yet throughout the bulk of Mailer's major work, one is much more aware of the conflict between the desire for existential freedom and the need to experience a sense of cultural continuity, which one can have only by establishing a connection with one's origins. It is precisely this conflict that comes to a focus in Mailer's treatment of the problem of the father, a problem that produces many of the conflicts and much of the violence that are dramatized in Mailer's characters. There is, for example, father hatred—dramatized against a background of false values and in some cases paternal violence—in the stories of Cummings, Croft, Hearn, Deborah Rojack, and D. J. Jethroe. In *Ancient Evenings* there is Nef-khep-aukhem's murderous betrayal of his son, Menenhetet Two, after his biological paternity has been superseded by the spiritual paternity of the Pharaoh Ptah-nem-hotep. And there is fatherlessness in the stories of Mikey Lovett, Sergius O'Shaugnessy, Marilyn Monroe, and in a sense, Gary Gilmore, whose father once left his wife, Gary, and Gary's older brother in a restaurant, saying that he had to get some change, and was not seen again by them for three months. In all of these cases Mailer is certainly reflecting Hemingway's conclusion that mature existential consciousness begins with separation from the father. Yet, notwithstanding his strong identification with romantic alienation, Mailer is insisting just as forcefully that the need for cultural continuity survives this separation. Indeed, it is intensified by it. And if one is unable to establish the necessary cultural link between generations to make possible the transmission of significant values, psychological and moral expatriation becomes tantamount to life-denying exile. Nowhere does Mailer make this point more dramatically than in *Ancient Evenings*, where Menenhetet Two's survival in the Land of the Dead depends upon his ability to maintain a connection to the life-sustaining myths of his culture through his filial relationships with Menenhetet One and Ptah-nem-hotep. Of course, Mailer made much the same point early in his career in the stories of Mikey Lovett and Sergius O'Shaugnessy through their respective apprenticeships with McLeod and Eitel. For in each case the older man clearly acts as a surrogate father who is able, despite his own failures, to communicate to his "son" moral values and ideals that form the basis for political and artistic commitment. Within this context Lovett's narcissistic isolation and Sergius's impotence signify not so much sexual problems as the sterile, self-limiting condition of the cultural orphan. Just as disturbing of course is the situation of the son or daughter who is victimized by the father. As Mailer dramatizes in the stories of Deborah Rojack and D. J. Jethroe, if one is unable to escape the influence of the brutal father and draw upon an alternative source of values, one may well be doomed to imitate, and perhaps even surpass, the brutality that one hates.

It is precisely this alternative in the aftermath of Rusty's betrayal that D. J. is seeking when he and Tex leave camp at night to go off together into the Arctic wilderness. But before they can hope to discover a new source of values, they must first attempt to rid themselves of the corruptions of corporate America. As a result, they decide to perform what D. J. self-consciously terms "a purification ceremony" (175), abandoning their weapons to confront the wild without protection. In the course of their existential expedition into raw nature, the boys learn that "it's terrifying to be free of mixed shit" (184). They know what it is to be alone, experiencing too the sharpening of the senses that is one of the psychological rewards for enduring the awe and dread of a direct confrontation with the powers of the North.

Yet as D. J.'s pseudoscientific explanation of the subliminal communication of modern madness suggests, there is finally no escaping the debilitating effects of Corporation Land. According to D. J., human impulses are subject to the mysterious laws of electromagnetism, chemistry, and psychic phenomena, which include the principle that frustration turns impulses into telepathic crystals. Thus D. J. envisions the polar icecaps as colossal manifestations of the collective frustration of the human race. Yet, as telepathic receivers, the icy poles constitute "the Encyclopedia of Cataclysmic Knowledge" (159), for in opposition to the electromagnetic field of the earth, D. J. posits "the Magnetic-Electro fief of the dream," the domain of all unconscious communication. As D. J. notes, "when you go into sleep, that mind of yours leaps, stirs, and sifts itself into the Magnetic-Electro fief of the dream, hereafter known as M. E. or M. E. F., you are a part of the spook flux of the night like an iron filing in the E. M. field (otherwise glommed as e. m. f.) and it all flows, mind and asshole, anode and cathode, you sending messages and receiving all through the night." (170). Since opposites attract, all unconscious communications go right to the poles, with the sweet dreams and nightmares of North America ending up at the Brooks Range. Thus one realizes that Alaska's frozen wilderness has become the battleground for a contention of ultimates. On the one hand, there are the concentration of M. E. F. madness and the despoliation effected by the technological hunters, which has driven many of the animals into a perverse insanity, while, on the other hand, there is in those parts of the wilderness that remain undefiled a godlike yet beastly immanence of overpowering grandeur.

As a result of such complications, critics have differed greatly in interpreting the novel's conclusion.[4] The problem lies in identifying the ethical significance of the boys' mystical encounter with a deadly yet divine force in nature and relating the lesson to their subsequent enthusiasm over the immediate prospect of fighting in Vietnam. D. J. and Tex experience their beastly revelation in the dead of night while camping out miles away from any other human being. At this point their senses are most acute. Three hours before, in the beauty of the late evening sunset, D. J. perceived "the sorrow of the North," which "brought by leaves and wind some speechless electric gathering of woe" (196). Now he and Tex are as close as they can get to being purified of "mixed shit." In this condition the boys observe the aurora borealis as it begins to flash in the sky above, communicating to them the real presence of a beastly god whose magnetic force is drawing them to leave camp and walk utterly defenseless into the frozen wilderness, where they would "disappear and die and join that great beast" (202). In this moment of truth Tex's and D. J.'s relationship expresses itself in a conflict of erotic and aggressive urges. Insofar as each represents the other's alter ego, together composing in Jekyll-and-Hyde fashion the two parts of one split personality, the urges that they experience are most significantly expressions of the fundamental nature of the human personality itself, revealing the instinctual desires to copulate and to kill, which lie at the root of human action. These instinctual aims in fact represent the human manifestation of the principle in nature that the godly beast expresses in the words, " 'Go out and kill— fulfill my will, go and kill' " (203). The statement expresses nothing less than the principle of survival, which is naturally regulated by the equity of the hunt and diametrically opposed to the cowardly practice of technological overkill, which typifies modern warfare and which predominated in Vietnam.

As Robert Solotaroff rightly argues, the boys' encounter with this immanent god constitutes "an authentic moment"[5] in which they understand killing as part of the cycle of nature. At the same time they pledge themselves to each other in blood brotherhood, forming a bond that reflects their common commitment to fulfill the will of the beast by killing with courage and a sense of equity and only out of the necessity to survive. As the "authentic moment" lapses, however, and the boys are again exposed to the electronic madness of America, this primitive ideal is debased, becoming instead a desire for the cannibalistic joy of the kill, that is to say, the perverse and ultimately self-destructive pleasure of killing for its own sake rather than out of the necessity to survive. The debasement of D. J. and Tex, as well as their primitive ideal, parallels the defilement of America as Virgin Land and New World Garden movingly described in the "Terminal Intro Beep and Out." Like "that sad deep sweet beauteous mystery land of purple forests, and pink rock, and blue water, Indian haunts from Maine to the shore of Californ," D. J. and Tex have been "gutted, shit on, used and blasted" by "all the woe and shit and parsimony and genuine greed of all those fucking English, Irish, Scotch and European weeds, transplanted to North America" (205). It is quite clearly as a result of such maddening abuse that D. J. perversely translates the violent imperative of the godly beast into the ejaculation "Vietnam, hot damn" (208). Thus one realizes that the novel itself rejects both technological mass murder and cannibalistic blood lust. It affirms instead the kind of liberating individual violence that Mailer sanctions in "The White Negro" and *An American Dream*, violence that is an expression of the soul's struggle to survive, the kind of violence that in *Why Are We in Vietnam?* is dramatized as being pure, instinctive, and god-like. One realizes too that with this novel, Mailer pressed his advocacy of violent left radicalism to its limit. Having reached this extreme, Mailer was now ready to alter his strategy of critique and begin explicitly identifying himself with the conservatism that constitutes an important minority element in "In the Red Light." At the same time he would take great delight in paradox-ically continuing to support the left, with the significant differ-ence that he would now be skeptical of violence and revolution. And so it is that the startling conclusion of *Why Are We in Vietnam?* in a sense clears the way for the appearance of Norman Mailer as America's one and only left conservative, advancing an ideology that would help create a new direction for his work, one that would challenge the assumptions of the millennial imagina-tion by forcing them into a direct confrontation with the limits of history.

Chapter 8

The Armies of the Night:
Mailer as Participant

Like "The White Negro," *The Armies of the Night* marks a significant turning point in Norman Mailer's career. In this book Mailer abandoned the traditional novel for the hybrid form of the nonfiction novel, substituting for the alienated protagonists of his earlier works a fictional comic character named "Mailer" who attempts, with a good deal of self-conscious reluctance, to discover a significant form of political protest and participate in a historic event of national importance. These aesthetic innovations nicely complement Mailer's affirmation of left conservatism, for they move into the dramatic foreground the chronic problem of political participation, which was abandoned in triumphant despair as a matter of romantic principle by fictional heroes embodying the views of the alienated radical left. As Ihab Hassan notes with misdirected admiration, the alienated romantic protagonist's "inevitable defeat is the source of his greatest pride."[1] Mailer's left conservatism rejects the ironic pride and heroism of victimization, forcing whenever possible a confrontation with history. Mailer's nonfiction novel provides the vehicle for this confrontation, raising the question of the extent to which the expression of American millennial ideals has been limited by history while challenging the imagination to achieve the paradoxical goal of creating a context for romantic possibilities within society itself.

These concerns demand, of course, that one attempt to discover the meaning of historical issues and events. For Mailer,
such a task falls quite naturally within the province of the novelist
when objective sources of information prove unavailable or inconclusive or when an understanding of the issue or event requires a revelation of the national character. The need for a
novelistic revelation of the national character in understanding
the October 1967 march against the Pentagon serves as the raison
d'être of *The Armies of the Night*. So it is not surprising that Mailer
would attempt in the book to expose the chronic inability of the
corporate news media to express a historical truth that is not
self-evidently revealed by the superficies of public rhetoric and
behavior. He initiates this attempt on a personal basis, taking the
incredible comic risk of opening *Armies* with *Time* magazine's
scathing portrait of his drunken, obscene address at Washington's Ambassador Theater before a group of several hundred
people opposed to the Vietnam War, an account that concludes
with a brief, sarcastic reference to Mailer's arrest two days later
for bolting across a military police line during the march against
the Pentagon. Reprinting the blurb serves as an effective device
for stimulating one to read on in search of further entertainment,
but the danger, of course, is that the portrait will be accepted at
face value, with the ineradicable image of Mailer the fool presiding over the entire book. Mailer took the risk of leaving this
impression because the *Time* account provided him with the
perfect opportunity to use the media's caricature of Norman
Mailer as a point of departure for transforming himself into a
fictional "comic hero" (53) whose sometimes outrageously foolish
and egotistical behavior is belied by an acute consciousness of his
own foibles, signifying that, as a novelist, he is "in command of a
detachment classic in severity" (54).

According to Mailer, such a character provides the best possible point of view for examining the march on the Pentagon. For
the march was an ambiguous event fraught with absurd incongruities, reflecting in general the nature of twentieth-century
America and more particularly America's involvement in Viet-

nam. If a reliable report on the march will never be forthcoming, it is still possible to attempt to create a compelling and trustworthy personal narrative of the event by viewing it through the eyes of a comic character whose absurdities, incongruities, and disproportions reflect the psychology of the event itself. As the reader grows familiar with the incongruities of this character, he learns at the same time to identify and compensate for the character's subjectivity, which is comically reflective of Mailer's own. By combining such familiarity with a knowledge of the existing facts on the march as well as a comparison of conflicting reports of what actually transpired, the reader may finally uncover the meaning of the march against the Pentagon and in so doing gain a complex understanding of the divisions existing in America at the time as a result of the war in Vietnam.

The reader is able to achieve an intimate identification with Mailer because, unlike most comic characters, he is not flat but instead possesses considerable depth. As the comic characteristics of Mailer unfold in the beginning of the book, the fullness of his flawed humanity likewise reveals itself. The result, as the comedy and sympathetic humanity grow together, is one of Norman Mailer's most brilliant creations.

Dominating the early pages of the book is Mailer's comic ambivalence over whether to participate in the march at all. Informing this ambivalence is an acute consciousness of public image as well as an unrelenting commitment to self-scrutiny. At the outset Mailer confesses that "he had in fact learned to live in the sarcophagus of his image—at night, in his sleep, he might dart out, and paint improvements on the sarcophagus. During the day, while he was helpless, newspapermen and other assorted bravos of the media and the literary world would carve ugly pictures on the living tomb of his legend" (5–6). The idea that Mailer's authentic self is trapped, Draculalike and helpless, within the sarcophagus of his public image is clever, endearing, and not a little misleading. As I have suggested, one of Mailer's primary purposes in *Armies* is to substitute an elaborate self-fiction for the media's demeaning image of him. Ironically, the insistence that Mailer is largely at the mercy of his public image provides the perfect rhetorical ploy for changing that image. It immediately creates sympathy for Mailer while building upon the sense of comic vulnerability that was created by reprinting the *Time* magazine portrait. As a result, he has already prepared the reader to accept a radical transformation of the Mailer persona. For he quickly inverts the image of Mailer as the strident self-advertiser, sensationalist, and tireless prophet of risktaking to reveal the contrasting image of the wounded man who is comically fearful of perpetuating his reputation as "a loser." Thus when Mitchell Goodman calls to enlist him in the Pentagon protest and Mailer is reticent, one immediately understands. Goodman's previous attempt at symbolic protest by sponsoring a walkout at the National Book Awards earlier that year had more or less fizzled because of a wavering commitment among the literati, and Mailer, the presumptive loser, perhaps could not afford to support someone "whose instinct for the winning move was not—on the face—spectacular." Of course, even while embracing Mailer's unaccustomed reticence, one is meant to see that the real reason for his hesitation is simple unadulterated fear. Mailer, who was boycotting the awards in protest for having never been nominated, wonders for the reader's benefit if he would have had the courage to walk out of them in protest against the war. And when Goodman mentions that the ultimate goal of the Pentagon protest is "'to try to invade the corridors of the Pentagon during office hours and close down some of their operation'" (8), Mailer's private response is a comic act of heresy against the existential code of the risktaker:

Mailer received such news with no particular pleasure. It sounded vaguely and uneasily like a free-for-all with students, state troopers, and Hell's Angels flying in and out of the reports—exactly the sort of operation they seemed to have every other weekend out on the Coast. He felt one little bubble of fear tilt somewhere about the solar plexus. (9)

Of course, Mailer finally agrees to participate. But the fears remain. A few weeks later, arriving in Washington for the march, he entertains the fantasy, stimulated by the chilly October breeze, that he could conceivably be dead in two days, a fantasy that thoughts of the power of the government and talk of the possible use of paratroopers do nothing to diminish.

It is precisely by focusing on such fears and inconsistencies that Norman Mailer gives his comic character dimension. In so doing, he presents the anti-heroic alter ego of the existentialist risktaker, a man whose constantly shifting personality is the expression of a multiplicity of conflicting demands and intentions. As Mailer admits, "the architecture of his personality bore resemblance to some provincial cathedral which warring orders of the church might have designed separately over several centuries, the particular cathedral falling into the hands of one architect, then his enemy." As a result, "boldness, attacks of shyness, rude assertion, and circumlocutions tortured as arthritic fingers working at lace, all took their turn with him" (17).

Mailer's identification of himself in *Armies* as a left conservative serves as the perfect ideological extension of such a paradoxical personality. The opening pages of the book are replete with the colorful and energetic statement of conservative positions, each of which is calculated to attack one's preconception of Mailer as the Hip left radical. One learns that the man who once dubbed himself General Marijuana is now opposed to drugs, for his use of them has succeeded only in giving him "Swiss cheese for memory" (6) and "the illusion he was a genius, as indeed an entire generation of children would so come to see themselves a decade later out on celestial journeys of LSD" (5). One learns too that Mailer's long-held biases against liberal academics, homosexuality, masturbation, unisex psychology, and guilt-free copulation have now assumed even greater proportions in his imagination even as his commitment to violence and his belief in revolution have diminished. Now, as a revolutionary manqué, he finds himself with an animus toward hippies and young idealists, whom he sees as "utterly lobotomized away from the sense of sin" (14). Of course, it is with the hippies, young idealists, and liberal academics that Mailer has publicly aligned himself, and it is they who will serve as his comrades as he marches against the Pentagon. But the alliance is uneasy at best, ever subject to the tensions perpetually at work within Mailer himself. This uneasiness is particularly evident when Mailer arrives at a pre-march party "given by an attractive liberal couple" (13). Harboring a score of reservations about the psychology, politics, and style of the liberal academics at the gathering and wishing to avoid predictably awkward cocktail party exchanges, Mailer takes refuge in huddling with Robert Lowell, whom he imagines shares the same political self-image:

if they were doomed to be revolutionaries, rebels, dissenters, anarchists, protesters, and general champions of one Left cause or another, they were also, in private, *grands conservateurs*, and if the truth be told, poor damn emigre princes. They were willing if necessary (probably) to die for the cause—one could hope the cause might finally at the end have an unexpected hint of wit, a touch of the Lord's last grace—but wit or no, grace or grace failing, it was bitter rue to have to root up one's occupations of the day, the week, and the weekend and trot down to Washington for idiot mass manifestations which could only drench one in the most ineradicable kind of mucked-up publicity and have for compensation nothing at this party which might be representative of some of the Devil's better creations. (18)

Read within the context of one's preconceived image of Mailer as well as later revelations of his attitudes in *Armies*, this passage is highly suggestive of the many layers of ambivalence and contradiction that constitute Mailer as a comic character. Once the possessor of a revolutionary vision, he is now "doomed" to be numbered among the rebels; though still identifying himself publicly with the forces of protest and change, in private he is a *grand conservateur*; though capable elsewhere in *Armies* of professing his great faith in democratic man, here he is clearly as suspicious as James Fenimore Cooper of the leveling tendencies of democracy; and though "willing if necessary (probably) to die for the cause," he is irritated that his participation in a potentially chaotic protest threatens to spoil his weekend plans, which, one later learns, include most prominently a wicked New York party.

Such flamboyant contradictions as these prepare one to expect almost anything of Mailer, and he certainly does not disappoint. In fact he even warns one that his normal quotidian personality has been known to transform itself spontaneously into a wild egomaniacal "Beast," an image that immediately recalls the drunken, obscene Norman Mailer of the *Time* magazine piece. Yet when the Beast does appear at the Ambassador Theater, he is decidedly different from the one-dimensional *Time* caricature. Though actually more outlandish in the highly detailed comic account presented in *Armies*, he is now clearly a sympathetic figure. One already feels quite intimate with the many internal contradictions of the quotidian Mailer, having enjoyed the humor and candor with which he has, however calculatedly, exposed his own foibles to public scrutiny. And given the tendency for omniscience to engender forgiveness, when the Beast reveals himself at the Ambassador, one understands and accepts. Though he may appear to be simply a bullying, foul-mouthed drunk who commandeers the stage to draw attention to himself, in reality he is a serious man, a would-be teacher, a philosopher with high ideals and aspirations. Undeterred by the fact that prior to addressing the crowd he has clumsily urinated upon a darkened lavatory floor, he chooses to admit the faux pas to his audience, using the self-confessed embarrassment as a convenient point of departure for an object lesson on the redemptive capacity of the human spirit. As Mailer affirms in language that is marvelously suggestive of the fool's gold of drunken associations,

man might be a fool who peed in the wrong pot, man was also a scrupulous servant of the self-damaging admission; man was therefore a philosopher who possessed the magic stone; he could turn loss to philosophic gain, and so illumine the deeps, find the poles, and eventually learn to cultivate his most special fool's garden: *satori*, incandescence, and the hard gem-like flame of bourbon burning in the furnaces of metabolism. (31–32)

Now all of this is quite comic yet poignant too in light of Mailer's acknowledgment that he has far too often been written off as a loser and in view of his corresponding need to be taken seriously, a need best expressed in his affectionate envy of Robert Lowell, who seems silently to condemn Mailer's Ambassador Theater antics with "one withering glance . . . saying much, saying, 'Every single bad thing I have ever heard about you is not exaggerated'" (41). Yet even more poignant is the growing implication that Mailer's character serves as a comic reflection of a uniquely American tragedy of aspiration that has repeated itself throughout the nation's history, unfolding time and again with fateful inevitability out of the heritage of a tortured Puritan psychology, which pits the faith that Americans are God's Chosen People against the knowledge that all humanity is fallen and depraved. Mailer, the self-admittedly flawed, perennial seeker of greatness, sees in the hollows of Lowell's cheeks the physical signs of the spiritual erosion caused by the clash of transcendent imperative and self-limiting knowledge, for "the hollows speak of the great Puritan gloom in which the country was founded—man was simply not good enough for God" (33).

The hope of *Armies* is that this judgment may not be final. Perhaps America may be good enough. Perhaps without denying the truth of its limitations it may yet transcend all internal conflict and conduct itself in a manner that is worthy of God's Chosen People. Yet, as in the case of Mailer, the dialectical protagonist who becomes the book's representative American, often one is primarily aware of the divisions. For Vietnam has exposed the horrible gap between American myth and American history, further polarizing the nation along the lines of every conceivable difference, driving to self-defensive, antagonistic extremes young and old, left and right, middle class and working class, and black and white.

From Mailer's point of view the march on the Pentagon becomes a bloody pageant play that dramatizes these national oppositions. Mailer repeatedly identifies the symbolic nature of the protest, emphasizing its medieval aspect. The protesters are "Crusaders" (92) or, as Mailer christens the Ambassador Theater audience, "'fellow carriers of the holy unendurable grail'" (38).

The Pentagon itself was chosen as the focal point of the protest because it "symbolized the military might of the Republic." The purpose of the march was "not to capture" the Pentagon "but to wound it *symbolically*." Nevertheless, "the forces defending that bastion reacted as if a symbolic wound could prove as mortal as any other combative rent. In the midst of a technological century, close to its apogee, a medieval, nay, a primitive mode of warfare was reinvigorated, and the nations of the world stood in grave observation" (54). At the same time, however, Mailer insists upon the real consequences of this symbolic event, for the march is "'at once a symbolic act and a real act'" (47) in which the anti-war protesters are putting both body and soul on the line, "going out to attack the hard core of technology land with less training than armies were once offered by a medieval assembly ground" (92).

For Mailer the march becomes the epitome of an existential situation since neither the marchers nor the government knows what the outcome of the protest will be. And from the outset of *Armies* he stresses the sense of danger and unknown consequences that attends the march in particular and opposition to the war in general. There is, of course, Mailer's own fearful reticence at participating in the march itself, at pledging to take part in income tax protest, and at aiding men who choose to burn or turn in their draft cards. Moreover, as Mailer suggests, the protesters themselves are taking even greater risks. At a draft protest on the steps of the Justice Department on the day following his Ambassador Theater exploits, Mailer observes that the resisters are "committing their future either to prison, emigration, frustration, or at best, years where everything must be unknown" (74). The commitment of these men inspires in Mailer a new, uncharacteristic modesty as well as a new respect. For he realizes that some of the draft protesters would have to be numbered among the liberal academics whom he avoided and secretly deprecated at the party the evening before. Now witnessing their quiet courage enforces in him the lesson that "there was no escape. As if some final cherished rare innocence of childhood still preserved intact in him was brought finally to the surface and there expired, so he lost at that instant the last secret delight he retained in life as a game where finally you never got hurt if you played the game well enough" (78). Thus the draft resisters have a double effect on Mailer. They return him to both the hated, long-abandoned humility of his youth and the exigencies of his existential ethic, which demand that he take the risk of confronting the government with the expectation of arrest and so defeat fear and heal his own internal divisions by performing the very act that might hold the most fearful consequences. The real object of Mailer's political protest is, of course, not the inevitable arrest but confrontation— challenging the government to prevent him and the other protesters from invading the Pentagon. And it is precisely this emphasis on confrontation, risk, and activist protest that distinguishes Mailer's political action from the romantic self-sacrifice exemplified by Hearn's decision to resign his command, a decision that Ihab Hassan praises as ironically redemptive.

Mailer's self-admittedly modest act of courage and the courage of thousands of other Pentagon protesters serve in the book as moral examples. They suggest that a deeply divided nation with a historic obligation to atone for its failure to live up to its millennial ideals might heal its divisions and atone for past sins and failures of courage by taking the risk of publicly expressing total opposition to the Vietnam War, which more than anything else in American life since the enslavement of the blacks and the genocidal slaughter of the Indians had come to represent all that was wrong with the country. Once again Mailer sees the burden of America's guilt reflected in Robert Lowell, who "gave off at times the unwilling haunted saintliness of a man who was repaying the moral debts of ten generations of ancestors" (83). He sees the country's guilt likewise, however, in both the recent failures of the old left opposition and the hypocrisy of the entrenched governmental and corporate authority. On the one hand, according to Mailer there was the left's "sound-as-brickwork-logic-of-the-next-step" (85), which had succeeded only in splintering America's progressive political movements into dozens of impotent factions or in coopting the left's integrity by associating it with establishmentarian anti-communism and politically innocuous national labor unions. On the other hand, there was the governmental and corporate authority that knew well the rhetoric of morality and used that knowledge to present lies as truth, its public deception now pervading American culture, dominating its politics, its economy, its education, and its entertainment. It was this authority that had sought to fashion the minds of the sixties youth. Yet with the most perceptive of the young the authority had failed, failed precisely because it did lie. In this failure Mailer finds a cause for faith. And so in *Armies* Mailer places his faith, however qualified and tentative, in the politics of these young Americans who, seeing through the lies of the authority and rejecting the formulaic strategy of the old left ideologues, committed themselves to a radical new left protest that sought to discover its shape existentially in the act of protest itself. As Mailer notes, "the aesthetic of the New Left . . . began with the notion that the authority could not comprehend nor contain nor finally manage to control any political action whose end was unknown."

Of course, even as he invests his faith in this existential political aesthetic, believing that it might give promise of a rebirth of mystery in American public life—the sense of mystery having expired for him since the assassination of John F. Kennedy—Mailer emphasizes that the deep divisions in the American character have a long, complicated, and bloody history. They will not be healed by a weekend's protest. Indeed, he describes the march as the "first major battle of a war which may go on for twenty years," and in retrospect it is clear that Mailer might as well have left his timetable open. For the war has continued, unresolved, right up to the present day. Appropriately, he suggests the history and depth of the divisions within America and the agonizing difficulty of healing them by invoking as the presiding spirit of the march the "ghosts of the Union dead" (88). "The Armies of the Dead" live for Mailer, and for Lowell too, as they prepare to march in protest against the Vietnam War, and one of the effects of Mailer's recurring references to the Civil War is to resurrect the myth of American heroism and aspiration, bringing the past into the present and so revealing that the nation's commitment to the ideals of freedom and equality has always been tested through conflict. In so recovering American history, Mailer is directly countering the awful American denial of the past, which composes the ignorant underside of American innocence and of which the hippie protesters, ironically garbed in the costumes of history, are as guilty as the government they detest.[2] Thus Mailer confesses that he is "haunted by the nightmare that the evils of the present not only exploited the present, but consumed the past, and gave every promise of demolishing whole territories of the future. The same villains who, promiscuously, wantonly, heedlessly, had gorged on LSD and consumed God knows what essential marrows of history, wearing indeed the history of all eras on their back as trophies of this gluttony, were now going forth (conscience-struck?) to make war on those other villains, corporation-land villains, who were destroying the promise of the present in their self-righteousness and greed and secret lust (often unknown to themselves) for some sexotechnological variety of neo-fascism" (93). Later he is plagued by further questions about the American antipathy toward the past as expressed by the reckless attack by both the hippies and the government against nature, again asking with a transcendentalist reverence for the organic cycle of death and rebirth is "the past being consumed by the present? by nuclear blasts, and blasts into the collective living brain by way of all exploding acids, opiums, whiskies, speeds, and dopes?—the past was palpable to him, a tissue living in the tangible mansions of death, and death was disappearing, death was wasting of some incurable ill. When death disappeared there would be no life" (123).

In addition to placing the march within the context of the history of conflict in America and criticizing the American bias against history, Mailer's recurring invocation of the Civil War also reveals the deep well of patriotism from which his bitter criticism of America has always sprung. As Richard Poirier has noted concerning American literature, "there is perhaps no other literature quite so patriotic because none is so damning of the failure of a country to live up to its dreams and expectations. Like others who are aware of the fantastic human resources of which America has failed to make proper use, Mailer has an unquenchable affection for the energy, the wildness, the undeveloped possibility that is part of the American scene even at its shabbiest."[3] In perhaps no work since Whitman's "Democratic Vistas" is the embattled relationship of the serious American writer to America so apparent as in Mailer's *Armies*. And, as Mailer admits, it is really the sense of America in conflict that brings to the fore the full mix of one's emotions about the country. Walking in the front line of the march, he realizes that

the sense of America divided on this day now liberated some undiscovered patriotism in Mailer so that he felt a sharp searing love for his country in this moment and on this day, crossing some divide in his own mind wider than the Potomac, a love so lacerated he felt as if a marriage were being torn and children lost . . . here, walking with Lowell and [Dwight] Macdonald, he felt as if he stepped through some crossing in the reaches of space between this moment, the French Revolution, and the Civil War, as if the ghosts of the Union Dead accompanied them now to the Bastille. (113)

Representing all that threatens Mailer's love of America and his romantic vision of what the country could be if only it lived up to its millennial ideals is the Pentagon itself, the ultimate example of the totalitarian architecture that Mailer has persistently condemned. As Mailer observes, the Pentagon is "the true and high church of the military-industrial complex," the "blind five-sided eye of a subtle oppression which had come to America out of the very air of the century" (113–14). The confrontation reinforces Mailer's sense of the rightness of his lifelong opposition to American totalitarianism. He feels "a confirmation of the contests of his own life on this March to the eye of the oppressor, greedy stingy dumb valve of the worst of the Wasp heart, chalice and anus of corporation land, smug, enclosed, morally blind Pentagon, destroying the future of its own nation with each day it augmented in strength" (114). And as always in Mailer's work, confrontation serves as an act of self-definition, revealing existentially the degree of personal growth in one's ability to overcome fear and act with the courage to stand by one's beliefs and values. By this standard Mailer realizes that he has grown. The fear that he feels is palpable and intimate. His flaws and weaknesses remain. But though Mailer again admits with self-deprecating humor his desire to get arrested early so as to be able to attend that wickedly attractive New York party, though he acknowledges the concern that the march will either prove pointlessly anticlimactic or culminate in bloody, perhaps even mortal, combat, and though much to his embarrassment he begins at one point to flee in fear and confusion at the sight of the panic-stricken retreat of a group of National Liberation Front protesters, he is able finally to act with courage and conviction, in effect challenging the government to defend its morally untenable prosecution of the war in Vietnam.

Sprinting through the ranks of the military police line, running alone toward the Pentagon—under the amusing misconception that comrades Lowell and Macdonald are following close behind—Mailer undergoes a rite of passage that anticipates the coming of age of the demonstrators who would maintain their positions before the Pentagon through a night, a day, and part of another night in the face of random arrests and brutal beatings marked by the disproportionate victimization of women. Mailer, the man of warring personalities who has never "had a particular age" but has instead "carried different ages within him like different models of his experience" (9), now knows a moment of psychological and moral integration: "He felt his own age, forty-four, felt as if he were finally one age, not seven, felt as if he were a solid embodiment of bone, muscle, flesh, and vested substance, rather than the will, heart, mind, and sentiment to be a man, as if he had arrived, as if this picayune arrest had been his Rubicon" (138).

In addition to this private confirmation of manhood, Mailer's arrest yields political and literary benefits. For it allows him to infiltrate "the land of the enemy" and obtain a prisoner's inside view of the government's attempt to neutralize the anti-war protest and punish the demonstrators. Thus he is able to look behind the mask of democratic order and "see" the enemy's "face," thereby gaining a sense of the character of the Americans who are engaged in the bureaucratic quelling of dissent. Mailer feels the barely restrained violence of the military police—suggesting "the cold clammy murderous fury of all cops at the existential moment of making their bust" (131)—then observes, minutes later, the "cold professional studied indifference" (139) of the soldiers and marshals standing about a Pentagon reception area. Mailer also has a rather vicious but nevertheless amusing encounter with a neo-Nazi who was arrested along with the anti-war demonstrators. Mailer and the Nazi engage in an intense staring contest, which, concluding in a Mailer victory, ushers in an obscene exchange of ethnic insults. But the confrontation is abruptly halted by a U.S. marshal ideally built for the job of enforcement, with "the body and insane look of a very good rangy defensive end," a complexion "pocked with the big boiling craters of a red lunar acne," and eyes that flame with the intensity of a "blowtorch" (143, 144). Suitably impressed with the marshal's threatening presence, Mailer imagines that the man is impervious to retaliatory attack, for "there seemed no place to hit him where he'd be vulnerable; stone larynx, leather testicles, ice cubes for eyes. And he had his Marshal's club in his hand as well. Brother! Bring back the Nazi!"

Mailer's character sketch of the marshal is but one of the many memorable portraits that appear in *Armies* and help make it such lively reading. Certainly one comes away from the book with a lasting sense of Mailer's ability almost at will to capture with wit and humor the essence of a personality, whether his subject happens to be Robert Lowell, Dwight Macdonald, Paul Goodman, or an anonymous marshal. But of greatest significance is Mailer's ability to develop out of the character sketch a series of associations that reveal with lyrical brilliance the character of contemporary America itself. This gift is never more apparent than in Mailer's observations on the marshal and his colleagues as they guard him and the other demonstrators before busing them off to the U.S. post office in Alexandria, Virginia, where they will be temporarily detained before being transported to a workhouse in Occoquan twenty miles away. Mailer sees the indomitable marshal as a lover of action caught "in that no man's land between the old frontier and the new ranch home" (144). After speculating on the marshal's redneck hatred of the demonstrators and his strongly held conviction that the real threat to America is communist inspired, Mailer moves on to his own critique of America, expressing the contrary conclusion that the evil in the country was endemic rather than transported from the Soviet Union, "that the best in America was being destroyed by what in itself seemed next best, yes American heroism corrupted by American know-how" (145). After observing the faces of the marshals who are standing outside the detention bus, Mailer notes that "they emitted a collective spirit which, to his mind, spoke of little which was good, for their eyes were blank and dull, that familiar small-town cast of eye which speaks of apathy rising to fanaticism only to subside in apathy again" (151). Mailer is reiterating here the view of "In the Red Light" and *Why Are We in Vietnam?*, which insists that the center of the nation is no longer sane. Something had shifted in the middle-American mind, and the madness was seeking an outlet in the war in Vietnam.

This middle-American insanity is graphically portrayed in Mailer's brief sketch of the Vegas-crazed Grandma with orange hair, which appears as a kind of surrealistic, black comic interlude in the midst of Mailer's ruminations on the marshals. Grandma's obsession with the slot machines renders her incapable of acknowledging the atrocity of Vietnam even though a burned Vietnamese child has been wheeled right up to her as she gambles in the Las Vegas casino. For Mailer, Grandma is frightening precisely because she is typical. The surrealistic style of the short sketch suggests hyperbole but in fact acts as an explosive device that blasts to the surface a representative moral dislocation, the result of a warping combination of ignorance, greed, provinciality, frustration, prejudice, pent-up rage, hatred, lust for violence, and gross insensitivity to human suffering. As Mailer maintains, "one did not have to look for who would work in the concentration camps and the liquidation centers—the garrison would be filled with applicants from the pages of a hundred American novels, from *Day of the Locust* and *Naked Lunch* and *The Magic Christian*, one could enlist half the Marshals outside this bus, simple, honest, hard-working government law-enforcement agents, yeah! There was something at loose now in American life, the poet's beast slinking to the marketplace." According to Mailer a feverish insanity, a horrible potential for mad violence had always been a part of rural American life, but its spirit had largely kept within the shadowed nooks and dusty attic corners of the old country manse, which Hawthorne knew so well, going abroad only at night, traveling on the wind yet ever encompassed by the gothic atmosphere of the village itself. But now the psychic insulation of the rural village was gone. Now the "small towns were disappearing in the bypasses and the supermarkets and the shopping centers" (152). Now the madness of nineteenth-century American gothic romance had gotten loose, quitting both the boundaries of the small town and the "neutral territory" of fiction, looking to establish a new habitat and discover new violent satisfactions in the mainstream of American life:

the nightmares which passed on the winds in the old small towns now traveled on the nozzle tip of the flame thrower, no dreams now of barbarian lusts, slaughtered villages, battles of blood, no, nor any need for them—technology had driven insanity out of the wind and out of the attic, and out of all the lost primitive places: one had to find it now wherever fever, force, and machines could come together, in Vegas, at the race track, in pro football, race riots for the Negro, suburban orgies—none of it was enough—one had to find it in Vietnam; that was where the small town had gone to get its kicks. (153)

At home in this new America of superhighways, supermarkets, and instant electronic communication, which feeds the familial paradigms of TV network sitcoms into millions of the nation's living rooms, are the freshly scrubbed middle-American high school boys and girls who listen in incomprehension to the political chants of the demonstrators as the prison bus rolls through the intersections of suburban shopping centers. Looking remarkably like members of those same TV families, the teenagers rekindle Mailer's sense of the responsibility of the major American writer to try to span the divisions of the country, expressing a vision of existence that, despite its complexity, could somehow compete with the facile views of life ground out by the various organs of government and mass media. The paradoxical demand of such an ambition suggests to some extent Hawthorne's desire to duplicate the popularity of the sunny sketch writers of his day while yet testifying to the ubiquity of evil. Indeed, awareness of the near to impossible magnitude of the task leads Mailer to recall that "he had written a good essay once about the failure of any major American novelist to write a major novel which would reach out past the best-seller lists to a major part of that American audience brainwashed by Hollywood, TV, and *Time*. Yes, how much of Fitzgerald's long dark night may have come from that fine winnowing sense in the very fine hair of his nose that the two halves of America were not coming together, and when they failed to touch, all of history might be lost in the divide. Yes, there was a long dark night if you had the illusion you could do something about it, and the conviction that not enough had been done. Or was it simply impossible—had the two worlds of America drifted irretrievably apart?" (157–58).[4]

Mailer's sense of an America divided and his feelings of alienation from the greater part of the country that he loves surface yet again when he observes a turnkey at the U.S. post office. In Mailer's view the man "was more American than anyone had a right to be, that high worried forehead, narrow receded mouth, white hair, those innocent blue eyes capable of watching an execution (only to worry about it later) and the steel-rimmed spectacles. Narrowness, propriety, goodwill, and that infernal American innocence which could not question one's leaders, for madness and the boils of a frustrated life resided beneath. No, he would not want to hear Mailer's arguments on why we should get out of Vietnam, no, he would shake his head and cluck his tongue and say, 'It's an awful war, I know, but I guess all wars are awful, and it's a shame, but our boys have to fight them I suppose'" (169). In preparing to present these arguments in a chapter entitled "Why Are We in Vietnam?" Mailer reflects on his own political position, calling attention to the irony that in having drawn upon the resources of both left and right ideologies, he had succeeded in isolating himself from both political camps. "There was," he admits, "no one in America who had a position even remotely like his own" (180). Nevertheless, the most interesting implication of Mailer's left conservatism is the possibility that one can advance a radical critique of the social-political establishment and yet remain within society, appealing to rather than isolating oneself from elements on both the left and the right.

Mailer's arguments against the war are intended to make such an appeal. Using a tactic reminiscent of his invocation of Edmund Burke to attack Barry Goldwater's conservative credentials in "In the Red Light," Mailer calls upon conservative standards to evaluate the justice of U.S. involvement in Vietnam. On this basis, beginning "at the root," he argues that a war is bad and its prosecution immoral if one's nation exploits an obscene advantage in arms and materiel and engages, partly as a result of this advantage, in the daily, indiscriminate slaughter of the women and children it presumes to defend, forcing the relocation of those who by chance have survived. A war is bad too, insists Mailer, if there is "no line of battle or discernible climax," if it requires "an inability to reason as the price of retaining one's patriotism," and if it gives "no prospect of improving itself as a war," failing to offer "the possibility that further effort will produce a determinable effect upon chaos, evil, or waste." At the same time, Mailer's solution to the disaster of U.S. involvement in Vietnam is decidedly left, decidedly radical: it is quite simply to "pull out of Vietnam completely. Leave Asia to the Asians" (185) without knowing if it would go communist, believing at any rate that a "submersion of Asia in Communism was going to explode a shock into Marxism which might take half a century to digest" (186) and that the more communism expanded, the more its problems would become. In the final analysis, the "real difficulty might be then to decide who would do more harm to Asia, Capitalism or Communism. In either case, the conquest would be technological, and so primitive Asian societies would be uprooted. Probably, the uprooting would be savage, the psychic carnage unspeakable. He did not like to contemplate the compensating damage to America if it chose to dominate a dozen Asian nations with its technologies and its armies while having to face their guerrilla wars" (187).

Having made his argument in earnest, Mailer returns, however, to the pessimistic conclusion that such views could never reach those schizophrenic Americans who were fundamentally divided in their deepest beliefs and loyalties, pledging their absolute faith in both Christian mystery and corporate logic, a division that recalls the profound moral dislocation of Grandma with orange hair. In this context Mailer recalls the futility of his discussion with a middle-aged southern guard at Occoquan in which he tried to voice why he and the other demonstrators were opposed to the war:

You could use every argument, but it was useless, because the guard didn't want to care. If he did, he would be at war against the cold majesty of the Corporation. The Corporation was what brought him his television and his security, the Corporation was what brought him the unspoken promise that on Judgment Day he would not be judged, for Judgment Day—so went the unspoken promise—was no worse than the empty spaces of the Tonight Show when you could not sleep. (189)

Mailer's left-conservative condemnation of the Vietnam War and his conclusion that the U.S. must immediately withdraw bring into focus the moral obligation that impels the political activism of Mailer and the other demonstrators. Clearly, the absolute obscenity of Vietnam demands absolute opposition. The moral complications of giving expression to such an obligation, especially when one is already imprisoned, become painfully apparent to Mailer when he encounters beat pamphleteer, rock musician, and fellow prisoner Tuli Kupferberg. Kupferberg asserts that cooperating with the government in any way on the issue of Vietnam is immoral. One should therefore refuse to comply with the government's precondition for release from Occoquan, namely the demand to stay away from the Pentagon for at least six months. Mailer rightly perceives that, however courageous, taking such a stand would commit one to an openended series of increasingly dangerous and ultimately self-destructive risks that would lead one, despite one's radicalism, back down the self-sacrificing liberal road of the victim-hero who collaborates in oppression by defeating himself. In this way prison would become "an endless ladder of moral challenges. Each time you climbed a step, as Kupferberg just had, another higher, more dangerous, more disadvantageous step would present itself." To avoid self-destruction, "sooner or later, you would have to descend." Mailer's initial response to this moral dilemma, however, is decidedly uncharacteristic of him. For he concludes that the "first step down in a failure of nerve always presented the same kind of moral nausea" (195). Coming from the man who has offered himself as the paradigmatic risktaker, the man who prides himself above all on the ability to make fine moral distinctions in the substance and style of his existential choices, such a sweeping generalization is singularly unworthy. As Robert Solotaroff states, such a conclusion "argues against the cult of courage that has nourished Mailer and his work for so many years. . . . If all nausea is the same and the defeat which will cause the nausea is inevitable, then there is really no prevailing reason for behaving bravely, or, in fact, for not behaving in a consistently cowardly fashion."[5]

Mailer's lapse from the demands of his own existential faith is, however, only momentary. After being dealt, because of his notoriety, the comparatively stiff sentence of thirty days in prison (with twenty-five suspended), Mailer is released on his own recognizance, pending appeal, and experiences at the moment of freedom a corresponding "liberation from the unending disciplines of that moral ladder whose rungs he had counted in the dormitory while listening to Kupferberg" (212). He knows then that "all effort was not the same, and to eject oneself from guilt might yet be worth it, for the nausea on return to guilt could conceivably prove less: standing on the grass, he felt one suspicion of a whole man closer to that freedom from dread which occupied the inner drama of his years, yes, one image closer than when he had come to Washington four days ago" (212–13). Mailer is then inspired to give a statement to the press in which he concludes with the rather cryptic pronouncement that "'we are burning the body and blood of Christ in Vietnam. Yes, we are burning him there, and as we do, we destroy the foundation of this Republic, which is its love and trust in Christ'" (214). The climactic remark makes perfect sense to the reader of *Armies*, who is privy to Mailer's private ruminations on the conflict between Christianity and the corporation. But at the time, in the absence of any such gloss, the remark was merely an invitation to ridicule, and Mailer was duly accommodated by a *Washington Post* reporter, who, as the spiritual double of the *Time* magazine character assassin, rendered the comment absurd by juxtaposing it against the fact that "Mailer is a Jew" (215).

Thus in the conclusion of Book One of *Armies*, the reader is brought full circle in observing the comic misadventures of the public Mailer. But now that public image is superseded by the reader's knowledge of Mailer as a man who has undergone a private rite of passage that liberates him at once from the guilt of past failures and the disproportions of comedy. As a number of critics have noted, "The Steps of the Pentagon" dramatizes the education of Norman Mailer, or more precisely, the education of the comic character known as Mailer.[6] It is this newly elevated Mailer who serves as the narrator of Book Two, offering to the reader who has become intimate with Mailer's biases a trustworthy and coherent point of view on the march that can counter the collective inaccuracies of the mass media. At the same time the proleptic relationship of Mailer's own education to the collective rite of passage depicted in Book Two prepares one to read this section of *Armies* as both the corrective history and the collective novel that Mailer intends. For one comes to realize that Book Two does have a protagonist, and it is none other than America itself. Indeed, Mailer's contention in *Armies* is that it is finally the character of America with all of its historic divisions that is undergoing a spiritual transformation as a result of the clash between the government and the Pentagon demonstrators, especially those who persisted in their protest until the very end.

For those demonstrators, many of them young representatives of a disaffected urban middle class, the thirty-two-hour vigil before the Pentagon held all the promise of an existential act— offering them the possibility of forging a new identity while gaining an increased sense of freedom and power, stolen, so Mailer insists, from the psychological resources of the working-class soldiers who confronted them. As Mailer notes, "surrounded on the plaza and on the stairs, [the demonstrators] could have no idea of what would happen next, they could be beaten, arrested, buried in a stampede, most of them were on the mouth of their first cannon, yet for each minute they survived, sixty seconds of existential gold was theirs" (259). Like Mailer, the demonstrators were engaged in a comparatively modest act of courage. Yet in each case the decision to place oneself at risk to defend a moral principle reflects an essential change in character. More important, since in each case the private rite of passage was undergone in defense of the nation itself, in defense, that is, of a vision of America threatened by the Vietnam War, the demonstrators' heroism carries for Mailer "the echo of far greater rites of passage in American history." In one of the most brilliant lyrical passages in *Armies*, Mailer identifies the historic meaning of the Pentagon protest, hearing in it

some refrain from all the great American rites of passage when men and women manacled themselves to a lost and painful principle and survived a day, a night, a week, a month, a year, a celebration of Thanksgiving—the country had been founded on a rite of passage. Very few had emigrated here without the echo of that rite, even if it were no more (and no less!) than eight days in the stink, bustle, fear, and propinquity of steerage on an ocean crossing (or the eighty days of dying on a slave ship) each generation of Americans had forged their own rite, in the forest of the Alleghenies and the Adirondacks, at Valley Forge, at

New Orleans in 1812, with Rogers and Clark or at Sutter's Mill, at Gettysburg, the Alamo, the Klondike, the Argonne, Normandy, Pusan—the engagement at the Pentagon was a pale rite of passage next to these, and yet it was probably a true one, for it came to the spoiled children of a dead de-animalized middle class who had chosen most freely, out of the incomprehensible mysteries of moral choice, to make an attack and then hold a testament before the most authoritative embodiment of the principle that America was right, America was might, America was the true religious war of Christ against the Communist. (280)

In the religious witness of the demonstrators, which opposes these principles of debased millennialism, Mailer perceives a significant, though subtle, change in the character of America itself, a radical shift back to the millennial ideals that inspired the pioneers who founded the country and left their legacy of courage. At the very least he hopes that the courage and perseverance of the demonstrators, epitomized by the noncooperation of the Quakers who lay naked "on the cold floor of a dark isolation cell" (287), has earned the nation forgiveness. Yet Mailer likewise suggests that, in perfect keeping with the ambiguity, indeed the profound moral schizophrenia of our times, the nation has also moved with the same significance and subtlety in the opposite direction as a result of the clash at the Pentagon. For, as he observes, "there are negative rites of passage as well." As an example, he quotes a Pentagon spokesman who is able to comment with perfect totalitarian indifference about charges of government brutality, saying " 'our action is consistent with objectives of security and control faced with varying levels of dissent' " (284). The language is worthy of Orwell's *1984* and suggests that an event such as the march on the Pentagon does indeed have the partial effect of further confirming the authority in the ruthless prosecution of its policies while consolidating its hold over a significant part of the nation. Indeed, as Mailer admits, the march succeeded in temporarily increasing Lyndon Johnson's popularity while bringing down upon the protesters the condemnation of much of the press.

Thus in "The Metaphor Delivered," the concluding section of Book Two, Mailer suggests that the only certainty is that America is indeed undergoing a transformation of character as a result of Vietnam, a transformation both advanced and epitomized by the march against the Pentagon. At stake is the very nature of America's millennialism as the nation moves toward embracing one of two radically opposed mythic identities. As Raymond A. Schroth puts it, the choice is between "America as the new Eden, the primitive paradise that must keep itself innocent, and, at the same time, set an example for the world" and America as "the new Israel," the militaristic debasement of its faith in itself as God's Chosen People, "the land of Joshua rather than the land of Adam, God's kingdom destined to be his Empire."[7] The conflict between these two visions of America continues unabated. It is both the conflict of our time and the great unresolved conflict of American history. In *Armies* Mailer creates for the reader an enduring image of that mythic conflict. In so doing, he has succeeded in writing his finest work to date, a work that fulfills the epic ambition of the American novel, balancing the nation's hopes and fears while revealing how the force of personal endeavor and the shaping of individual identities help to form the as yet unformed and ever mysterious identity of a nation that persists in believing in the truth of its millennial dream.

Chapter 9

Mailer's Nonfiction (1968-1972): The View of the Outsider

I

In *The Armies of the Night* political participation makes possible both personal and collective growth so that finally hope emerges out of the deepest sense of alienation and division. Of course, it is not the existence of some hope in *Armies* that makes it Mailer's finest work. Indeed, the contention that a work of art must somehow suggest a possible road to redemption reflects a critical bias that is wholly without foundation. The crucial test of greatness for any work, including *Armies*, is its ability to synthesize experience. In *Armies* the hope, highly qualified and tentative, emerges primarily as an epiphenomenon of Mailer's synthetic achievement, which depended upon his ability to participate in every sense in the march and draw inspiration from the symbolic significance of the event itself.

For Mailer, however, the moment of personal and political integration is fleeting. In the four books following *Armies*—in *Miami and the Siege of Chicago*, *Of a Fire on the Moon*, *The Prisoner of Sex*, and *St. George and the Godfather*—Mailer, himself, remains the outsider. Indisputably, on the issues of sex and women's liberation the exotic hybridity of Mailer's left conservatism is in fullest bloom. In *The Prisoner of Sex* he therefore succeeds, despite the appearance of engagement, in standing utterly by himself, defining a position that is at once romantic, existential, mystical, moralistic, and essentially reflective of no one's beliefs but his own. Similarly, in the books of reportage the central concern becomes the difficulty of participation, which gives rise to the corresponding problems of understanding and sympathizing dependent as they are on the possibility of experiencing through one's own engagement an epiphany of the imagination that can conceivably yield a synthetic image of America.

It has become something of a critical commonplace to argue that these books of reportage are less successful than *The Armies of the Night*. But in view of the injustice of using an author's finest achievement as a critical weapon to bludgeon his other works and in view of the persistent problem of participation, it is far more precise to maintain that for Mailer the details of the conventions and the moon launch threatened to remain intractable. And their potential intractability becomes a story in itself, the compelling story of Mailer's uncomfortable relation to these historic events. In the final analysis, though unresolved questioning may be less satisfying than a wholly integrated vision, it may be no less significant or representatively American. At any rate it is clear that for Mailer there was no choice. In the troubled years that are chronicled by these books he had indeed become the deeply divided and questioning American who would have to remain emotionally and ideologically outside of the events that he observed.

II

At the outset of *Miami and the Siege of Chicago* Mailer's question is fundamental: what exactly is going on at the 1968 Republican Convention in Miami Beach? In this city of extremes that are subtly suggestive of the political polarization at work within the nation itself, in a city where the "the air conditioning is pushed to that icy point where women may wear fur coats over their diamonds in the tropics,"[1] the truth seems to Mailer to be hidden somewhere beneath the opaque surface of events. Real passion and conflict are covered over, concealed by the public facade of Republican party politics just as the Florida jungle has been covered over by macadam.

Despite the fact that the convention leaves Mailer in the position of grasping at journalistic opportunities, he is able to discern a significant change in the millennial faith of the Republican delegates. Like the Goldwaterites of the 1964 San Francisco convention, the 1968 Republican delegates believed in America as "the world's ultimate reserve of rectitude," indeed as the "final garden of the Lord." And as Mailer maintains, though this faith was "never articulated by any of them except in the most absurd and taste-curdling jargons of patriotism mixed with religion" (33), it was nevertheless deeply rooted, for at bottom these Republicans "believed in America as they believed in God—they could not really ever expect that America might collapse and God yet survive, no, they had even gone so far as to think that America was the savior of the world, food and medicine by one hand, sword in the other, highest of high faith in a nation which would bow the knee before no problem since God's own strength was in the die." In 1964 Republican fervency had grown to fanaticism as the conviction of America's righteousness had resurrected beatific visions of Manifest Destiny that could establish a spiritual-political hegemony over much of the world. But, as Mailer notes, the Vietnam War had given the lie to such dreams of power and influence. As a result, "the high fire of hard Republican faith was more modest now, the vision of America had diminished" (34). According to Mailer many of the Republican delegates had even come to the realization that their service to God's Country, America, was no longer wanted. And it is through his perception of both the delegates' acknowledgment of this rejection and the transformed character of Republican faith that Mailer is able to identify the underlying purpose of the 1968 convention: having suffered through the diminishment of their millennial vision of America, the delegates were gathering in Miami Beach to nominate a man who could in some way "bring America back to them, their lost America, Jesusland" (36).

This man was, of course, none other than Richard Milhouse Nixon. As Mailer points out, Nelson Rockefeller, with his highly suspect liberal agenda, could hardly hope to personify such dreams. Nixon, on the other hand, had built his career by pandering to every self-righteous militaristic prejudice that could help sustain the millennial vision of America's primacy. As one might expect, for Mailer, Nixon is the very incarnation of the Prince of Darkness. Indeed, Mailer admits that he had

disliked him intimately ever since his Checkers speech in 1952—the kind of man who was ready to plough sentimentality in such a bog was the kind of man who would press any button to manipulate the masses— and there was large fear in those days of buttons which might ignite atomic wars. Nixon's presence on television had inspired emotions close to nausea. There had been a gap between the man who spoke and the man who lived behind the speaker which offered every clue of schizophrenia in the American public if they failed to recognize the void within the presentation. Worse. There was unity only in the way the complacency of the voice matched the complacency of the ideas. It was as if Richard Nixon were proving that a man who had never spent an instant inquiring whether family, state, church, and flag were ever wrong could go on in secure steps, denuded of risk, from office to office until he was President. (41–42)

Despite this scathing indictment Mailer is willing to entertain the absurd possibility that by 1968 Nixon may have begun to undergo a substantial change in his political image such that one might witness at any public appearance the images of old Nixon and new Nixon phasing in and out with the shifting demands of his rhetoric. There was, of course, in 1968 much talk in the media about the appearance of a new Nixon, a more sympathetic, honest, and dignified Nixon, a man chastened by defeat and broadened in scope by the multiform rigors of a remarkable political comeback. As we all know by now, and as many observers knew in 1968, there was no new Nixon at all. New Nixon was the old Tricky Dick refurbished according to the specifications of a slick public relations concept of what would ride in 1968. As Robert Solotaroff suggests, Mailer was drawn to indulge in speculation over the possible appearance of a new Nixon precisely because the "Republican convention offered . . . no opportunity for dramatic action and so few [opportunities] for dramatic thought."[2] Notwithstanding the cogency of this point, one must note that Mailer's unresolved questioning of the nature of Nixon's character does fulfill an important thematic purpose. For it serves as another way of expressing the point that the significance of the 1968 Republican Convention had not yet emerged, that it was concealed beneath the surface of events in Miami, and that it would finally be revealed through the outcome of the delegates' search for "their lost America." And the delegates' hope was, of course, depending in large part on Nixon himself.

The conjunction of Mailer's two focuses—namely the delegates' millennial vision of America and the presumptive enigma of Richard Nixon—is expressed most strikingly in Mailer's analysis of the rhetoric of Nixon's acceptance speech. As Mailer notes, Nixon plays upon every conceivable patriotic sentiment and cliché—exhorting his fellow Republicans to "'win this one'" (76) for Ike "the Gipper" Eisenhower; suggesting that contemporary violence was an unworthy sequel to America's storied past, which includes heroic deaths "'in Normandy and Korea and Valley Forge'"; praising in debased Whitmanesque rhetoric the virtue and heterogeneity of "'the great majority of Americans'" who "'give drive to the spirit of America . . . life to the American dream . . . steel to the backbone of America'"; pledging in fateful phrase "'to bring an honorable end to the war in Vietnam'" and achieve a friendly rapprochement with the peoples of all lands while rededicating the U.S. to "'a revolution . . . that will never grow old, the world's greatest continuing revolution, the American Revolution'" (77–78). As Mailer observes, Nixon then "went on to call for progress, and reminded everyone that progress depended on order. He was of course in these matters shameless, he had no final passion for the incorruptible integrity of an idea; no, ideas were rather like keys to him on which he might play a teletype to program the American mind. And yet the American mind was scandalously bad—the best educational system in the world had produced the most pervasive conditioning of mind in the history of culture just as the greatest medical civilization in history might yet produce the worst plagues" (78). These ironies provide Mailer with a suggestive rhetorical basis for reiterating that Nixon's ultimate effect on America was as yet inscrutable, for perhaps good could come from a Protean politician who projected a series of new and old images upon a still gullible electorate. Perhaps "if the Lord Himself wished to save America, who else could he possibly use for instrument by now but Richard Nixon?" (78–79).

Nixon concludes his speech by scandalously echoing the visionary rhetoric of Martin Luther King, claiming to "'see a day'" (79) arriving of millennial peace, brotherhood, and well-being in America and sentimentally recalling his own cherished childhood dreams that were now on the verge of becoming a reality not only through the self-sacrifice and caring of "'a father who had to go to work before he finished the sixth grade . . . a gentle Quaker mother with a passionate concern for peace . . . a great teacher . . . a remarkable football coach . . . courageous wife . . . loyal children'" but finally through the patriotic efforts of millions of Americans. It is for reasons such as these that Nixon believes "'so deeply in the American dream.'" Finally, in the spirit of such faith, Nixon calls upon Americans "'to help [him] make that dream come true for millions to whom it's an impossible dream today,'" promising that through his leadership "'the long dark night for America is about to end.'" For the "'time has come for us to leave the valley of despair and climb the mountain'" (80). Then Americans will "'see the glory of the dawn of a new day for America, a new dawn for peace and freedom to the world.'" With the exception (one now knows) of Ronald Reagan, no one could have articulated the Republican faith better. Yet as Mailer suggests, Nixon's rhetoric was horribly divorced from reality, for "out in Miami, six miles from Convention Hall . . . the Negroes were rioting, and three had been killed and five in critical condition as Miami policemen exchanged gunfire with snipers" (81).

Mailer's reference to the Miami riot provides the perfect transition to his coverage of the Democratic Convention in Chicago, where anti-war demonstrations and a police riot would command center stage. For Mailer, the rioting exemplifies Chicago's talent for providing "honest spectacle" (90)—in this case, a spectacle as unabashedly brutal, Mailer suggests, as the methods of the butchers in the Chicago slaughterhouses, which he describes with such marvelous explicitness and gusto as part of his boldly idealized opening description of the city. Nevertheless, "if Miami had masked its answers" (82) so that Mailer could arrive at no secure conclusions, honest Chicago would complicate questions of allegiance, engagement, courage, and authentic moral witness through the chaos of its overwhelming street drama.

The crucial question of moral witness is first sounded with typical Mailer eccentricity through his admission of the belief that his own marital infidelity may have added some feather's weight of support to the forces of evil in a morally synchronous universe, thus helping to tip the scales against Robert F. Kennedy and bring about his assassination. Robert Solotaroff calls Mailer's consideration of his own complicity megalomaniacal,[3] and many people would certainly agree. Passing silently over this psychoanalytic diagnosis, I would offer the defense that as usual with Mailer there is considerable integrity to be found in his speculative thinking if only one is able to look beyond the obvious eccentricity. For Mailer is really responding to Kennedy's murder with a heightened sense of personal responsibility reminiscent of the Puritans, suggesting that all of one's choices, however personal and seemingly insignificant, do have serious moral content and that it is the moral quality of each of our lives that shapes the moral quality of the nation. Thus, according to Mailer, all Americans shared responsibility for the turmoil of the 1960s, if only through their noninvolvement and moral lassitude.

Having reiterated the obligation of engagement, Mailer finds

himself in a rather uncomfortable position as he observes the
Democratic Convention in Chicago, for he discovers that he can
wholeheartedly support neither the Democratic establishment
nor the demonstrators in the streets. At the convention the Democratic leadership, the leadership that had perpetrated an unspeakable escalation of the war in Vietnam, was preparing to
annoint Hubert Humphrey as its candidate despite the fact that
he had not tested that candidacy in the primaries. Moreover, as
Lyndon Johnson's vice-president, Humphrey was virtually bereft
of "political property," that is, in Mailer's terminology, almost
wholly without the means to barter for votes—wholly without
power or political identity except through his relation to Johnson.
Thus Humphrey had been unwilling to break with Johnson and
the Democratic center on the war in Vietnam. Indeed, he had
staunchly supported Johnson's determinedly hawkish policies
despite the fact that such a position was tantamount to political
suicide. Moreover, as Mailer suggests, Humphrey would not
oppose the war "for the most visceral of reasons—his viscera were
not firm enough to face the collective wrath of that military-
industrial establishment he knew so well in Washington . . . he
was not ready to tell the generals that they were wrong. Peace they
might yet accept, but not the recognition that they were somewhat
insane—as quickly tell dragons to shift their nest" (113).

Clearly for Mailer, Humphrey was the very archetype of the
morally compromised liberal politician who announces with
boundless enthusiasm the coming of a government-sponsored
social panacea, the announcement merely part of the rhetoric of a
political career built with the support of corrupt labor unions and
a party machinery that can always deliver the votes of the poor.
Such a deep division of purpose suggests that, like Nixon, Humphrey was incapable in his speeches of locating anything more
palpable than the platitudes of July Fourth celebrations. As
Mailer notes, Humphrey "simply could not attach" his words "to
any reality" (124). Indeed, according to Mailer, Humphrey might
even be more likely than Nixon to lead the country over the brink
of perdition.

In view of his absolute detestation of the Democratic establishment, one might think that Mailer would strongly identify with the activist opposition of the Chicago demonstrators. But the reservations that Mailer expressed about the anti-war youth in *The Armies of the Night* have now in "The Siege of Chicago" become even more pronounced. Focusing on the hippies and Yippies in Lincoln Park, Mailer repeatedly refers to the demonstrators as "children" or "kids." To Mailer the hippie values of peace, free love, and mind expansion through psychedelics reflect a philosophy that is at once naive and nihilistic. From Mailer's point of view the hippies' radically democratic vision of life leads to an elimination of meaning through the denial of all distinctions.

Nevertheless, Mailer had overcome similar doubts the previous year in Washington and chosen to march. The crucial difference is that now for Mailer in Chicago there is no symbolic center to the protest. No Pentagon looms in the distance to give urgency to one's activism, enboldening one to lay one's body on the line, now in this particular time and place.

Mailer's ambivalence thus becomes the real story of "The Siege of Chicago," giving rise to repeated self-questioning of his courage to act. And in truth Mailer, whether as journalist or activist in abeyance, is all too often out of the action. Having chosen not to confront the police, Mailer finds himself at parties during the first two attacks against the demonstrators. Later he watches, as he admits, in safety from the nineteenth floor of the Hilton as the police attack the demonstrators in the streets below. And when the opportunity presents itself to march in protest with a group of delegates from the convention center to the Hilton, Mailer decides not to participate. As a result of such disengagement, he develops a bad conscience and an intimate sense of his own expanding fear, acknowledging not only the fear of acting but a fear of the direction that the country is taking. At bottom he is afraid of losing "even the America he had had, that insane warmongering technology land with its smog, its superhighways, its experts and its profound dishonesty. Yet, it had allowed him to write. . . . and a profound part of him (exactly that enormous literary bottom of the mature novelist's property!) detested the thought of seeing his American society—evil, absurd, touching, pathetic, sickening, comic, full of novelistic marrow—disappear now in the nihilistic maw of a national disorder" (186–87).

Plagued by doubts and fears, Mailer realizes that "he would be driven yet to participate or keep the shame in his liver" (188). Mailer's compensatory actions turn out, however, to be ineffectual. In fact, one is distinctly reminded of Mailer's maneuvering at the end of "Ten Thousand Words a Minute" when he commandeers the stage prior to a Sonny Liston press conference as a minor act of challenge and bravery to make up for having, in his own view, failed to provide Floyd Patterson with sufficient psychic support in his championship fight against Liston. In "The Siege of Chicago," with a similar regard for the compensatory value of personal testing, Mailer attempts to remove the guilt of inaction by inspecting in military fashion a group of national guardsmen who have been called out to help quell the demonstrations. Then with newly acquired respect for the demonstrators for having survived so many battles, Mailer acknowledges their heroic potential and pledges to try to organize a march of at least 300 delegates, but he has no luck in bringing the plan to realization. Finally with one anticlimax following quickly upon the other, Mailer is arrested twice within the span of a few minutes as a result of a pair of minor confrontations. Thus one realizes that the dramatic development of "The Siege of Chicago" is precisely the opposite of *The Armies of the Night*. Whereas *Armies* proceeds from comic display to modest heroic action, "Chicago" moves from guilty inaction to comic anticlimax, with Mailer's ambivalence and self-questioning dominating the mood.

III

Mailer's ambivalence also predominates in *Of a Fire on the Moon*. Mailer begins his account of the 1969 Apollo 11 moon flight by recalling Ernest Hemingway's suicide eight years earlier, suggesting that if the death of the greatest romantic of the age did indeed reveal that in these times even the most courageous and death defying of us would finally be overcome by personal demons, then it was possible that the romantic imagination was itself dying as well. In Mailer's words, "it was conceivable that man was no longer ready to share the dread of the Lord."[4] In that event "technology would fill the pause" (4), attempting to subdue through reductive reason and corporate will the sense of dread that humanity, bereft of romantic longing and inspiration, could no longer endure.

In this way Mailer establishes the context for considering the moon launch in particular and the technological exploration of space in general. Throughout *Fire* he repeatedly, indeed obsessively, raises the question of whether the effect of landing on the moon and venturing into space will be good or evil, expressing the opposition between romantic imagination and technological development by way of the divine conflict that serves as the informing myth for all his ethical inquiries: invoking the ultimate terms of his existential theology, Mailer asks "was the Space Program admirable or abominable? Did God voyage out for NASA or was the Devil our line of sight to the stars?" (80). Of course, technology is virtually always under attack in Mailer's work as an essentially Faustian enterprise that seeks to dominate nature through the blind assertion of a totalitarian will. As he remarks in *Fire* on the eve of the moon launch as part of a moving meditation on a once pristine America, "the country had been virgin once, an all but empty continent with lavender and orange in the rocks, pink in the sky, an aura of blue in the deep green of the forest— now, not four centuries even spent, the buffalo were gone, and the Indians; the swamps were filled; the air stank with every exhaust from man and machine" (82).

Nevertheless, despite Mailer's long-time detestation of technology, he remains ambivalent toward the space program and the flight of Apollo 11. On the one hand, he considers that in traveling to the moon, man will be trespassing upon the heretofore uninvaded domain of romance, mystery, and magic, threatening in the process to transform the haunt of Diana into a profane space station. Thus Mailer fears that the expedition might well represent the first stage of technology's final assault on the romantic spirit, opening the prospect of a sterile future in which wholly technologized human beings, unconscious of the existence of transcendent values, colonize the stars. On the other hand, Mailer acknowledges that a journey to the moon is intrinsically heroic. He is drawn to that element of heroism in the Apollo launch and hopes that it may have the effect of ennobling the mission. Perhaps then Apollo 11 will mark the beginning of a truly mythic quest. Perhaps despite its historic opposition to romance, mystery, and magic, technology might yet serve as the profane instrument of a divine vision of expanding possibilities, sending into space a race of New Adams to explore an illimitable New World of which America was but the microcosmic type.

Partly as a reflection of his double attitude toward the moon mission, in *Fire* Mailer lives within the persona of Aquarius. As the title of chapter 1 suggests, he is a man who has suffered "a loss of ego." Having finished fourth in a field of five candidates running for the Democratic nomination for mayor of New York, he is now "weary of his own voice, own face, person, persona, will, ideas, speeches, and general sense of importance. He felt not unhappy, mildly depressed, somewhat used up, wise, tolerant, sad, void of vanity, even had a hint of humility" (5–6). A "somewhat disembodied spirit" (6), he has learned through experience "to live with questions" and "has never had less sense of possessing the age. He feels in fact little more than a decent spirit, somewhat shunted to the side. It is the best possible position for detective work" (4).[5]

Certainly it seems that Mailer as Aquarius has adopted the perfect attitude to approach his investigation of the moon launch, for throughout its course there is never any hope of participation, and he is almost always feeling separate from the institution, the people, and the event that he is attempting to cover. For Mailer, visiting the NASA Manned Spacecraft Center outside Houston is like winding one's way through the halls of the Pentagon, where, as he notes in *Armies*, it is "impossible to locate the symbolic

loins of the building" (229). At the MSC, Mailer could see
everything and learn nothing essential. He could receive ready
answers from NASA personnel to all his questions, and still
nothing of importance would be revealed. But perhaps most
elusive of all are the personalities of the Apollo 11 astronauts
themselves. Neil Armstrong, Edwin Buzz Aldrin, and Michael
Collins seem men of profound contradictions, "technicians and
heroes, robots and saints, adventurers and cogs of the machine"
(313), men whose personalities seem not at all to fit the heroic
dimensions of the mission. Indeed, in Mailer's view, as the
ultimate representatives of technological man, the astronauts
incorporate many of the contradictions of the twentieth century
itself, a century that is both reductively rational and wildly
insane, both humanitarian and genocidal. As Mailer notes, "the
century would create death, devastation and pollution as never
before. Yet the century was now attached to the idea that man
must take his conception of life out to the stars. It was the most
soul-destroying and apocalyptic of centuries. So in their turn the
astronauts had personalities of unequaled banality and apocalyptic dignity" (47). Incongruity also inheres within the moon flight
as a historic event. At a press conference Wernher Von Braun
describes the moon launch as "'equal in importance to that
moment in evolution when aquatic life came crawling up on the
land'" (72–73), while in a newspaper interview he elevates the
enterprise to the level of a search for God by affirming that
"'through a closer look at Creation, we ought to gain a better
knowledge of the Creator'" (79). Yet for Mailer the technological
displacement of the spirit of adventure and the utter absence of
charisma in the astronauts themselves leave an emotional void at
the center of the event, which, Mailer insists, again typifies the
character of the century itself. For the "horror of the Twentieth
Century was the size of each new event, and the paucity of its
reverberation" (34). Moreover, the sense of emptiness is unavoid-
ably suggested in the barren setting of the launch. Indeed, at
Cape Kennedy "the abandoned launch towers and the hot lonely
ocean breeze opened vistas of the West," while reminding Mailer

"of how many of the most important events in America seemed to take place in all the lonely spaces" (52). Observing the crowds of people camping out in the countryside surrounding Cape Kennedy, Mailer senses an air of expectation and excitement as the hour of the launch approaches. But to Mailer the mood signifies the naive American propensity to be galvanized by a single idea in addition to reflecting an appetite for all that is new, big, and sensational. Mailer attributes such characteristics to the absence of long-standing American cultural traditions. He considers that "perhaps some instinct in American life had been working all these decades to keep the country innocent, keep it raw, keep it crude as a lout, have it indeed ready to govern the universe without an agreeable culture to call its own—for then, virgin ore, steadfastly undeveloped in all the hinterworld of the national psyche, a single idea could still electrify the land. Culture was insulation against a single idea, and America was like a rawboned lover gangling into middle age, still looking for his mission" (70). And as he notes in response to Von Braun's "quietly apocalyptic" banquet room speech before a group of corporate executives, "out of his big bulk and his small voice he would offer miracles. That was his knowledge of America, no mean knowledge. Prosperity satisfies those who are rich in culture. But in lands where the geography like the people is filled with empty space, then faith in miracles is the staple of the future" (77).

Of course, Mailer himself is without such naive faith, and as a result of its impersonal aspect, he remains emotionally detached from the moon mission until the very moment of the launch when the brute beauty and force of the fiery and at first soundless liftoff effect for him a mythic transformation in the slowly ascending spacecraft. At that moment it reveals itself to be "white as the white of Melville's Moby Dick, white as the shrine of the Madonna in half the churches of the world." Then, seconds later, the blast of the rocket reaches Mailer and the other onlookers, overwhelming them with "an apocalyptic fury of sound equal to some conception of the sound of your death in the roar of a drowning hour, a nightmare of sound" (100).

The actual landing on the moon prompts Mailer to exclaim "what a new fact! Real as the presence of immanence and yet not located at all" (113). But once the reality establishes itself, Mailer is depressed. Not only did the touchdown of Apollo 11 on the lunar surface apparently fail to loose a retaliatory curse, but the success of the mission suggested that the establishmentarians had proven the efficacy of their world view, leaving romantics in the terrestrial dust. NASA had proven that technology could triumph where Prometheus had failed. It could smash taboos, invade the sanctuary of romance, mystery, and magic, and steal the fire of the gods, all without consequence. In Mailer's view once reason has conquered all primitive fears, insanity emerges in the garb of the commonplace. Such has been the legacy of technology in the twentieth century, expediting the extermination of the Jews and threatening to perpetrate the ultimate holocaust through the development of nuclear weapons. Thus in the twentieth century the "real had become more fantastic than the imagined. And might yet possess more of the nightmare." In the aftermath of such ruminations Mailer no longer knows what to think or feel. The ethical significance of the moon mission itself remains ambiguous, and he feels cast "adrift" (141).

Mailer's response to this predicament is "to make a first reconnaissance into the possibility of restoring magic, psyche, and the spirits of the underworld to the spookiest venture in history, a landing on the moon" (131). In the long middle section of *Fire*, using as a model the repetitive methods of science itself, Mailer advances his romantic cause by reviewing the entire story of the moon mission. In so doing, while revealing in extensive detail his ability to master the principles of aerospace technology and engineering, he propounds several typically idiosyncratic but brilliantly suggestive theories that serve as romantic alternatives to rationally reductive explanations of experience, insisting that the strangeness and complexity of the world can never be adequately accounted for by a strictly rationalistic epistemology.

Because Mailer is interested in discovering the unconscious intent of the moon mission, he attempts to redefine the significance of dreams. Rejecting as inadequate and reductive the Freudian view that dreams are essentially wish fulfillment fantasies, Mailer argues that they may in fact serve as simulations, psychic experiments into possible courses of action, revealing complications and dangers that may have been only barely perceptible to one's conscious self.

Having propounded this existential theory, Mailer draws an analogy between the significance of dreams and the underlying purpose of the moon mission. The conceptual underpinning of the analogy is Mailer's long-held belief, first broached in "David Riesman Reconsidered," that there is an unconscious as well as a conscious direction to society and its institutions. In Mailer's view the U.S. space program would serve as the quintessential example of the double intent of social institutions, with NASA's frustratingly formulaic explanations of the purpose of space exploration functioning as so much ideological and rhetorical protection against the dread-inducing ambiguities of undertaking a journey into the limitless unknown. Thus Mailer speculates "that our voyage to the moon was finally an exploration by the century itself into the possible consequences of its worship of technology, as if, indeed, the literal moon trip was a giant species of simulation to reveal some secret in the buried tendencies of our history" (161). And though it may have seemed at first that the gods of magic failed to respond to this renewed challenge of technology, Mailer insists that there is much not only in the moon mission itself but also in the history of technological development, not to mention the mysteries that lay at the epistemological borders of physics, to suggest that magic does exist, that the laws of cause and effect may at times be inexplicably suspended, and that indeed there may even be a psychology of machines whereby in "some all but undetectable horizon between twilight and evening" a machine "is free to express itself, free to act in contradiction to its logic and its gears, free to jump out of the track of cause and effect" (162). Moreover, Mailer argues that the simplicity of radio communication testifies to the distinct possibility of telepathy, observing that if one considers "the existence of natural receivers, of organic radios in every square mile of earth and God knows what unknown forms of psychic electricities still undetected by any instrument of measure but radiated in messages between every insect, blade of grass, and tree, the possible existence then of the earth as one giant communications bank of invisible transmitters and receptors!—it was enough to knock a technologist on his ear if he began to think too much of the psychology of machines" (167).

In such a manner Mailer labors hard to create a universe that is an animistic paradise of unruly spiritual forces and cacophonous psychic communications, a universe in which the transcendental will of material objects shapes their physical forms so that form becomes a revelation of essence. This is clearly the world in which Norman Mailer lives. Unfortunately the astronauts are off somewhere else. Even Mailer recognizes this fact. He knows that the astronauts would dismiss his theories as crackpot. So although he has succeeded in reaffirming his faith in romance, mystery, and magic and struggled as successfully as anyone could in "restoring magic, psyche, and the spirits of the underworld" to the moon mission, Mailer realizes that he cannot change the conscious personalities of the astronauts themselves or overturn the ascendancy of the computer and its binary system of logic, which eliminates from consideration whatever cannot be quantified. Nor can he deny the establishmentarian astronauts their success. Protected by a mind-boggling redundancy of circuits and machinery, lobotomized from any "outrageous sense of adventure," the astronauts had nevertheless landed on the moon and, in so doing, taken the first step in projecting their own persistently prosaic, computer-ridden view of life out across the stars. Thus according to Mailer the "Wasps," "the most Faustian, barbaric, draconian, progress-oriented, and root-destroying people on earth" (10), had won, at the very least, an important battle in their perpetual war against the forces of romance and rebellion. It was the first stirrings of this realization that had prompted Mailer to embark on his defense of the romantic imagination. And when, upon returning from Houston to Provincetown, he is embarrassed in a restaurant by the booming, comically obscene voice of his drunk friend, Eddie Bonetti, Mailer hears echoing within himself an unspoken "voice large and endless in its condemnations of himself and all the friends of his generation and the generations which had followed" (440), leveling

an indictment of the ways they had used their years, drinking, deep into grass and all the mind illuminants beyond the grass, princelings on the trail of the hip, so avid to deliver the sexual revolution that they had virtually strained on the lips of the great gate. They had roared at the blind imbecility of the Square, and his insulation from life . . . but now it was as if the moon had flattened all of his people at once, for what was the product of their history but bombed-out brains, bellowings of obscenity like the turmoil of cattle . . . while the Wasps were quietly moving from command of the world to command of the moon, Wasps presenting the world with the fact after prodigies of discipline, while the army he was in, treacherous, silly, overconfident and vain, haters and despisers of everything tyrannical, phony, plastic and overbearing in American life had dropped out, goofed and left the goose to their enemies. Who among all the people he knew well had the remotest say on the quality of these lunar expeditions whose results might yet enter the seed of them all with concentrates worse than their collective semen already filled with DDT. An abominable army. A debauch. (440–41)

Throughout the summer of the moon landing Mailer is plagued by a sense of endings: 1969, the end of the decade, seems like the *fin de siècle*; his marriage to Beverly Bentley is dissolving about him; and the marriages of many long-wedded Provincetown couples are ending as well. With the summer winding to a close in "the land of the Pilgrims and the cod," the place that was "the beginning of America for Americans" (461), Mailer and many of his friends and neighbors gather for the burial of an old car. The broken-down old auto is representative of earth-bound technology and, by extension, of a time, now past, when the morality of technological development might be affirmed or denied with more assurance and less ambiguity. As the car, however, is transformed from a worn-out heap of machinery into a half-buried, paint-bespattered "artifact" entitled "Metamorphosis"—the "first machine to die with burial in the land of the Pilgrims and the cod" (464)—the sense of romantic possibilities emerges once again. As Robert J. Begiebing observes, "the scene" implies "that regeneration may yet reside in turning mechanism into life and art."[6] Moreover, both the car and the burial suggest a time when the possibility that human beings could be born, live, and die in colonies in outer space seemed as remote as the dimmest star. In that bygone time, Mailer laments, there was, as there may not be in some future colony in space, "a nice balance of food consumed and material used" (465) and a sense of natural balance and equanimity in the way that human beings lived and died.

It is perhaps the suggestion that such a transformation is possible that allows Mailer to feel justified in affirming to some degree the astronauts' flight to the moon, an affirmation that he in fact wished to make all along because of the heroic conception of such a flight. Thus when he returns to the MSC to see for himself the moon rock that the astronauts brought back with them from their mission, he does not ascribe to it the ominousness that he saw earlier in a Magritte painting of a rock, which was hanging in the foyer of a Houston mansion, a painting that "hung from the wall like a severed head" and intimated that "the world of the future was a dead rock, and the rock was in the room" (133, 134). Now instead he, Aquarius, a "Nijinsky of ambivalence," views this actual specimen of moon rock with warmth, seeing in it both age beyond comprehension, perhaps "three billion years or more," and at the same time eternal youth and the promise of "the subtle lift of love which comes up from the cradle of the newborn" (472). And so in the closing pages of *Fire* he gives the moon mission his highly qualified approval, deciding that he would

in some part applaud the feat and honor the astronauts because the expedition to the moon was finally a venture which might help to disclose the nature of the Lord and the Lucifer who warred for us; certainly, the hour of happiness would be here when men who spoke like

Shakespeare rode the ships: how many eons was that away! Yes, he had come to believe by the end of this long summer that probably we had to explore into outer space, for technology had penetrated the modern mind to such a depth that voyages in space might have become the last way to discover the metaphysical pits of the world of technique, which choked the pores of modern consciousness—yes, we might have to go out into space until the mystery of new discovery would force us to regard the world once again as poets, behold it as savages who knew that if the universe was a lock, its key was metaphor rather than measure. (471)

Despite this eleventh-hour affirmation—really an affirmation of exploration, new beginnings, and the poetic imagination and in no way an endorsement of technology—one is most aware in *Fire* of Mailer's deep-seated distrust of technological development, a distrust that reflects the essence of his left conservatism. For on the one hand it is born not only of Mailer's romanticism and his opposition to the established governmental order but also of his belief in the importance of preserving the natural, organic order of life and his desire to return to a time when human beings lived in mythic harmony with nature. It is in part this belief and this desire that have led Richard Poirier to the at first surprising judgment that Mailer's "cultural conservatism . . . smacks always of agrarianism" and to the perceptive conclusion that the past that Mailer seeks to recreate is mythic in nature and therefore "elusive of any historical location.[7] These concerns, which are central in *Fire,* animate as well Mailer's highly idiosyncratic discussion of women's liberation in *The Prisoner of Sex* and help to suggest that Mailer's much criticized attitude toward women has very little to do with typical male chauvinism. At the same time, Mailer's association of women's liberation with technology, artificiality, and totalitarian simplification and his insistence that women embrace their biologically determined roles as mothers testify to the fact that, despite the appearance of being at the center of a public debate, in *The Prisoner of Sex*, as a result of the singularity of his left-conservative argument, Mailer again becomes the outsider.

IV

Mailer associates women's liberation with technology because in his view the movement advocates the use of modern techniques to free women from the need to conceive and gestate and argues that women will never enjoy full equality with men until they are liberated from motherhood. Thus according to Mailer the introduction of new contraception and abortion techniques serves as the technological prelude to the development of artificial wombs. To indicate the currency of such an idea among women's liberationists, Mailer quotes both Dana Densmore and Ti-Grace Atkinson, whom he calls "the Chief Engineer of Women's Technology . . . the Surgeon-General of the female Armies of Liberation." Atkinson argues, for example, that the "'first step that would have to be taken before we could see exactly what the status of sexual intercourse is as a practice is surely to remove all its institutional aspects: We would have to eliminate the functional aspect. Sexual intercourse would have to cease to be Society's means to population renewal. This change is beginning to be within our grasp with the work now being done on extrauterine conception and incubation'" (65).

According to Mailer such a development would help to eliminate meaningful differences between the sexes rather than creating true equality. Significantly, Atkinson argues that "'in order to improve their condition, those individuals who are today defined as women must eradicate their own definition. Women must, in a sense, commit suicide, and the journey from womanhood to a society of individuals is hazardous'" (66). In Mailer's view Atkinson's utopian "society of individuals" is essentially totalitarian, denying complexity and variety even as it pursues its ideal of liberation. As Mailer notes, "it was the measure of the liberal technologist and the Left totalitarian that they exhibited the social lust to make units of people" (129).

Mailer, of course, totally rejects such utopian dreams of social engineering, particularly if they conceive of the ascendancy of androgynous or unisexual attitudes and styles of behavior. As I have noted in my discussions of both his definition of totalitarianism and his unique integration of existential and transcendentalist points of view, Mailer is forever concerned with elaborating differences while discovering new complexities and meanings. And for him meaning can be understood only in terms of dialectical relatedness. Thus Mailer opposes contraception not only because its use anticipates the development of artificial wombs but because, in preventing conception, it diminishes the human significance of the sexual act. Similarly he condemns abortion as both the murder of human potential and the technological violation of mystery, though he supports a woman's right to choose because, as he argues in *St. George and the Godfather*, control over one's body is a basic human right and the decision of whether or not to bear a child is "an act of self-recognition," revealing a woman's loyalty to either "'the recollection of magic'"[8] or her own practicality.

For Mailer, the sexual act is primarily the revelation of meaning through the passionate intercourse, indeed the erotic play, of opposites. Mailer first expressed this view in *The Deer Park* and gave it full articulation in "The White Negro" through his discussion of "the apocalyptic orgasm." In *The Prisoner of Sex* he reiterates it in the affirmation that "the come was the mirror to the character of the soul as the soul went over the hill into the next becoming" (88). And it is from this Hip perspective that in the section entitled "The Advocate," while engaging in a lengthy defense of Henry Miller and D. H. Lawrence against the feminist attack of Kate Millett, Mailer praises Miller's insistence on antagonism and polarity, quoting Miller's remark that "'the loss of sex polarity is part and parcel of the larger disintegration, the reflex of the soul's death and coincident with the disappearance of great men, great causes, great wars'" (125). The statement is pure Miller and pure Mailer. In fact, Miller embodied earlier in his work Mailer's own idea of a true democratic equality that is a celebration of differences, a celebration of the right, indeed the need, for all of life to continue stubbornly to assert its own unique value. For this reason "Miller was a true American spirit. He

knew that in a nation of transplants and weeds the best was always next to the worst" (104). Similarly, Mailer praises Lawrence
for containing within himself "a cauldron of boiling opposites"
(137), and he affirms Lawrence's central theme that transcendent
experience through love and sex is achieved only by people
delivering "themselves 'over to the unknown.' No more existential statement of love exists, for it is a way of saying we do not
know how the love will turn out" (147–48).

Mailer's insistence that sex have meaning and that meaning be
defined as dialectical relatedness explains his long-standing
biases against masturbation and homosexuality. In Mailer's view
masturbation suggests meaninglessness because it is essentially
an act of self-pleasure. To see it then as acceptable, let alone the
equal of heterosexual intercourse, is to cast a vote for the absurd.
Mailer's case against homosexuality proceeds from closely related ideas and apprehensions. He believes that without differences in gender there is no possibility of establishing a dialectical sexual relationship. As a result, he insists deplorably
upon denying the legitimacy of homosexuality. Unfortunately for
Mailer the superficial absence of sexual differences prevents him
from perceiving the obvious presence of a psychological dialectic
arising out of the opposites contained within the personalities of
each of the persons involved in a sexual relationship, whether it
be homosexual or heterosexual.

Of course, in addition to such biases Mailer's transcendentalist
passion for meaning leads him to find significance in every nook
and cranny of creation as well as in almost every conceivable
situation, thereby producing some of his most exotic ideas. In *The
Prisoner of Sex* he argues, for example, that perhaps the embryo
can determine its sex, that at one time women had the power to
choose when they would conceive, and that the ovum may be a
woman's "artistic creation" (194), a distillation of her essential
being and experiences. Such ideas outdo even Whitman. And
they are certainly easy to ridicule, especially from the standpoint
of technology. As feminist Mary Ellmann notes in reference to
Mailer's metaphysical investigation into the significance of hu-

man waste, "'it will not be admitted, by Mailer, that even the bowels move without personal meaning, the sewers reek with messages. . . . One is reminded of the fundamental grimness with which Norman Mailer thinks of every pickle and ice-cream cone as an index of intestinal morality'" (25). But such glib cynicism betrays a failure even to try to understand the romantic integrity of Mailer's ideas and purpose, which again is to preserve the sense of meaning in life, a sense that according to Mailer is constantly under siege. As Mailer argues, "no thought was so painful as the idea that sex had meaning: for give meaning to sex and one was the prisoner of sex—the more meaning one gave it, the more it assumed, until every failure and misery, every evil of your life, spoke their lines in its light, and every fear of mediocre death. Worse. It was not an age to look for meaning in one's acts—a dread of the future oozed from every leak in the social machine—unless the future could be controlled" (213–14).

Having criticized the relationship between women's liberation and technology and defended meaning against the totalitarian tendencies of modern life, Mailer tries his best to conclude by assuring women of his good will toward them. He still insists that a woman's "'prime responsibility . . . probably is to be on earth long enough to find the best mate for herself, and conceive children who will improve the species'" (231). But he argues that "women must have their rights to a life which would allow them to look for a mate. And there would be no free search until they were liberated" (232–33). And so "finally, he would agree with everything they asked but to quit the womb" (233). Of course, feminists could in no way accept Mailer's insistence on the primacy of a biologically determined role, especially if that role might some day be superseded through technological advances. So despite Mailer's attempt in the closing pages of *The Prisoner of Sex* to arrive at a rapprochement with women—reflecting what was at this point in his career the still unachieved synthetic goal of his left conservatism—he remained, as Joyce Carol Oates has observed, "the central target of the fiercest and cruelest of Women's Liberation attacks."[9] At the same time, Mailer's closing benediction of women's liberation does nothing at all to alter the singularity of his views on the subject. And so at the conclusion of *The Prisoner of Sex* Mailer remains the ideological outsider, the very substance and style of his engagement alienating him from the forces of both the left and the right.

V

Partly as a sign of his left-conservative alienation and partly as a reflection of his continuing involvement in questioning the direction of America, in his next book, *St. George and the Godfather*, Mailer again identifies himself as "the modest and half-invisible" (310) Aquarius. Even more than the Republican gathering four years earlier, the 1972 Democratic Convention lacks the kind of political drama that moves toward a climax, releasing one from the throes of endless questioning. The candidates themselves, for example, arouse little interest. Of them all, George Wallace provides whatever small hope for drama may exist. For the assassination attempt, which has left him paralyzed, seems to have served as some arcane experiential antidote to the virulence and rabidity of his public image. Now that image has been softened, rendered even a hint sympathetic. Now Wallace addresses his audiences with all the decorated dignity of a wounded war veteran, while his rhetorical style reflects the well-modulated, inexplicit racism of America's disgruntled center. Nevertheless, like the ghost of a guilty past that refuses to be put to rest, Wallace still "brings with him the clank of chains down in the dungeons of the moon-reaching blood-pumped crazy American desire" (319), the desire that enforces the good old-fashioned permutations of hate, fueling the nation's racism, militarism, and anti-communist crusades.

Meanwhile Hubert Humphrey and George McGovern project the excitement of a pair of political clerics. At the end of his career "Father Hubert" is like "a Renaissance priest of the Vatican who could not even cross a marble floor without pieties issuing from his skirt" (322). For his part front-running "Reverend" McGovern emanates the aura of a saint blessed with charisma "not of personality but of purpose" (324, 326). Thus Mailer concludes that McGovern is the leader of "a clerical revolution, an uprising of the suburban, the well-educated, the modest, the reasonable, and all the unacknowledged genetic engineers of the future" (327).

Of course, in practical political terms McGovern and his delegates were hopelessly ineffectual from the start at appealing to the majority of American voters. The young, idealistic Mc-Govern delegates, with faces reflecting none of the corruption of the old party politicians, were constitutionally incapable of producing the circuslike spectacle which was a specialty of the deposed Democratic machine and which could attract at least the passing interest of much of the American public. Nor were they or their candidate able to appeal to the patriotic piety of "the wad," Mailer's term for the Nixon "Silent Majority." As Mailer notes, "in America, the country was the religion" (374). And the rhetoric of McGovern's acceptance speech seems to assume such faith as it calls for the nation to "'come home,'" to return, that is, to the innocence and purity of "'the affirmation that we have a dream'" (375). As McGovern would soon discover, however, the nation thought that it was already at home with Richard Nixon and the Republicans, where, as Mailer indicates, it could know high church American righteousness while enjoying the full benefits of complete moral concealment.

The consummate skill with which Richard Nixon engages in moral concealment serves in fact as the focus of Mailer's account of the 1972 Republican Convention in Miami. It is appropriate therefore that he prefaces his report on the Republicans by brooding over the implications of his recent luncheon interview with Henry Kissinger, the grand master of moral rationalization and bureaucratic gamesmanship. Unfortunately, like virtually every other member of the press, Mailer falls prey to Kissinger's intellectual siren song.[10] Mailer admits that he likes Kissinger and suggests that Nixon's National Security Adviser was a man "who worked in the evil gears and bowels and blood left by the moral schizophrenia of Establishment, but still worked there . . . for good more than ill" (399). Mailer partly redeems himself for this hideous lapse of perception by admitting that the interview made him begin to doubt "the value of the act of witness" (398). Indeed, he is suspicious, as well he should be, of his initially positive response. As Mailer puts it,

> how could one pretend that Kissinger was a man whose nature could be assessed by such a meeting; in this sense, he was not knowable—one did not get messages from his presence of good or evil, rather of intelligence, and the warm courtesy of Establishment, yes, Kissinger was the essence of Establishment. . . . If there was a final social need for Establishment, then Kissinger was a man born to be part of it and so automatically installed in the moral schizophrenia of Establishment, a part of the culture of moral concealment. (398–99)

Kissinger's ability to maintain the appearance of accessibility while remaining essentially inscrutable personifies the character of the convention itself. For the 1972 coronation of Richard Nixon was decidedly "an exhibit without suspense, conflict, or the rudiments of narrative line" (400). Indeed, its very success depended upon these qualities, for among the narratives begging to be told were the account of America's saturation bombing of Southeast Asia during Richard Nixon's four years as president and the disclosure of the full truth about the Watergate break-in. Of course, it is precisely because of the degree of control and the totality of moral concealment that the Republican convention is able to assume an interest, an intensity, and even a hint of sinister fascination, all of which the Democratic convention wholly lacked. At the same time it provides for Mailer "the first sustained clue he has ever had to the workings of Richard Nixon's mind and *his* comprehension of America, and it is a mark of Aquarius' own innocence that he has never recognized until now how Nixon's vision might be conceivably more comprehensive than his own" (444). Mailer realizes that "Nixon was the artist who had discovered the laws of vibration in all the frozen congelations of the mediocre," understanding "that this inert lump which resided in the bend of the duodenum of the great American political river

. . . had indeed its own capacity to quiver and creep and crawl and bestir itself to vote if worked upon with unremitting care and no relaxation of control" (424–25).

While there were intimations of the religious at the Democratic Convention, the Republican Convention under the direction of Richard Nixon would become the political equivalent of a worship service. Presiding over the ceremony is the spirit of television incarnated in Nixon himself. As Mailer observes, Nixon, "the Eisenstein of the mediocre and the inert" (458), is "the first social engineer to harness and then employ the near to illimitable totalitarian resources of television" (457), creating an event emptied of all real content, an event that "would possess *no* history—since there would be no possibility for anything unsettling to happen in the hall. Therefore the *history* of this convention would exist immediately, but in the world, not the hall—the communication itself would be the convention" (456). In this way Nixon proved that television's vaunted ability to bring the world into one's own living room was essentially a fake. For it was possible for an event to be televised from start to finish and still conceal its truth from most Americans.

In *St. George and the Godfather* Mailer refers time and again to the Vietnam War, thereby applying constant moral pressure to expose the enormity of the Republican evasion of the truth. Significantly, Ronald Reagan obliquely states the rationale for continuing the war in Vietnam through Vietnamization when he affirms that "'this nation will do whatever has to be done so long as one American remains in enemy hands.'" As Mailer observes, Reagan's statement reflects "the fetishism of American blood" (480), suggesting that extraordinary, even apocalyptic violence is justifiable if it gives hope of protecting American interests or saving American lives and that America's priority in 1972 was not to stop the killing in Southeast Asia but to stop the killing of Americans. As Mailer emphasizes, the great danger of such a belief is that it encourages a nation "to avoid all responsibility" (481). Such criticism is, of course, utterly foreign to the "Silent Majority" of Americans as they witness the Republican ceremony of faith. Their unwavering support, given puerile expression by the mindless histrionics of the Young Voters for the President, as well as the ineffectuality of both the McGovern Democrats and the demonstrators in Flamingo Park testify to Nixon's election-year success at shaping an image of America that was completely divorced from the war-torn reality. His ability to shape such an image is reflected in the cynicism of his acceptance speech in which he insists that America seeks "'lasting peace in the world'" (497) and refers with the sympathy of a political opportunist to the diary of Tanya, a Russian child who lost her entire family during the battle of Leningrad in World War II. In an attempt to counter such horrible cynicism, Mailer graphically reveals what peace-loving America is doing to the children of Southeast Asia by juxtaposing against Nixon's reference to Tanya the parallel situation of "T'Nayen en Dhieu":

> For the last five weeks the airplanes have been coming over.
> On the first day Uncle Nguyen was killed. Three days later, my brother Nang Da.
> Last week Aunt Vinh Tan was killed together with my baby sister Minou.
> Yesterday Papa bled to death.
> Today Mama burned to death.
> All are dead. Only T'Nayen writes this. (498)

As Mailer suggests in his preface to *Some Honorable Men*, the 1976 collection of his writings on presidential conventions, the drama of America's political life has become increasingly covert. And though he argues that even in 1972 one could still "try to believe in history as the product of forces more or less open to the vision of skilled observers" (xi), his accounts of the 1968 and 1972 conventions and his report on the moon launch all really emphasize the opposite point, namely that the conflicts of history were already quickly receding from the view of critical observers. Thus for Mailer, as the decade of the 1970s began to unfold, the forces of alienation were multiplying, with a sense of division emerging out of the inscrutability of historical causes, the hypocrisy of moral concealment, and the paradoxes of his own left-conservative philosophy. If alienation from America would have to remain his subject or at least his imaginative point of departure, it was natural for him to try to charge it with renewed interest. And so in his writings throughout the rest of the decade and into 1980, Mailer returns to considering the relationship between romance and alienation. He, therefore, abandons his Aquarian modesty and focuses on the combination of charisma and estrangement in such figures as the movie star, the boxer, and the psychopathic criminal.

Chapter 10

From *Marilyn* to *The Executioner's Song:* Charisma and Estrangement

One can find no better statement in all of Mailer's work of the tragic conjunction of charisma and estrangement, of romance and alienation, of transcendental promise and irredeemable loss than in the opening pages of *Marilyn*. After describing Marilyn Monroe as "every man's love affair with America," the legendary movie star who, above all others, was enshrined in the imagination as "the sweet angel of sex," Mailer confronts the reader with the crashing, inevitable conclusion, the brute fact intruding on one's consciousness with the shock of a personal loss involuntarily recalled at one's happiest moment on the nicest day of the year, the memory opening one to the long train of images that accompanies a lifetime of loss. Mailer writes that "sex was, yes, ice cream to her. 'Take me,' said her smile. 'I'm easy. I'm happy. I'm an angel of sex, you bet'" (15). Then he hits the reader with the unavoidable fact:

What a jolt to the dream life of the nation that the angel died of an overdose. . . . Her death was covered over with ambiguity even as Hemingway's was exploded into horror, and as the deaths and spiritual disasters of the decade of the Sixties came one by one to American Kings and Queens, as Jack Kennedy was killed, and Bobby, and Martin Luther King, as Jackie Kennedy married Aristotle Onassis and Teddy

Kennedy went off the bridge at Chappaquiddick, so the decade that began with Hemingway as the monarch of American arts ended with Andy Warhol as its regent, and the ghost of Marilyn's death gave a lavender edge to that dramatic American design of the Sixties which seemed in retrospect to have done nothing so much as to bring Richard Nixon to the threshold of imperial power. "Romance is a nonsense bet," said the jolt in the electric shock, and so began that long decade of the Sixties which ended with television living like an inchworm on the aesthetic gut of the drug-deadened American belly. (15)

In Mailer's view Marilyn's death was, like Hemingway's, a type of "the deaths and spiritual disasters" of the 1960s, threatening romantic faith and diminishing his image of America. For Mailer's unrequited romance with Marilyn parallels his "love affair with America." For him, as for her early photographer André de Dienes, she suggested unlimited possibilities as the "Girl of the Golden West" (55), giving rise to the fantasy that sex with her could bring deliverance and redemption. Indeed, "she gave the feeling that if you made love to her, why then how could you not move more easily into sweets and the purchase of the full promise of future sweets, move into tender heavens where your flesh would be restored" (15). She became a myth, and that myth was more real, more charged with meaning, than the reality of her life. Mailer describes her as "the last of the myths to thrive in the long evening of the American dream" (16). And like America she was complex, enigmatic, Protean—her shifting personality virtually impossible to fix in the imagination except in terms of its multi-form oppositions. For Marilyn was a living contradiction, her personality founded upon ultimately irreconcilable conflicts. Indeed, as Mailer states,

In her ambition, so Faustian, and in her ignorance of culture's dimensions, in her liberation and her tyrannical desires, her noble democratic longings intimately contradicted by the widening pool of her narcissism (where every friend and slave must bathe), we can see the magnified mirror of ourselves, our exaggerated and now all but defeated generation, yes, she ran a reconnaissance through the Fifties, and left a message for us in her death, "Baby go boom." Now she is the ghost of the Sixties. (16–17)

In *Genius and Lust*, his 1976 anthology of Henry Miller's writings, Mailer states that "genius may depend on the ability to find a route between irreconcilables in oneself."[1] Yet as Mailer notes in *Marilyn*, "exceptional people (often the most patriotic, artistic, heroic, or prodigious) had a way of living with opposites in themselves that could only be called schizophrenic when it failed." And how rare is that genius of personality who can chart such a course for a lifetime! Obviously there are limits. And when one finally reaches those limits, one may experience, as Mailer suggests, a shattering of all those disparate selves that reveals the horror of the void that one's life had always fought against.

One can, of course, chart the public course of such a life, employing the established techniques of conventional biography. But, as Mailer argues, if one hopes to come close to discovering the heart of the mystery of such a divided personality, a personality that assumes the psychic dimensions of myth, one will have to explore beyond the petty tyranny, false securities, and, when all is said, the inevitable contradictions and ambiguities of fact. One must become what Mailer calls a "psychohistorian" (19) or novelist biographer for whom facts become imaginative points of departure, springs for the novelistic imagination to enter intuitively into the complexities of human character. Embracing this approach, Mailer commits himself in *Marilyn* to "a *species* of novel ready to play by the rules of biography." Mailer states the rules explicitly: in his novel biography

no items could be made up and evidence would be provided when facts were moot. Speculation *had* to be underlined. Yet he would never delude himself that he might be telling a story which could possibly be more accurate than a fiction since he would often be quick to imagine the interior of many a closed and silent life, and with the sanction of a novelist was going to look into the unspoken impulses of some of his real characters. At the end, if successful, he would have offered a literary hypothesis of a *possible* Marilyn Monroe who might actually have lived and fit most of the facts available. (20)

In taking the novelist's path to the heart of the mystery of Marilyn, Mailer ventures characteristically romantic and expansive interpretations of her personality. And in doing so, he is careful to provide the essential defense against the reductive cynicism of his many critics, arguing "that the reductive voice speaks with no more authority than the romantic," for "it is also an unproved thesis" (23). Mailer's own romantic thesis is many-sided and provocative. For example, he introduces into the equation the possibility of multiple lives, suggesting that Marilyn's driven and divided personality may have been partly the result of the psychological and moral legacy not only of her ancestors but also of her own previous existences. The suggestion reflects Mailer's increasing interest in the idea of karma, which resurfaces in *The Fight*, *The Executioner's Song*, and *Tough Guys Don't Dance* and which serves as an elaboration of Mailer's eschatological existentialism, with its emphasis on moral economy and its relation of death and judgment.

If the search for an understanding of Marilyn leads Mailer to extend long-held existential ideas, it also quite naturally raises again for him the question of the psychology of the orphan. In Mailer's view although Marilyn carried with her the psychological and moral debts of the past, as the "fatherless child" (248), she was left by the very circumstances of her birth without a sense of cultural continuity. Her rootlessness therefore becomes a magnification of the predicament of all modern men and women whose search for identity and meaning begins with the recognition that they have been left with no place from which to begin, no place but the unknown self that they wish to discover.

According to Mailer it may have been the orphan's search for identity, along with the driving ambition to put her "signature upon existence," that led Marilyn into acting. As he notes, "a child who is missing either parent is a study in the search for identity and quickly becomes a candidate for actor (since the most creative way to discover a new and possible identity is through the close fit of a role)." But Mailer quickly adds that "the origins of insanity can be glimpsed in wild and unmanageable ambition" (22). And what could be a more ambitious imaginative act, a more daring mixture of life and art, than the attempt to assume a series of disparate roles, each with its own psychological dangers and complexities, in the buried, barely acknowledged hope that, by giving life to such characters, one might discover at last a new coherence and power or at the very least escape temporarily from the chaos of one's own life into what might seem the less threatening chaos of an imaginary role? Of course, such an escape is no solution to the problem of identity. For one must eventually return to oneself. And as Mailer makes clear in both the biography and *Of Women and Their Elegance*, his 1980 imaginary memoir of Marilyn in which he combines fact and fiction while attempting to enter her own point of view, the secret to sanity is not so much finding a way to live through a single personality as it is allowing for internal communication among one's conflicting selves. The more romantic, extreme, and charismatic the personality, the more difficult such communication becomes. In the end, as Marilyn's short life and the romantic tragedies of the 1960s dramatize, the complexity often proves overwhelming, and one is left with a sense of estrangement that, as *An American Dream* suggests, drives one to the extremes of murder or suicide—toward murder as a doomed purge of self-defeat or suicide as a self-destructive leap at salvation, a preemptive act of desperation that seeks to preserve whatever of value is left in the belief that "an early death is better for the soul than a slow extinction through a misery of deteriorating years" (Mar. 173).

Mailer is, of course, acutely aware of the dangers that attend upon the life of the romantic, charismatic, and deeply troubled personality, a life whose expansion into myth seems so often inextricably bound up with a fateful movement into violence, madness, and death. But as Mailer suggests through his discussion of karma and the psychology of the orphan, complexity and conflict constitute the psychic birthright of such a personality. For the romantic and charismatic human being, character is indeed fate, the fate of having to lead an existential existence. For such a person there are no dispensations, no protections. Life is embattled from the start, and one's code and style of life emerge out of the embattlement, the existential code and style providing both a way of attacking life and a mode of defense.

It is within this context that one can best understand Mailer's long-time obsession with boxing. In Mailer's view a movie star such as Marilyn Monroe embodies the essential mystery of the romantic personality with its often destructive attraction to extremes. But the boxer suggests a way of surviving while he explores the rich complexities of that attraction. In other words the boxer becomes for Mailer a type of the existentialist. He is the isolated artist-hero who can survive only by revealing the "genius" of balancing "on the edge of the impossible" (F 185), an image suggested by Mailer's observation of Muhammad Ali as he successfully battled against George Foreman from the precarious vantage of the ropes throughout the better part of their 1974 championship fight. And more than any other fighter it is Ali, "America's Greatest Ego. . . . the swiftest embodiment of human intelligence we have had yet,"[2] who personifies Mailer's existential view of boxing: according to Mailer boxing is not only "a rapid debate between two sets of intelligence" (EE 7) but an activity embodying an "unstated religious view" (PP 247) of life that "looks upon death as a condition which is more alive than life or unspeakably more deadening" (PP 245). Moreover, it implicitly affirms the Hip argument "that violence may be an indispensable element of life" (PP 246), that in fact courageous and creative violence acts as "a defense against the plague, against that plague which comes from violence converted into the nausea of all that nonviolence which is void of peace." For Mailer then, while boxing may not be "a civilized activity," it belongs to the best part of "the tradition of the humanist," showing "a part of what man was like," revealing "his ability to create art and artful movement on the edge of death or pain or danger or attack," and expressing much "about the subtleties of human style."

Mailer is, of course, describing boxing at its best: as an epic battle of complex forces that intensifies experience and lends both a mythic and an existential sanction to violence. But as he has come increasingly to admit, violence is most often simply a part of the plague. This realization is already implicit in Mailer's observation in "Ten Thousand Words a Minute" that existential violence is a reflection of "the culture of the killer who sickens the air about him if he does not find some half-human way to kill a little in order not to deaden all" (PP 247). Mailer has in fact confronted quite often in his career that sickening of the air. For it constitutes the essential ambience surrounding Sam Croft and at times Marion Faye. It emanates from the hipster who beats in the brains of a candy-store keeper or embraces the nihilism of the storm trooper, and it infects D. J.'s farewell dinner at the conclusion of *Why Are We in Vietnam?* Above all, it establishes the mood of *The Executioner's Song*, for Gary Gilmore seems at times to be none other than the charismatic real-life incarnation of all of Mailer's destructively violent and estranged fictional characters.

Mailer's nonfiction novel of Gilmore's life and death by execution unfolds with deceptive simplicity in a style that competes with the best of Hemingway yet is truly Mailer's own, revealing with amazing versatility the points of view and colloquial language of the burnt-out moral drifters and strait-laced law-abiding Mormons of Book One as well as the brigade of lawyers, judges, media people, and hucksters who fill the pages of Book Two. The narrative begins with a brief sketch of Gilmore and his cousin Brenda trying to conceal an innocent childhood transgression, for in climbing to the top, Brenda has broken off a branch of one of Grandma's prized apple trees. The story then moves quickly ahead to reveal that Gilmore is a man who has spent almost his entire adolescent and adult life in institutions, progressing from reform school to the Oregon State Penitentiary to a maximum security prison in Marion, Illinois. As Gilmore states in a letter to Brenda, being in prison is like being exiled to another world. He writes that "it would be totally alien to you and your way of thinking, Brenda. It's like another planet. . . . Being here is like walking up to the edge and looking over 24 hours a day for more days than you care to recall" (7–8).

Gilmore's letter sets forth the theme of estrangement and alienation that dominates the book while anticipating all the complications and dangers of his own release from prison. Within the first month of that release, Gilmore reveals in dozens of ways his total estrangement from society and his fundamental incapacity to cooperate with people or even comprehend the basic ground rules of a variety of simple social situations. At J. C. Penney's he remarks pathetically to Brenda, "'Hey, I don't know how to go about this. Are you supposed to take the pants off the shelf, or does somebody issue them to you?'" (24). Playing poker with new-found acquaintances, he cheats flagrantly. He delights in telling graphic prison tales of sex, violence, and degradation, talks obscenely at the top of his lungs during a movie at a local theater, and is sexually aggressive and violently abusive toward women. His sexual frustration and rage are always ticking away, threatening to explode. His two blind dates serve as cases in point. On the first outing he makes premature sexual overtures to Lu Ann Price and later threatens to strike her when she suggests he get out of her car and persists in lecturing him. And when Marge Quinn, his companion on the second date, fails to respond to subsequent phone calls or a belligerently insistent late night visit to her house, a drunken Gilmore responds by smashing the windshield of her car after unsuccessfully trying to tip over the vehicle with the help of an inebriated Ricci Baker, the brother of Nicole, who will soon become Gilmore's girlfriend.

As Mailer makes clear, however, Gilmore's estrangement is simply a criminal manifestation of what for many of the young men and women of Book One is an insuperable condition of life. If Gilmore's future, with all its overriding limitations, was confirmed by adolescent lawlessness and imprisonment, their lives were equally limited and their sense of estrangement established by early, and, in some cases, multiple marriages. In fact, it seems that most of the young people of Book One were married as teenagers and separated or divorced before they could have possibly had any idea of what a stable and substantial adult relationship is. The best example is Nicole, who has been married four times and has two children before she is out of her teens. The first marriage is at fourteen to "a big immature clunk" (94) by the name of Jim Hampton. Of Hampton she notes that "he didn't have a job so they were living on unemployment. He wouldn't go to work, but really knew how to use a fingernail file on Coke machines" (95). The relationship lasts only until she happens to encounter sometime drug dealer Jim Barrett, who will become her second husband. The couple originally met prior to Nicole's first marriage while she was involved for two days and nights in orgiastically servicing an acquaintance and his entire circle of friends. A third marriage to the seriously paranoid Kip Eberhardt is a brief nightmare. A fourth marriage lasts two weeks. Like Nicole, the far more stable Brenda has also had four marriages, the first at sixteen. Other examples of marital division include Ricci Baker and his wife Sue; Nicole's cousin Sterling Baker and his wife Ruth Ann; and Nicole's neighbor, Kathy Maynard, whose story is particularly disturbing. Kathy is married at sixteen. After three months of marriage, her seventeen-year-old husband commits suicide before her eyes, stabbing himself in the stomach. Two weeks later, having remained drunk since her husband's death, she marries a man she met for the first time at the funeral. She lives with him for only a few weeks, and after she leaves, he forms a relationship with her best girlfriend.

Interestingly, with a naturalistic perception that recalls his view of the daunting power of nature in *The Naked and the Dead*, Mailer suggests that the aimlessness and desolation that plague so many of these people are partly a spiritual inheritance of the West itself. Indeed, in *The Executioner's Song* the traditional symbolism of the West is inverted, suggesting not limitless possibilities and the transcendental freedom of "the hero in *space*" but the imaginative paralysis that comes when one feels like an outcast whose fate it is to live in the middle of nowhere. Lu Ann Price hints at this desolation in a conversation with Gilmore: "The desert was at the end of every street, she said, except to the east. There, was the Interstate, and after that, the mountains. That was about it" (28).

What quickly emerges out of Mailer's portraits of these people is a powerful sense of the overwhelming moral chaos of their lives.

Gilmore's personal mix of psychopathy and evil does, of course, partake of this chaos, but its aggressive criminality and hatefulness clearly distinguish it from the more benign aimlessness of such people as Nicole, Ricci, Hampton, Barrett, Kathy Maynard, Kip Eberhardt, and Nicole's harmless but deeply disturbed sister April. They are truly the beat legatees of the spiritually and politically exhausted hipsters, hippies, and left radicals whom Mailer derides at the conclusion of *Of a Fire on the Moon*. For them life is a series of non sequiturs, a series of discontinuous turn ons and turn offs that lead from nothing to nothing. As April puts it, "'every day . . . is the same. It's all one day. . . . You have to get them used up'" (219). Given such a view, one's only alternative is to embrace the nihilism and despair of trying to get whatever pleasure one can right now since one moment leads pointlessly to the next and nothing matters.

At the center of this moral chaos stands Nicole. For the confusion and trauma of her four marriages are reflected in all the details of her life. She is haunted by the memory of having been sexually abused as a child by her late Uncle Lee, seems bent upon sleeping with every stray dog of a man, is institutionalized at thirteen, and ingests drugs with total abandon. Certainly there is great spirit, strength, and resilience in Nicole. Indeed, she has the necessary freedom of spirit to fulfill Mailer's idea of the true existentialist. But her liberated spirit has expressed itself only in terms of indiscriminate indulgence, which leads ironically, as one exerts less and less control, to a diminution of freedom. As Nicole herself realizes, one can violate the moral economy of life for only so long. For this reason when she first meets Gilmore and discovers that she is actually pursuing the man, she feels scared: "it was the thought of getting mixed up with another loser. She felt it was bad to float through life. You might have to pay too much the next time around" (77).

Nicole is feeling frightened too by the intensity of her feelings for Gilmore. The two of them in fact become obsessed at first sight, for they are drawn to each other by the overwhelming force of mutual desperation. The relationship is therefore highly charged, and from the start one knows that, rather than providing a refuge from chaos, it is doomed to drive both of them to further extremes. In fact, the course of the relationship veers wildly, moving through intimacy and good times, impotence battled through marathon sexual sessions forced by Gilmore, violent confrontations and threats, Gilmore's occasional physical abuse of Nicole, and finally separation. In Gilmore's case the turmoil of the relationship triggers that murderous rage of evil which has always lived inside him and which has been threatening to explode ever since his release from prison. Thus he turns to murder as a despairing purge of a lifetime of rejection and alienation that has now come to a focus in the apparent loss of Nicole.

By chance on the evening of the first murder Gilmore finds himself in the company of April. April's profound disorientation and mindblown surrealistic associations remind one of young Vardaman Bundren's mad psychological connections in *As I Lay Dying*. Vardaman believes that his mother is a fish, and April, when she is experiencing a psychotic episode, is equally convinced that if she cannot get a new guitar string, her grandmother will die. She also proclaims that she has "'always wanted to be a pig'" (223) and insists in all paranoid seriousness that "'the FBI look in on houses to see if people are committing crimes. Through the TV, you know'" (225). April's psychotic mutterings provide an insanely lurid counterpoint to Gilmore's utterly random, irrational, psychopathic, yet coldly sane murders. Mailer captures the combination of cold sanity and psychopathy in Gilmore through a simple yet brutally realistic description of his murder of Max Jensen. Leaving an oblivious April in his van, Gilmore walks over to the gas station where Jensen is working. After robbing the station, Gilmore forces Jensen to lie down on the bathroom floor:

Gilmore brought the Automatic to Jensen's head. "This one is for me," he said, and fired.

"This one is for Nicole," he said, and fired again. The body reacted each time. (223–24)

The following night at a motel located next to his Uncle Vern Damico's house, Gilmore repeats the crime, shooting motel manager Ben Bushnell in the head after forcing him to lie on the floor of his office. After he is apprehended, Gilmore himself provides the best description of the randomness of the murders while revealing through his chillingly detached language the essential psychology of the psychopath. Lieutenant Nielsen, the interrogating officer, presses Gilmore for his reasons for going to the motel and the gas station:

> "Well," said Gilmore, "the motel just happened to be next to my uncle Vern's place. I just happened on it."
> "But the service station?" said Nielsen. "Why that service station in the middle of nowhere?"
> "I don't know," said Gilmore. "It was there." (288)

In stark contrast to Gary Gilmore's psychopathy and the overwhelming moral chaos of the lives of so many of the young people in Mailer's book stands the weary but indomitable stoicism of Gilmore's mother, Bessie. Certainly the limitations of life have come crashing down just as forcefully and indifferently on Bessie as they have on her son, Gary. As the granddaughter of a Mormon convert, she inherited the pioneer belief in expanding possibilities that motivated her grandfather to go west, pushing "a cart across the plains with all his belongings, one of an army of Mormons pushing their little wagons up the canyons of the Rockies because there was not enough money in the Church that year for prairie-wagons, and Brigham Young had told them, Come anyway, come with handcarts to the new Zion in the Kingdom of Deseret" (315). Now, however, for her there is no expectation that life can be better. Her future is fixed in the silence and isolation of her plastic trailer, where she swelters in the summer and freezes in the winter. Contemplating her predicament, with a husband and a son dead, another son condemned to execution, and two remaining sons gone away, she does not know why she has been left utterly alone. As Mailer notes, "she did not know how much was her fault, and how much was the fault of the ongoing world that ground along like ironbanded wagon wheels in the prairie grass, but they were gone" (496). What she does know is that now for her there is only the companionship of memory. She cherishes the memory of herself as "a farm girl who wouldn't work in the sun and wore large sun hats and long gloves," as a natural-born ballerina who got A+ in her high school dance class, and as the "Queen of the Golden Green Ball at church" (317). She cherishes the memory too of sitting

for hours looking at the beautiful peak she called Y Mountain because the first settlers had put down flat white stones on its flank to make a great big white "Y" for old Brigham Young. Once, when she was a child, she was looking at Y Mountain and her father came over and Bess said, "Dad, I'm going to claim that for my very own," and he said, "Well, honey, you've got just as much right as anyone else, I guess," and walked off, and she thought, "He gave me his consent. That mountain belongs to me." Sitting in the trailer, she said to the good friend who was her memory, "That mountain still belongs to me." (319)

For Bessie memory is truly her "best and only friend . . . the only touch to soothe those outraged bones that would chafe in the flesh until they were a skeleton free of the flesh" (318). Until that day all Bessie can hope for is the ability to continue to endure, an ability epitomized a few years before her son's murders by her response to the news that Gary had committed armed robbery: "when she found the story" in the newspaper "she cried till she was sick. One more river in the million tears she had cried over Gary" (311). Indeed, as Bessie tells herself after visiting a twenty-two-year-old Gary at the Oregon State Correctional In-stitution and as she tells herself again after learning of Gary's two murders, "'I am the daughter of the very first people who settled in Provo. I am the granddaughter and great-granddaughter of pioneers on both sides. If they could live through it, I can live through it'" (314).

A number of women in *The Executioner's Song* reflect this same stoic attitude. As Joan Didion notes, "they are surprised by very little. They do not on the whole believe that events can be influenced. A kind of desolate wind seems to blow through the lives of these women."[3] One thinks of Marge Quinn's resignation to the fact that Gilmore has smashed her windshield: "she let it go. It was one more unhappiness at the bottom of things" (57). One also recalls the reaction of Kathryne Baker, Nicole and April's mother, to coming home and finding April the night after the Jensen murder "enthroned like a zombie in the kitchen chair": "'I can't do anything about it,' Kathryne said to herself. She was just thankful the child was home. It was one more wall Kathryne was holding up with her life" (238). One more river, one more wall, one more unhappiness—these words might serve as the epigraph to Mailer's book. They might also describe to a degree Nicole's attitude toward life, for the inner strength that she exhibits does contain an ineradicable element of stoicism that has enabled her to endure a lifetime of male abuse. But again that stoic fortitude has been diverted toward a self-destructive objective, namely sustaining her relationship with the condemned Gilmore. For once Gilmore is jailed, convicted, and sentenced to die, the obsessiveness of the relationship deepens, and as it does, Gilmore gains an increasingly powerful hold over Nicole, who will now do absolutely anything to prove her love for him. In fact, Gilmore becomes more and more demonically manipulative as his futile, despairing, and incredibly selfish desire to possess Nicole assumes control of his being. When Nicole, who is tiring of promiscuity, begins to suggest that she would like to try being faithful to him, Gilmore takes advantage of the suggestion to attempt to lock Nicole into lifelong psychological slavery to him and his memory. His voice echoes in her mind: "'Don't fuck those cocksuckers. It makes me want to commit murder again. If I feel like murder it doesn't necessarily matter who gets murdered—don't you know that about me?'" (351). Later in a letter he makes the demand for lifelong celibacy even more directly, using as additional leverage the insidious argument that violation of the vow of chastity would force him to seek extinction in the afterlife.

As if turning Nicole into a celibate votary worshiping throughout her life at the shrine of his memory were not enough, Gilmore further tests her loyalty and love by trying to convince her to join him in a suicide pact. Yet when the two of them do agree to attempt to kill themselves, while Nicole obviously tries to take her own life through a drug overdose, Gilmore suspiciously ingests a less than lethal dose of drugs right before his morning cell check virtually guaranteeing that he will not die. As a result, one is left wondering at the distinct possibility that Gilmore first wanted to have the satisfaction of knowing that Nicole had indeed become his sacrificial virgin before keeping his part of the deadly bargain.

The singlemindedness, force of personality, and flair for the dramatic that Gilmore exhibits in manipulating Nicole are likewise responsible for turning his capital case into a story of national interest. Before his conviction and sentencing, he has no desire to die, tries to convince psychiatrists that he was not wholly responsible for the killings, and demands that his court-appointed lawyers provide him with a strong defense. Once convicted, however, Gilmore adamantly advocates his own execution. In so doing, he is undoubtedly motivated by his contempt for prison life. But he is perhaps also moved by some desire to pay for what he did, by a belief in a life beyond death, and, as journalist Barry Farrell suggests, by the pressure of the publicity that he himself generated. Gilmore puts his position bluntly after learning of the first stay of execution:

Don't the people of Utah have the courage of their convictions? You sentence a man to die—me—and when I accept this most extreme punishment with grace and dignity, you, the people of Utah want to back down and argue with me about it. You're silly. (521)

Though Gilmore claims that he has no desire for publicity, such a statement is virtually guaranteed to create it. Thus the media circus begins, and in detailing the crowd of reporters and hucksters that descended upon Provo to compete against each other in "Merchandising Gary Gilmore's Dance of Death,"[4] Mailer does a good job of showing how thin the line is between journalism and exploitation. In fact, sometimes the line does not exist at all, for serious reporters may easily find themselves drawn into the chaos of trying to get a piece of the action, not to mention the fact that even those with the most passionate dedication to the truth are still in the final analysis merchandising that truth. Among the clear-cut exploiters is Dennis Boaz, the "more organic than thou" (639) hippie ex-lawyer who originally intrudes upon the situation without any real credentials to advocate Gilmore's right to die and ends up trying to make money in any way that he can, even self-importantly trying to sell to David Susskind the story of his own involvement in the case. As one might expect, there are also *The National Enquirer* and *The New York Post*, champions of the lurid headline and the disappearing fact, as well as Universal Pictures, which will buy the rights to Gilmore's story only if he is executed. In addition there is corporate-hippie Geraldo Rivera of "Good Morning America," whose despicable hypocrisy journalist Robert Sam Anson exposes in a memorable description: "directly in front of the prison building," moments before the execution, "Geraldo Rivera, attired in black leather jacket and jeans and looking cool, the way only Geraldo Rivera can look cool, is shouting into his mike. 'Kill the Rona segment. Get rid of it. Give me air. You'll be able to hear the shots. I promise. You'll be able to hear the shots'" (975). As for the majority of the other media representatives, they inhabit the never-never land of "people" journalism, with its love of the facile, photographic image and its corporate indifference to serious analysis.

Mailer's treatment of the media's highly questionable involvement in the story of Gary Gilmore broadens and deepens the theme of estrangement that dominates Book One. Mailer's westerners suggest the sickening divisions that live within us all, divisions that are reflected in the current epidemic of broken marriages, the absence of any clear sense of direction, and the widespread loss of faith in any idea or value beyond the self. Increasingly in the face of all the public and private moral chaos of recent years even the most conventional and complacent of middle-Americans have had to confront the horrible possibility that life in general and their own lives in particular might break

down one fine day into a discontinuous series of pointless conflicts. To this disturbing vision of contemporary life, Mailer adds
through Book Two's eastern voices the suggestion that there is
also a division in America between the chaos of public and
private life. The media people who cover Gilmore's execution
seem to descend upon Provo like invaders from an alien world.
For the most part their essentially predatory objectives conflict
violently with the personal intentions of the people who are
intimately involved in Gilmore's life, people who are simply
trying to get on with their lives despite a near to overwhelming
sense of pain and loss. One is left finally with the image of
America as a complex, multileveled society that is madly working
at cross-purposes with itself in the absence of any communication, understanding, or sympathy.

The focus of the moral ambiguities attending the media's
coverage of Gilmore's execution is Lawrence Schiller, the man
who finally did secure the rights to Gilmore's story, contracted
with Mailer to write the book, and eventually produced the movie
for which Mailer wrote the screenplay (all of which points up the
fact that, although it was written after Gilmore was dead and the
uproar had subsided, *The Executioner's Song* is nevertheless
implicated in the moral questions that arise when the grief of
private tragedies is exposed to public scrutiny). At the time of the
Gilmore case Schiller's reputation was horrible. Despite a highly
successful career as a photographer and some worthwhile
documentary work, he was viewed as "a carrion bird" (718), a
merchandiser of death, having advanced his fortunes in part by
interviewing the dying Jack Ruby and publishing a book on Susan
Atkins, one of the members of Charles Manson's family of mass
murderers. Mailer exposes Schiller's flaws but is largely sympathetic toward him. In fact, he often views Schiller's shortcom-
ings with some of the same humor and affection that he had in the
past reserved for "Mailer" and Aquarius. In addition to admiring
the professionalism of Schiller's hustling, Mailer apparently saw
in Schiller's problematic reputation a reflection of the wanton
misunderstanding that has plagued his own public image. But if

some of Mailer's admiration is self-serving, it is also based on what seems to be a legitimate distinction between Schiller and so many of the other media people. One is, of course, finally left in the position of trusting Schiller's own personal testimony as interpreted by Mailer, but it does appear that, by producing serious journalism instead of sensationalistic trash, Schiller and his collaborator Barry Farrell do for the most part avoid joining the ranks of the exploiters. Both men are able to gain an intimate understanding of Gilmore and his predicament, and both agonize over the morality of their involvement in the story. In fact, after a diarrhetic catharsis, Schiller experiences a moment of truth in which he decides to forge a new sense of integrity by turning down a whole slew of deals, including Rupert Murdoch's *New York Post* offer of $125,000 for an eyewitness report of Gilmore's execution.

Interestingly, as one views the condemned Gilmore through the eyes of Schiller, Farrell, and above all Mailer, one sees that Gilmore is also able to grow into a new sense of dignity, for he is capable of courage as well as grace under pressure. Considering what his response might be to encountering "a reincarnated Benny Bushnell," he says, "I don't fear it. Fuck fear. I may meet Bushnell—if I do, I will *never* avoid him. I recognize his rights" (692). Explaining to his Uncle Vern why he wants him to witness the execution, Gilmore reveals a real awareness of the importance of the manner in which one confronts death, saying, "'I want to show you. I've already shown you how I live . . . and I'd like to show you how I can die'" (982). Indeed, the day before he dies, he maintains the same strength of will: "I don't feel any fear right now," he says. "I don't think I will tomorrow morning. I haven't felt any yet" (889). And just before his execution, when asked by Warden Smith if he has a final statement to make, Gilmore looks at Vern and simply says, "'Let's do it.'" In Vern's view it was the "most pronounced amount of courage . . . he'd ever seen, no quaver, no throatiness, right down the line" (984).

In the closing pages of *The Executioner's Song*, one begins to feel death like an actual presence while knowing with an ever-increasing strength of conviction that Gilmore's execution, or for that matter the execution of any human being, is nothing but a legally sanctioned murder, "blood atonement" (953), as ACLU lawyer Judy Wolbach realizes. Mailer's use of realistic detail, reminiscent of Truman Capote's description of the hangings of Richard Hickock and Perry Smith in *In Cold Blood*, rips apart any pretense of legitimacy about the idea of execution, communicating the sense that Gilmore was taken off to a dirty factory and shot for the good of us all. As Mailer notes, when Schiller, one of Gilmore's invited witnesses, entered the death room, "he could not quite believe what he next observed. For the seat of execution was no more than a little old office chair, and behind it was an old filthy mattress backed up by sandbags and the stone wall of the cannery. They had rammed that mattress between the chair and the sandbags, a last-minute expedient, no doubt, as if, sometime during the night, they had decided that the sandbags weren't enough and bullets might go through, hit the wall, and ricochet" (980). In confirmation of the tawdry pointlessness of it all, Mailer leaves one with the image of reporters in the aftermath of the execution combing the death scene like scavengers, "swarming over the chair, the sandbags and the holes in the mattress, creatures of an identical species feeding, all feeding, in the same place" (992).

In addition to revealing once again the deep sense of estrangement in American life while exposing the exploitative nature of the mass media and the brutal pointlessness of capital punishment, *The Executioner's Song* also brings into focus Mailer's own aesthetic and political division of commitment, which has resulted from the paradoxical fact that while becoming increasingly conservative he has nevertheless remained essentially a romantic. Of course, the term left conservative suggests as much, and paradox has always been Mailer's favorite intellectual companion. Nevertheless, some choices are mutually exclusive, just as some aesthetic and political strategies, though once effective, can outlive their usefulness. The continuing commitment of left-conservative Mailer to the alienated romantic protagonist presents itself as a case in point. Within the historical context of the 1940s, 1950s, and 1960s, one could embrace the image of the alienated romantic protagonist as a powerful expression of rebellion and dissent. During those years the Underground Man still posed an imaginative threat to all that Mailer has defined as totalitarian. And Mailer's own work bears testimony to the truth of this statement. But if the turmoil of the 1960s has taught any aesthetic and political lesson, it has surely been that, having made his assault on the system, the conventional alienated rebel, in life as well as in art, is either driven deeper into isolation, where the lure of destructive violence assumes a new attraction, or neutralized altogether, the very substance and style of his rebellion having been absorbed by the democratic pretenses of the system. Despite their brilliance and power and despite the fact that they are important contributions to the literature of alienated protest, *An American Dream* and *Why Are We in Vietnam?*, Mailer's two novels of the 1960s, suggest respectively the futility and the destructiveness of continuing isolation in the fates of their protagonists, with Rojack being forced to seek nonexistent new territories and D. J. being driven to embrace the violence of Vietnam. Moreover, Mailer as Aquarius suggests America's capacity to absorb protest in his condemnation of the alienated left at the close of *Of a Fire on the Moon*. In fact, to insist upon the aesthetic and political exhaustion of the alienated romantic protagonist is really to do nothing more than draw out some of the implications of Mailer's own criticisms of the left in his late-sixties and early-seventies nonfiction.

Mailer's characterization of Gary Gilmore confirms this exhaustion. Gilmore is certainly no paradigm of the romantic, although he does embody romantic attitudes and values through his charismatic force of personality, his emphasis on the importance of courage, his existential view of death, and his passionately extreme relationship with Nicole. But in Gilmore's estrangement from society, in his murderous and ultimately self-destructive violence, and in his death by execution, one can perceive the fate not only of the psychopathic criminal but of the alienated romantic rebel as well. Happily *The Executioner's Song* also implies the left-conservative alternative, although the fact that Mailer's left conservatism is a central element of the book has apparently eluded at least one reviewer. For Earl Rovit accuses Mailer in *The Executioner's Song* of "frantically depending on life, unmediated by the passionate imagination, to announce meanings which he so well knows only man can provide" and claims that the book fails to illuminate "those wellsprings of human behavior which we have come to expect Mailer to divine and disclose."[5] Rovit might as well ask for subtitles to a pantomime. In other words he completely misses the point. Mailer's left conservatism invests the entire book, and one could easily detail his position in *The Executioner's Song* on any number of issues raised by the action. For there is the same emphasis on courage, risktaking, moral economy, and the importance of maintaining differentiated values as well as an exhaustive criticism of the corporate media, establishmentarian hypocrisy, and destructive violence that one has come to associate with Mailer as a left conservative. The crucial difference between *The Executioner's Song* and Mailer's earlier nonfiction is that finally these views are incorporated into the narrative point of view and organization of the book itself rather than being pressed ideologically. As I suggested in chapter 1, in *The Executioner's Song* Mailer's radical critique of society emerges out of the operation of a synthetic imagination that is able to see society whole having established a standpoint of lonely comprehensiveness. As a result, his left conservatism finally succeeds in maintaining a dialectic among the conflicting segments of society rather than alienating itself from the forces of both the left and the right. Moreover, abandoning ideological argument for synthetic vision allows for the development of a new sympathy in Mailer, a sympathy that extends to so many of the people in the book but is certainly most affecting in Mailer's astonishingly poignant descriptions of the loneliness and stoic fortitude of Bessie Gilmore.

In *The Executioner's Song* there is a sufficiency to this approach that eliminates the need for ideological divisiveness. As I have noted, however, Mailer himself remains divided within. He remains attracted to both a left-conservative synthesis and the self-involved conflicts of romantic alienation. The juxtaposition of *Ancient Evenings* and *Tough Guys Don't Dance*, the two books marking Mailer's return to fiction, highlights this division.

In *Ancient Evenings* Mailer is able to bring into a complicated dialectical balance the most compelling concerns of his left conservatism, combining a sense of the importance of mythic imagination with a knowledge of the inevitability of existential isolation. Here more than anywhere else in his canon Mailer, as a literalist of the imagination, attempts to make the image actual through the integration of myth and history, an integration dramatized through the story of his ancient Egyptian narrator-protagonists Menenhetet One and Two. At the same time, however, with a power achievable only by an unflinching confrontation with tragic inevitability, Mailer depicts the historic supersession of his characters' beliefs. Thus he reveals the all but unbearable isolation produced by the loss of community. And in so doing, he is able to suggest the extraordinary existential demands placed upon the contemporary left-conservative protagonist, who would attempt to live at the center of a spiritually alien society.

Of course, in *Tough Guys* there is also isolation, but here the implications are quite different. Rather than dramatizing the isolation produced by the loss of a desirable community of spiritual values, Mailer details once again the plight of the alienated protagonist who lives by romantic necessity on the outermost reaches of contemporary American society. Limiting himself to the now familiar conflicts of romantic alienation, Mailer is able merely to suggest mythic backgrounds and the outlines of contemporary social and political reality while recreating much of the irrational world of magical connections that is the locus of *An American Dream*. As a result, the focus of his existential mystery remains the lone protagonist so that finally one is left with an empty emblem of romantic rebellion rather than a significant expression of left-conservative protest that attempts to speak its message within the heart of the society that it opposes while affirming the need to maintain a vital relationship between myth and history.

Chapter 11

Mailer in the 1980s:
Mythic Imagination and
Existential Mystery

Ancient Evenings is quintessential Mailer. In this novel virtually all of his most important themes appear, assuming in their Egyptian dress decidedly complex and elaborate forms. Thus rather than representing a departure from transcendental and existential materials, *Ancient Evenings* actually creates a context, approximating that unlocatable past beyond history, in which contemporary skepticism toward the supersensible may be suspended. In this way Mailer acquires a new freedom to explore his syncretic philosophy in all of its literalness and eccentricity. Indeed, *Ancient Evenings* reflects the mature fulfillment of a tendency in Mailer, evident since his development of a personal style and philosophy in writing "The White Negro," toward subordinating narrative interest to the attractions of point of view. In fact, in this novel Mailer's thoroughly American mythic imagination actually becomes the subject. As a result, in relation to the rest of his writings, *Ancient Evenings* assumes the paradoxical position of a climactic archetype that reveals both the imaginative sources of his work and its ultimate direction.

Extending his achievement in *An American Dream*, Mailer succeeds in *Ancient Evenings* in projecting a vision of existence that is both mythic and existential. In placing his narrator-heroes, Menenhetet One and Two, in the Land of the Dead, he for the first time dramatizes in mythic terms his morally exacting existential eschatology, which insists that one's ability to survive death depends upon the existential value of one's life, which in turns reflects the degree to which one has been committed to psychological and moral growth through risktaking. At the same time, the primary condition of existence in the Land of the Dead is a painful groping after identity that duplicates the confused subjectivity marking the birth of consciousness. As the novel makes clear, this problem of identity may be solved only by rediscovering one's connection to the mythic heritage of one's previous life. And, as in much of Mailer's work, the possibility of making a life-sustaining connection with one's heritage depends upon establishing a relationship with a father figure. For in Mailer's work it is the father, acting as guide and mentor, who holds the key to preserving cultural continuity while preparing the young initiate to survive amid the uncertainties of a hostile world. In *Ancient Evenings*, however, Mailer introduces into this problem a stunning complication. After suggesting throughout the book that belief in myth and reverence for the dead have undergone a decline during the lives of Menenhetet One and Two, he reveals that those lives have long since passed, that the spirits of Menenhetet One and Two have survived into an alien era, and that their beliefs no longer have any currency. As a result, they have been abandoned by time and are bereft of any communitarian support as they confront the cosmic uncertainty of existence in the Land of the Dead.

Mailer raises the problem of identity in the opening sentences of the novel by dramatizing the fundamental existential predicament: a consciousness exists, but it exists as a nascent subjectivity all but unknown to itself, its feeling and thought lacking in definition or context, its experience virtually inseparable from an all-encompassing condition of pain. It is from this absence of identity, confusing subject and object, that the inverted and disjunctive self-assertion of the novel's first sentence as well as the subsequent insistent questioning of nature and a possible self emanate:

> Crude thoughts and fierce forces are my state. I do not know who I am. Nor what I was. I cannot hear a sound. Pain is near that will be like no pain felt before.
> Is this the fear that holds the universe? Is pain the fundament? All the rivers veins of pain? The oceans my mind awash? . . .
> Is one human? Or merely alive?[1]

One gradually learns that these thoughts are arising from the still surviving consciousness of the late Menenhetet Two, who was during his brief life of twenty-one years (circa 1150–1129 BCE) a member of the Egyptian nobility. Considering the posthumous predicament of this ancient Egyptian in the context of Mailer's other novels, one is immediately struck by how much it reflects the uncertain existential situations of Mikey Lovett and Tim Madden, Mailer's other amnesiac protagonists. Like *Ancient Evenings*, both *Barbary Shore* and *Tough Guys Don't Dance* convey the powerful sense of consciousness emptied of identity in the lapse of memory. Of course, in each case the mnemonic root of the problem of identity suggests a possible solution: if one can restore memory, one may likewise restore a sense of self. But for this renewed sense of self to transcend the romance of alienation, enabling one to develop enduring values and goals directed beyond the self, the resources of memory must be extended to include the creation of a significant sense of myth and history.

In *Barbary Shore* Mikey Lovett creates a new sense of self by reclaiming his revolutionary understanding of history and embracing the rebellious commitment of the existential risktaker. As I have noted, Lovett makes these connections through his relationship with McLeod. As Lovett's spiritual and political mentor, McLeod bequeaths to the young man "the remnants of" his "socialist culture" while inspiring in Lovett the belated courage to oppose American and Soviet totalitarianism by becoming a fugitive political activist. The novel itself, however, argues against the efficacy of revolutionary socialism, while Lovett's political commitment clearly propels him outside of society. As a result, whether as the amnesiac writer or the fugitive political activist, Lovett remains in the role of the alienated romantic protagonist without an external locus of values more compelling than the interior imperatives of the isolate self.

The moral agenda of *Tough Guys* protagonist Tim Madden is even more personal. Though Madden's vital relationship with his father, Dougy, does represent a linking of generations and though this relationship is instrumental in restoring his sense of self, the central focus of the narrative is relentlessly inward. Thus the novel remains self-absorbed, as the significance of reclaiming the identity of an isolated consciousness reduces the significance of mythic, historic, social, and political concerns that could have created a true dialectic between that consciousness and the complexities of the contemporary American scene. As a result, while the novel succeeds in dramatizing Madden's self-renewal, it fails to bring that self into the center of society, leaving one instead with the aesthetically and politically exhausted image of a latter day bohemian writer cultivating his marijuana garden on the margins of contemporary American society.

In *Ancient Evenings*, however, there is a profound commitment to myth and history, emphasizing the central importance of cultural heritage and social relationship in creating a coherent identity. Although Menenhetet Two must finally endure the revelation that he is the posthumous survivor of a dead culture, the anachronism of his faith in no way undercuts its truth. Indeed, Menenhetet Two's sense of identity is restored by reestablishing his connection to this culture, a culture that fosters the religious view of life that equates myth and history. In fact, the equation of myth and history constitutes the core of the novel's messianic message, making what is Mailer's most powerful case for a transcendentalist alternative to atheistic humanism and a left-conservative alternative to the American innocent's dangerous denial of history.

Mailer's brilliant dramatization of the struggle of Menenhetet One and Two to survive in the Land of the Dead underscores the novel's deeply left-conservative orientation. Because they are paradoxically the posthumous survivors of an eclipsed culture, they become perfect embodiments of Mailer's left-conservative protagonist, who must work out his commitment to social relationship within the very society that has superseded the values of his cultural heritage. Thus in *Ancient Evenings*, by employing the dramatic irony of an enduring, anachronistic faith, Mailer is able to transmute the materials of the romance of alienation into a typal image of the conflict and isolation of his contemporary American left-conservative hero.

From the standpoint of this transmutation, Menenhetet Two's story becomes an existential journey from one condition of isolation to another. At the outset of the novel, having struggled to recall his name and a few details of his life and having confirmed the fact of his own death, Menenhetet Two is forced to acknowledge that he was abandoned in death by his mother, Hathfertiti. For she sold his rightful tomb and gave him a shabby burial, all but insuring that his grave would be robbed. Thus dispossessed and violated, he would be left to "wander homeless in Khert-Neter" (283) (the Duad or Land of the Dead), where he would have to face eschatological terrors and final moral judgment. There, with the vulnerability of a cultural orphan, he would meet the ultimate existential test: either he would justify the value of his life and survive or he would fail the test of truth and "die forever" (32), his evil heart having been devoured by Ammit, the Eater of the Dead.

Given the extremity of his predicament, Menenhetet Two is in dire need of a guide who can first prepare him for and then safely lead him through the treacheries of the underworld. Menenhetet Two finds his Virgil in the ghost of his great-grandfather, Menenhetet One. Initially the elder Menenhetet's demonic reputation and vaunted experiments into the darkest secrets of ritual and magic render his intentions suspect indeed. But it is precisely because of the breadth of his experience and the intrepidity of his existential investigations into all that is powerful and strange that Menenhetet One is able to serve as his great-grandson's guide in the Land of the Dead. Indeed, having lived four lives spanning the better part of two centuries (including three mystically self-fathered reincarnations), having been numbered among the nobility, and having among other occupations been twice a general as well as a high priest, a brothel-keeper, a wealthy businessman, and a student of magic, Menenhetet One has, like Odysseus, contended with gods and pursued existence as a continuous quest for mastery over the mysteries of life and death. He is therefore the perfect guide in Khert-Neter, the one most capable of fostering Menenhetet Two's chances for survival, not merely by helping him to negotiate the dangers of the underworld but more importantly by restoring Menenhetet Two's lost connection to his heritage, thereby creating a coherent identity that will help to insure his survival amid the uncertainties of the Land of the Dead.

As the elegant instrument of his great-grandson's spiritual education, Menenhetet One employs the art of storytelling, initiating the instruction with the myths of the gods. The overwhelming importance of such storytelling is immediately clear to the spiritually lost Menenhetet Two. As he admits,

> I could think of tales I had been told in my childhood about Isis and Osiris and others of those Gods from Whom we all began, but now, as if the depths of such stories were as lost and far apart from me as the wrappings of my organs in their Canopic jars, I sighed and felt as hollow within as a cave. While I could not say why I thought this was so, it seemed to me as if nothing could be more important than to know these Gods well, as if, indeed, They could fill all that was empty in my marrow and so serve as true guides to the treacheries I would yet have to face in the Land of the Dead. For I now remembered an old saying: Death is more treacherous than life! (39–40)

Menenhetet One's stories of the gods provide Mailer with a wonderful opportunity to dramatize the epic, animistic theology of heroism that has been such an important part of his transcendental existentialism since the late 1950s. The object of this education through storytelling is, of course, the survival of death, so it is altogether appropriate that Menenhetet One's stories center on Osiris, the god of the underworld and judge of the dead, who apotheosized the ancient Egyptian hope of corporeal immortality, having survived death and dismemberment by rising from the dead in his reconstituted body. In addition to this central theme of resurrection, the stories teach the importance of such complementary Maileresque virtues as the courage "to dare losing all" (66) and respect for the necessity of moral balance as well as a gnostic belief in the transvaluation of values. As Menenhetet One suggests in a voice indistinguishable from Mailer's metaphysician of the belly, in the lowest one may find the highest, for life germinates out of corruption and "part of time" is "reborn, by necessity, in shit" (72).

Structurally, the stories serve as a prelude to the central narrative of the novel: Menenhetet One's account of his four lives, originally related in the company of his granddaughter, Hathfertiti; her husband-brother, Nef-khep-aukhem; their son, Menenhetet Two; and, the Pharaoh, Ptah-nem-hotep, Ramses Nine, during a visit to the royal palace. As the spirits of Menenhetet One and Two reexperience the events of this evening, common sense differentiations of time and space disappear, having been replaced by an ancient Egyptian version of Mailer's "enormous present," an eternal moment of mythic imagination wherein all times merge into one, a discrete sense of place is no longer certain, and consciousness is shared through telepathy. The aesthetic payoff from the novel's submersion in mystical relativity is rich indeed. For Menenhetet Two's ability to enter the minds of those around him and share their innermost thoughts and desires creates the opportunity for a complex, Jamesian study of subtle shifts in point of view that are simultaneously part of the story itself and an immediate, internal response to it.

Menenhetet One's narrative of his four lives also succeeds in expanding the novel's theme of initiation. For his story serves not only as Menenhetet Two's moral and cultural education, reconnecting him to his forgotten mythic heritage, but as Ramses Nine's pharaonic education as well, instructing him through the heroic example of Menenhetet's own godlike mentor, Ramses Two.

Insofar as he experiences, as both god and man, all of the sufferings and aspirations of his people, whose lives depend upon his power and judgment, the pharaoh represents the ultimate dialectical character in Mailer's canon. Within this context the explanation of Ramses Nine's self-confessed need for moral education becomes quite clear. Despite his godlike status, as a man the beautiful, delicate, cerebral Ptah-nem-hotep remains brilliant but flawed, wholly lacking in the warlike virtues of his ancestor Usermare-Setpenere, the great Ramses Two, whose superhuman potency and force insured the vitality of Egypt throughout his reign of sixty-seven years. As a result, Ramses Nine is highly vulnerable to a military challenge of power that, if successful, would accelerate Egypt's cultural and political dissolution.

Acutely aware that he is living in an increasingly decadent time in which faith is in decline and the threat of rebellion is ever present, Ramses Nine hopes that Menenhetet One will serve faithfully, despite his ambition to become vizier, as a spiritual mentor who can communicate the regenerative wisdom of the ultimate pharaonic model, Ramses Two. In this way Menenhetet One assumes the role of father-mentor to both Menenhetet Two and Ramses Nine, offering in the narrative of his relationship with his mentor, Ramses Two, "'a story far better than any father ever gave a son'" (232). Thus one realizes that the expansion of the theme of initiation likewise expands the theme of the father as the key to cultural continuity, establishing an intricate series of "father-son" relationships that survive even death, relating past and present while anticipating the novel's ultimate definition of identity as an integration of the essential wisdom of succeeding generations.

Interestingly, Menenhetet One's relationship with Ramses Two dramatizes much of the highly charged ambivalence that lies at the heart of the archetypal father-son relationship, an ambivalence that encompasses both pure love and pure hatred. When Menenhetet first sees Ramses Two, he is profoundly moved by the transcendent beauty and godlike power and authority of the young pharaoh. As he admits, "'from that moment I understood the meaning of a young man's love: It is simpler than other emotions. We love those who can lead us to a place we will never reach without them'" (251–52). In the case of Menenhetet's early uncomplicated filial love for Ramses Two, the otherwise unreachable goal is clearly an experiential knowledge of heroic and godlike ideals. Indeed, as Menenhetet notes later in his story, considering the terrible dignity with which Ramses Two accepted his soldiers' presentation of severed Hittite hands in the aftermath of the epic battle of Kadesh, "'to be near him was to gain all knowledge of how a God might act when He is in the form of a man'" (356). Yet the ruthless exercise of these same transcendent attributes of power and authority can easily produce in the vulnerable filial lover the fever of pure hatred. Examples abound in Menenhetet's relationship with Ramses Two. The pharaoh sexually abuses Menenhetet as a carnal exercise of his sovereign prerogative; he exiles him as a punishment for the death of the royal lion Hera-Ra while slandering his reputation as a warrior; and he later relegates Menenhetet, notwithstanding his position as General-of-all-the-Armies, to the post of harem-keeper. As Menenhetet confesses in a wonderfully balanced expression of the emotional complexity of his relationship with Ramses Two, "I knew the terrible rage, so full of its own weakness, that children suffer, for I hated my Pharaoh, but such hatred was worthless, for I wished to be able to love Him. Indeed, I knew I did love Him, and it was hopeless. He would only love me less. How I wished to destroy Him" (505). This volatile mix of love and hatred ultimately expresses itself in sexual competition and political conspiracy, as Menenhetet plots with Nefertiri, the pharaoh's spurned queen, to overthrow Ramses Two and become pharaoh himself. Menenhetet's rebellious decision to try to assume the throne of Egypt and make Nefertiri his queen is a perfect example of Maileresque risktaking. But Menenhetet's sexual daring costs him his life, for he is slain dramatically while engaged with Nefertiri in the sexual act by her jealous and potentially patricidal son Amen-khep-shu-ef.

It is important to note that as Menenhetet One's story unfolds before his audience, the drama of Menenhetet Two's father-son relationships is likewise unfolding, and, if anything, his filial relationships are even more psychologically complex than the elder Menenhetet's. One learns that Menenhetet One, Ramses Nine, and Nhef-khep-aukhem each contributed in a mystical comingling of identities to Menenhetet Two's conception. In terms of this triple paternity, Menenhetet One represents Menenhetet Two's ancestral alter ego, serving with the stature of a pharaonic surrogate as both a moral guide and the primary connection to the young man's cultural heritage. Nef-khep-aukhem stands merely as the nominal father, contributing his seed without truly joining in the creation of the boy's soul. As Hathfertiti confesses to her son, "'Nef-khep-aukhem is your father and yet he is not'" (163). Ramses Nine is Menenhetet Two's godlike spiritual father, and he asserts the preeminence of his spiritual paternity over Nef-khep-aukhem's nominal, biological paternity when he chooses to take Hathfertiti as his queen. Since she is descended from Queen Nefertiri by way of her grandfather Menenhetet One, who succeeded in fathering himself in his fatal act of intercourse with Nefertiri, Ramses Nine will be able through union with her to move closer "to all that Menenhetet might know, nearer, therefore, to what He desires the most— which was to dwell in the heart of Usermare." At the same time, the paternity of Ramses Nine signifies that Menenhetet Two belongs to a divine lineage. As Menenhetet Two realizes, "I came from the Pharaoh, Ramses the Ninth, Who was, with all else, a God. So He was not only my father but of greater eminence, my *Father*, the Good and Great God, a man and a God" (538).

The pharaoh's assertion of his godly paternal eminence does, however, initiate a fatal turning point in the events of the evening and the life of Menenhetet Two, driving to the center of the action the specter of treachery and betrayal. Upon realizing that Ramses Nine has superseded his role as the young Menenhetet's father, Nef-khep-aukhem abruptly departs, leaving in his wake a powerful curse upon his former son. As Menenhetet Two observes, "my first father had lived in our house like he-who-is-without-a-dwelling, and like a ghost he had left. There had been the sound of no door to close behind him. Only a curse. I had just learned that it is the smallest men who leave the largest curses" (549). Later, the absence of Nef-khep-aukhem weighs upon the young Menenhetet "like the wrath of a ghost" (595). And inexorably the sense of protective harmony and communion created by Menenhetet One's story becomes undermined by the curse. Indeed, a breach develops between the elder Menenhetet and Ramses Nine, ostensibly over a disputed detail in Menenhetet's story. But the breach actually reflects a deep-seated fear of betrayal that has threatened from the outset of the evening to disturb the delicate balance in the relationship of Ramses Nine and Menenhetet One, a balance of trust and suspicion, dependency and authority. For Ramses Nine knows that Menenhetet's ultimate ambition has always been to become pharaoh himself. Thus if he were to appoint Menenhetet vizier in recognition of the value of his counsel, as demonstrated through storytelling and confirmed in his title of the Master of the Secrets of the Things that Only One Man Sees, then he would be empowering the most dangerous man in all of Egypt.

While this psychological drama is building, Nef-khep-aukhem is setting into motion an actual rebellion, stirring up two separate factions to usurp the power of Ramses Nine. In response to this challenge, Ramses Nine is forced to share his power with a leader of one of the factions in order to avoid a complete overthrow. And so in the end, Menenhetet One's storytelling is unable to be an effective instrument for gaining or consolidating political power, as the potency of its wisdom is subverted by distrust and treachery. Nor is the wisdom of his epic narrative able to help Menenhetet Two escape the fatality of his relationship with his "former" father, Nef-khep-aukhem. Years later, when both have become sexual rivals for the incestuous favors of Hathfertiti, Nef-khep-aukhem has the young Menenhetet murdered by hired thugs. Interestingly, by revealing the practical and political limits of Menenhetet One's narrative, the novel indirectly underscores the true spiritual and cultural efficacy of storytelling. For it suggests through Menenhetet Two's experience as the elder Menenhetet's initiate in the Land of the Dead that when the art of storytelling serves as the sacred medium for communicating the spirit of one's cultural heritage, it can truly effect a spiritual regeneration, renewing one's life through the enduring energy of the lives of those who have gone before.

And this essentially is the experience of Menenhetet Two, whose isolation in the powerfully evocative closing chapter of *Ancient Evenings* recalls the dark conclusion of Twain's *No. 44, the Mysterious Stranger*, in which the events of the narrative vanish in the stark revelation of a single mind, "a homeless Thought, wandering forlorn among the empty eternities."[2] Indeed, Menenhetet One's voice echoes with the solemnity of 44's final, solipsistic pronouncement as he reveals to Menenhetet Two that the world they have known is gone: "It is true," he said. "The Duad is no more than a ghost. But then you must understand that you have been dead for a thousand years. The Pharaohs are gone. Egypt belongs to others." (705)

Having indeed experienced the eschatological trials of the Land of the Dead as if they were nothing more than the insubstantial projections of a child's nightmare, Menenhetet Two fears that he may be deprived of the self-knowledge that comes only from true, existential testing. But for him there is salvation from both cosmic isolation and moral ignorance. Having shared Menenhetet One's story, having taken into himself the myth and history of his culture, Menenhetet Two knows that identity is indeed created out of an integration of the essential wisdom of succeeding generations. He knows too that the hope for survival depends upon the generational bond. Thus he realizes that "if the souls of the dead would try to reach the heavens of highest endeavor then they must look to mate with one another" and so risk sharing "the same fate" (707, 708). Impelled by this knowledge and faith, Menenhetet One and Two merge into a single, enduring spiritual identity that struggles toward corporeal rebirth. And thus the novel concludes, having succeeded in compressing into a single image of transcendental questing the central themes of Mailer's career.

Of course, one would not begin to make such monumental claims for *Tough Guys Don't Dance*. Here, Mailer's ambition is uncharacteristically modest, notwithstanding the easy virtuosity evinced by the well-publicized fact that he wrote such an entertaining novel in just a little over two months. In fact, *Tough Guys* is easily Mailer's least ambitious novel, especially if one measures novelistic ambition in Maileresque terms by the expanse of new imaginative territory that a work of fiction is able to explore. For the book clearly represents a romantic return to the well-charted existential landscape of *An American Dream*. Moreover, Mailer's protagonist Tim Madden is indisputably a spiritual kinsman of Stephen Rojack. Though there are many significant differences in the details of their situations, the two share remarkably similar relationships and experiences. Both are embroiled in debilitating love-hate relationships with estranged wives who are ultimately murdered. Rojack, of course, kills his wife Deborah, and the amnesiac Madden believes for a time that he may have murdered his wife Patty Lareine. Both protagonists are attracted to the idea of "the Blonde"; both contend with black amatory rivals; and both find true love in spiritually battered but enduring girlfriends. Both hear voices that assert the powerful ontological claim of the irrational, and both engage in wild displays of existential risktaking, with Rojack traversing Barney Kelly's parapet and Madden attempting to scale the phallic heights of the Provincetown Monument.

Tough Guys, however, is not without its own resources of imagination and originality. Most notable is the startling elegance of the conception governing the plot of the novel. For Mailer has attempted to integrate the amnesiac protagonist's problem of self-creation with the elements of a murder mystery. In so doing, he has created an existential mystery in which the attempt to piece together the solution to a murder is at the same time a search for identity. Thus with the ultimate crime serving as original sin, Mailer engages in a moral dialectic whereby the existential investigation of his protagonist's true relation to guilt transforms a psychological and spiritual dead end into a new beginning, creating the chance to embrace a true love relationship and begin a new life that is free of the dark and torturous burden of self-destructive choices.

In telling this story of self-regeneration, the novel takes as its point of departure the obliteration of its protagonist's memory and the desolation of his soul. Over the past several weeks since Patty Lareine left him, Tim Madden has been forced to confront the depths of obsessive desire. Counting the days since his wife's departure, he experiences all the horrors of addiction as his dependency on nicotine merges with his desire for Patty and the two needs coalesce in the certainty that addictive, self-destructive love leads to cancer and doom. Then on day twenty-five, he awakens from a drunken stupor to find that he cannot remember with any confidence the events of the night before, a night, he will soon discover, when someone, perhaps he, himself, committed a grizzly murder.

Interestingly, the self-absorbed bleakness and extremity of Madden's predicament are objectified by the psychogeography of the novel's Provincetown setting, a setting that has long haunted Mailer's imagination for its association with America's beginnings, its gloomy off-season solitude, and its potential to serve as the perfect scene for murder. It appears, for example, as the setting for an orgiastic, murderous party in the turgid and muddled fragment entitled "Advertisement for Myself on the Way Out," which also contains a good, brief description of the Upper Cape and the Pilgrims' landing that anticipates the pictorial language and historical sense of *Tough Guys*. One recalls too Mailer's statement in *Of a Fire on the Moon* that the horror of the Manson murders had come as no surprise to him since he had once planned to write a novel "about a gang of illumined and drug-accelerated American guerillas who lived in the wilds of a dune or a range and descended on Provincetown to kill" (461).

Provincetown's gloomy, brooding presence in *Tough Guys* represents the literary fulfillment of this long-time fascination. With the coming of the chilly New England fall, Provincetown's atmosphere is transformed. The colorful summer carnival has vanished, leaving behind an all but empty town turning "gray before one's eyes,"[3] a town so depopulated that, as Madden observes, "on many a shortening November afternoon you could have taken a bowling ball and rolled it down the long one-way lane of our narrow main street (a true New England alley) without striking a pedestrian or a car. The town withdrew into itself, and the cold, which was nothing remarkable when measured with a thermometer . . . was nonetheless a cold sea air filled with the bottomless chill that lies at the cloistered heart of ghost stories" (5–6). Indeed, the shape of the land itself is emblematic of the need to withdraw, for as one travels north up the Cape, nearing the end of the road, the land becomes a "long curving spit of shrub and dune that curves in upon itself in a spiral at the tip of the Cape" (6–7). Yet at the same time Provincetown suggests the promise of new beginnings, for the land itself is new, having "been formed by wind and sea over the last ten thousand years," a period that, as Madden notes, "cannot amount to more than a night of geological time." Thus it seems to him that Province-town's "sand flats still glistened in the dawn with the moist primeval innocence of land exposing itself to the sun for the first time." This same sense of mythic innocence is reflected in the fact that Provincetown is the place where America began. As Madden emphasizes, echoing the words of Aquarius in *Of a Fire on the Moon*, "it was not at Plymouth but *here* that [the Pilgrims] landed" (7) with their dreams of discovering a New World of expanding possibilities.

As I have suggested, the dual significance of Provincetown as both the desolate road's end and a still innocent place of new beginnings reflects respectively Madden's dire predicament and the potential for renewed life that ironically opens for him when in all the paranoia of amnesia he is forced to confront the incredible possibility that he may be a murderer. After awakening from his stupor on the twenty-fifth day since his wife's departure, Madden discovers that the passenger seat of his Porsche is covered with blood. As a result, he is forced to wonder at the distinct possibility that he was engaged in some form of violence the previous evening. He discovers that a murder has in fact been committed when he journeys to the Truro woods to move his marijuana stash at the highly suspicious suggestion of Provincetown Police Chief Regency, who claims to have a religious love for the weed and a friendly desire to protect Madden from the area's intolerant state troopers. In the horror of finding the severed head of a blond-haired woman beneath the roots of the tree where he has hidden his marijuana, Madden panics. He hurriedly shoves the head back beneath the tree without daring to look at the face of the victim. As a result, both he and the reader are left wondering at her identity. Could she be Jessica Pond, the middle-aged but still seductive traveler from California whom he first met on the previous evening, a woman who served, along with her companion, Lonnie Pangborn, as the object of a passing homicidal fantasy that Madden morbidly entertained? Or could the victim indeed be his estranged wife, Patty Lareine?

The discovery of the severed head sets into motion the novel's two levels of action—the obsessive inward movement that leads to the reconstitution of the protagonist's identity and the maddeningly complicated outward movement built upon an elaborate network of interrelated characters and synchronously connected events that leads to the solution of the initial murder and the revelation of a series of other killings. At times the two levels of action are nicely integrated, and one is almost equally engaged in both the problem of identity and Mailer's eccentric adaptation of the novelistic machinery of the whodunit. Perhaps the best example is Madden and the reader's shared need to find out who the initial murder victim is. For the reader the question serves as a source of suspense, while for Madden it poses an existential challenge that is experienced as an absolute moral imperative. Like Madden's climbing of the Provincetown Monument—or indeed Rojack's walk across the parapet or Croft's attempt at scaling Mt. Anaka—the return to the Truro woods is an existential test of courage that must be undergone before any future growth is possible. Madden describes quite eloquently his experience of this undeniable obligation:

> I had to go back and look upon the face of the blonde who was dead. Indeed, I must do it not knowing whether her end came from my hands or belonged to others. Will you ever comprehend me if I say that such knowledge, while crucial to my self-preservation—was I in danger of the law, or of all that was outside the law?—was still not what called me forth so much as the bare impulse to go: that came from the deepest sign I could recognize—the importance of the journey must be estimated by my dread of doing it. (82)

This paradigmatic Maileresque statement of the value of dread as a moral indicator of the existential importance of apparently irrational risktaking also suggests why a problem eventually develops with Mailer's attempt to integrate the question of identity with the solution to a murder mystery. For it is ultimately not Madden's relationship to the law or to those outside the law that matters but his relationship to himself. Indeed, as the novel unfolds, it becomes increasingly clear that Madden's story is essentially a romantic excursion into the alienated self. As a result, the existential action eventually begins to assert its preeminence over the action of the murder mystery so that the solution of the various crimes is finally anticlimactic. In other words, the murder mystery itself becomes increasingly functional, a literary instrument that facilitates the resolution of the problem of identity. Thus one's response to the disclosure of the various crimes and the revelation of the culprits is reduced to varying levels of surprise. One shares, for example, Madden's shock when, on his third trip to the Truro woods, he discovers the heads of both Jessica Pond (the first murder victim) and Patty Lareine. Indeed, the discovery makes for a good twist in the novel's plot. But one's response to Patty's demise is tempered by the fact that she is never on stage herself and lives for one primarily through Madden's observations and in relation to his psychological predicament. Moreover, one realizes that within the structure of the novel, she is merely an obstacle that must be removed if Madden is to begin a new life and find a true love relationship with his long-lost girlfriend Madeleine Falco. Similarly, one is surprised but not particularly moved by the revelation that Patty murdered Jessica over a real estate deal or that she herself was murdered by her preposterously named ex-husband, the bisexual Meeks Wardley Hilby III. Nor does one have a more complex response when Wardley commits suicide or when one learns that Police Chief Regency is married to Madeleine, was romantically involved with Patty, and is deeply implicated in the killing of Jessica Pond. Indeed, once the existential action has approached its inevitable culmination, the exceedingly complicated details of the murder mystery prove almost distracting.

Two of Mailer's secondary characters, do, however, generate considerable interest. Madden's father, Dougy, emerges as the ultimate "Tough Guy" who embodies with considerable humanity the heroic code of the existential hero. In fact, his legendary reputation as a model of manly virtue has served over the years, along with Patty's domineering ways, as an emasculating force in Tim Madden's life, giving rise to a fear of latent homosexuality. Dougy's assistance, though, in solving the mystery of the murders and the yeoman service he provides in disposing of the numerous corpses that have piled up by the novel's end help bring father and son close together. Significantly, the new understanding that Dougy and Tim achieve represents the only such reconciliation in Mailer's career-long examination of the problem of the father. Like Dougy Madden, Madeleine Falco also has significant depth and humanity. Combining genuine toughness and sensitivity, she is the true love that Madden rejected to pursue Patty Lareine as the personification of the "insatiable" (110) Blonde, an idea that, as he notes, corresponds to his image of an insatiable America. Moreover, Madeleine is capable of the kind of Hip moral radicalism that was epitomized by Rojack's murder of Deborah, for in the conclusion of *Tough Guys*, she kills the captured and ailing Regency, knowing that "crazy people in serious places had to be executed" (226), certain that Regency would prove an insuperable barrier to starting a new life with Madden. For his part, Madden must contend with the fact that murder has been necessary to allow him to live his new life. As Madden notes, his hard-won "stability of mind" does indeed rest "on the firm foundation of a mortal crime" (228). Unlike Rojack, however, Madden is allowed to hold on to his love, and the novel ends on a relatively sanguine note with Madden and Madeleine living together more or less contentedly in Key West.

This happy ending, of course, in no way diminishes the fact that *Tough Guys* is deeply entrenched in the alternative world of romantic alienation—this despite the fact that such a world has lost its political and aesthetic point. We all know now the futility of living imaginatively on the margin of society, the futility of living underground. For no matter how many lights we use to illuminate our subterranean sanctuary, we will simply be ignored. We will remain invisible.

As I have been arguing, however, Mailer himself has developed a far better alternative: to struggle to synthesize the most compelling elements of romanticism and conservatism. This new synthesis offers the possibility of creating within the novel new left-conservative figures of protest who would express within the limits of society the radical critique of the alienated romantic protagonist. A model for such a character already exists in Melville's Confidence Man, who exposes the lies and hypocrisies of society by assuming their forms. Another alternative would be to create a figure who would embrace the most dangerous and imaginative of political choices: burrowing under cover into the heart of the establishment in order to oppose it from within.

The implications of Mailer's left conservatism do demand that he pursue such a course. But to take this direction, Mailer would have to sustain a certain imaginative faith. He would have to continue to believe not only in the idea that society can change but also in the ability of his left-conservative protagonist to survive, a protagonist who, to do justice to the range of Mailer's political sensibility, would have to combine the persona of General Cummings, the existential vision of Stephen Rojack, and the communitarian commitment of Menenhetet One and Two. Charting a course through such incompatibles would surely require genius, but the reward would be the achievement of Mailer's ultimate goal: creating a synthetic vision of America that truly disturbs.

Conclusion

More than any other writer of his generation, Norman Mailer has made America his subject. Throughout his career he has written with an acute sense of the millennial assumptions that helped create from the very beginning of the country a uniquely American consciousness. These assumptions have created the myth of America, and, as Mailer has repeatedly shown, they are responsible for producing the amazing dialectic of extremes in American life so that indeed "the best of our history is coupled as in no other nation with much of our worst." In relating both the promise and the debasement of the millennial idea of America to the complexities of the contemporary American scene, Mailer has amassed a body of work that enjoys undeniable cultural centrality. He has therefore assumed at the very least the kind of significance that has always been attached to James Fenimore Cooper, whose work embodies the central conflicts in nineteenth-century American attitudes toward the competing values of nature and civilization. As this book has sought to establish, however, one can make much greater claims for Mailer's work. For Mailer has compiled far and away the most challenging and exciting body of work of any contemporary American prose writer. And it should finally be stated, in evaluating Mailer's writings, that his novels need not defer to his nonfiction. In other words the excellence of *The Armies of the Night* and *The Executioner's Song* and their success in extending the limits of both nonfiction and the novel in no way diminish Mailer's achievements in the traditional novel, which surely rival in stylistic variety and imaginative scope the efforts of any of his contemporaries. *The Naked and the Dead* stands as the preeminent World-War-II novel. *An American Dream* is an extraordinary embodiment of Mailer's existential vision of life as well as a thoroughgoing romantic critique of contemporary American society. *Why Are We in Vietnam?* is quite simply a comic tour de force. And *Ancient Evenings* is both Mailer's most ambitious novel and his most compelling dramatization of the confrontation between myth and history, exposing the existential fate of the mythic imagination when it has lost through the faithlessness of society its communitarian identity. One can add to these accomplishments the superiority of Mailer's personal reportage and his mastery of the lyrical essay, best exemplified in that most seminal of texts, "The White Negro."

Having pressed these claims, one must also say that Mailer's flaws are largely those of a great writer. Like Blake, Yeats, and Lawrence, he is at times ironically limited by the rigorous eccentricities of a comprehensive system of thought. At times too, as in *Barbary Shore* and *The Deer Park*, which remains, despite its faults, a fine novel, he attempts more than he can manage. But as I have shown, these attempts were crucial to the development of Mailer's style and the creation of protagonists who could embody a significant response to totalitarianism. Finally one can certainly find Mailer guilty of being obsessively repetitive in his themes, but such obsession lives at the very heart of American romanticism.

In the final analysis Mailer has revealed more about America than any of his contemporaries, having had the moral courage and artistic integrity to write about the threat of totalitarianism in the land of the free and the home of the brave. The sustained quality and range of his work place him well within the first rank of American prose writers that includes Faulkner, Melville, James, Hawthorne, Emerson, Hemingway, Fitzgerald, Twain, Poe, and Thoreau. The truth of this judgment will become increasingly evident as the controversies surrounding Mailer's life cease to divert attention from his work and his captious critics either pass into oblivion or become footnotes in the most ambitious of literary histories. In the meantime, assuming continued health and vigor, Mailer will no doubt extend his body of work, producing books that deepen our understanding of the relationship of American myth and American history while attempting to stand as creations "equal to the phenomenon of the country itself" (CC 99).

Notes

Introduction (pages 1–7)

1. John Locke, "The Second Treatise of Government: An Essay Concerning the True Original, Extent, and End of Civil Government," in *The Works of John Locke*, vol. 5 (London: Printed for Thomas Tegg, 1823; reprint, Aalen: Scientia Verlag, 1963), p. 366; as quoted by R. W. B. Lewis, *The American Adam: Innocence, Tragedy, and Tradition in the Nineteenth Century* (Chicago and London: The University of Chicago Press, 1955), p. 42.

2. F. Scott Fitzgerald, *The Great Gatsby* (New York: Charles Scribner's Sons, 1925), p. 182.

3. Milton R. Stern and Seymour L. Gross, eds., *American Literature Survey*, vol. 1 (New York: The Viking Press, 1962), p. xxii.

4. Norman Mailer, *Cannibals and Christians* (New York: The Dial Press, 1966), p. 98. All further references to *Cannibals and Christians* (CC) will be noted in parentheses in the text.

5. Norman Mailer, *The Presidential Papers* (New York: Berkley Pub. Co., 1976), p. vi.

6. Norman Mailer, *The Presidential Papers* (New York: G. P. Putnam's Sons, 1963), p. 26. All further references to this edition of *The Presidential Papers* (PP) will be noted in parentheses in the text.

7. For example, Robert Ehrlich's *Norman Mailer: The Radical as Hipster* (Methuchen, N.J., and London: The Scarecrow Press, 1978) is devoted entirely to discussing Mailer's existentialism by examining his involvement with the figure of the hipster. Ehrlich notes that "Mailer has equated the concepts Hip and existential" (viii), a point that is certainly well taken. But he then goes on to locate evocations of the philosophy of Hip in almost every passage that Mailer has ever written. In addition, Laura Adams' work reflects how Mailer's existentialism has actually influenced the criticism of his own books. See, for example, *Existential Battles: The Growth of Norman Mailer* (Athens: Ohio University Press, 1976), p. 9. One unfortunate effect of such a critical approach is that it fosters a cavalier attitude toward the necessary relationship between structure and content and suggests rather vaguely that Mailer's works are successful to the extent that they reveal that he has "grown" as a writer and influenced his readers. The question of whether or not Mailer's books stand as finished works of art becomes a matter of only secondary concern.

8. Adams also places a strong emphasis on what she refers to as Mailer's

"nonliterary performances." In fact, she defines as inadequate any critical approach that "cannot take account of Mailer's nonliterary performances and insists upon separating his disturbing public personality from his 'art'" (*Existential Battles*, pp. 8–9). In so doing, she is reflecting the influence of Richard Poirier's idea of "performance," which he defines "in part" as "any self-discovering, self-watching, finally self-pleasuring response to the pressures and difficulties" of all that inhibits human expression. See *The Performing Self* (New York: Oxford University Press, 1971), p. 12. For both Poirier and Adams, writing is most importantly a performance, that is, an act of self-creation. The inevitable effect of such a view is to place a disproportionate emphasis on the writer, himself, an emphasis evident in Adams' introduction to *Will the Real Norman Mailer Please Stand Up?* (Port Washington, N.Y., and London: Kennikat Press, 1974), her edition of a collection of critical essays on Mailer. Robert F. Lucid's discussion of Mailer as a public writer in the introduction to his edition of a collection of critical essays on Mailer, entitled *Norman Mailer: The Man and His Work* (Boston: Little, Brown and Co., 1971), also fixes attention on Mailer's personality. In fact, Adams' and Lucid's collections both include sections devoted to essays on Mailer's personality.

Other unfortunate tendencies of critics who concentrate on Mailer's personality include equating Mailer with his characters and taking cheap shots at Mailer, himself. One expects to read the *ad hominem* comments of reviewers in newspapers and mass market magazines, but it is disheartening to find serious critics involved in character assassination. Consider, for example, this remark by George Alfred Schrader in "Norman Mailer and the Despair of Defiance": "Like all romantics, Mailer is overcome with pathos. He would be omnipotent—and stabs his wife! His action would be comical if it were not so pathetic." In *Norman Mailer: A Collection of Critical Essays*, ed. Leo Braudy (Englewood Cliffs, N.J.: Prentice-Hall, 1972), p. 93.

9. Adams, *Existential Battles*, p. 9; also, see Lucid, pp. 15–18.

10. See Philip H. Bufithis, *Norman Mailer* (New York: Frederick Ungar Pub. Co., 1978), p. 2.

11. Samuel Holland Hux, "American Myth and Existential Vision: The Indigenous Existentialism of Mailer, Bellow, Styron, and Ellison," Ph.D. diss., University of Connecticut, 1965, esp. pp. 179–80, 194–208.

12. Richard Poirier, *Norman Mailer* (New York: The Viking Press, 1972), p. 3.

13. Stern and Gross, p. xxii.

14. Norman Mailer, *Advertisements for Myself* (New York: G. P. Putnam's Sons, 1959), p. 17. All further references to *Advertisements for Myself* (Adv.) will be noted in parentheses in the text.

15. Norman Mailer, *The Prisoner of Sex* (Boston: Little, Brown and Co., 1971), p. 56. All further references to this book will be noted in parentheses in the text.

16. Adams' approach unfortunately has this effect. On the other hand, Richard Poirier believes that the influence of literature on life "is always a good deal less than most historically or politically oriented readings of literature like

to suggest. It seems to me a worthy enough function for literature to illustrate how and against what oppositions significant possibilities for the self in contemporary life can be imagined" (*Norman Mailer*, p. 23).

17. Robert Merrill's *Norman Mailer* (Boston: Twayne Publishers, 1978) serves as an important corrective to criticism that focuses on Mailer's ideas apart from his art, concentrates on his personality, or suggests that his books are impressive only in part and do not stand as "realized works of art" (11). Merrill's book attempts to provide a "full-length aesthetic evaluation" of Mailer's work, focusing primarily "on questions of literary structure rather than 'theme'" (12). Merrill, however, uses the word "theme" rather loosely, equating a thematic approach to Mailer's work with criticism that focuses on Mailer's ideas apart from his art. Actually a thematic approach would by definition have to consider Mailer's ideas as they are elaborated within the structure of his individual works, and, as I indicate, this is precisely what I will do in discussing Mailer's treatment of America. In this way I will be placing the focus where it should be in Mailer studies while at the same time considering "questions of literary structure."

18. I refer here to such thematic studies as Adams' *Existential Battles*, Robert Solotaroff's *Down Mailer's Way* (Urbana: University of Illinois Press, 1974), Stanley T. Gutman's *Mankind in Barbary: The Individual and Society in the Novels of Norman Mailer* (Hanover, N.H.: University Press of New England, 1975), and Jean Radford's *Norman Mailer: A Critical Study* (New York: Barnes & Noble Books, 1975). Of these books, Solotaroff's provides the most illuminating commentary on Mailer's philosophy and politics, but his study does not include a sustained, detailed discussion of the full implications of their close and complex relationship.

Chapter 1 (pages 8–23)

1. As Norman Podhoretz notes in "Norman Mailer: The Embattled Vision," "the principle" of Cummings' and Croft's "behavior is a refusal to accept the limitations inherent in any given situation as final. . . . The trouble with [Lieutenant] Hearn and [Private] Valsen is their inability to transcend the terms of the given; they know perfectly well that these terms are intolerable, yet they cannot envisage any conditions other than the ones before their eyes, and therefore they are reduced to apathy, cynicism, and despair. Croft and Cummings also know that the terms are intolerable, but the knowledge acts as a stimulus to their energies and a goad to their imagination. Though the laws of nature seem to prohibit a man from climbing to the top of Mt. Anaka, Croft . . . dares to attempt the climb, while Hearn and Valsen shrug helplessly at the sight of the peaks: like liberalism itself, they lack the vision and the drive to push toward the top of the mountain" (Lucid, pp. 66–67).

2. Norman Mailer, *The Naked and the Dead* (New York: Rinehart and Co., 1948), p. 321. All further references to this book will be noted in parentheses in the text.

3. Ralph Waldo Emerson, *The Journals and Miscellaneous Notebooks of*

Ralph Waldo Emerson, Volume IV, 1832–34, ed. Alfred E. Ferguson (Cambridge: The Belknap Press of Harvard University Press, 1964), p. 141.

4. Poirier, *Norman Mailer*, p. 26.

5. For Mailer's criticism of *Barbary Shore*, see *Advertisements for Myself*, p. 94. Mailer's obsessive involvement with the materials of *The Deer Park* is amply evidenced in *Advertisements*, pp. 228–64. Mailer also expended considerable time and effort in adapting *The Deer Park* into a play.

6. As Richard Poirier states, "*The Naked and the Dead*, along with the two books immediately following, *Barbary Shore* and *The Deer Park*, are unlike Mailer's later works in that he had not yet learned how to suggest any possible heroic resistance to the encroaching forces of totalitarianism." Indeed, Mailer had not "yet imagined a hero with whose violence he [could] unabashedly identify himself" (*Norman Mailer*, p. 26).

7. Merrill, p. 69.

8. Solotaroff, pp. 180, 182.

9. Norman Mailer, *The Armies of the Night: History as a Novel/The Novel as History* (New York: New American Library, 1968), p. 53. All further references to *The Armies of the Night* (Arm.) will be noted in parentheses in the text.

10. Steven Marcus, "An Interview with Norman Mailer," in Braudy, pp. 29, 30.

Chapter 2 (pages 24–41)

1. Robert Alter, "Norman Mailer (1923–   )," in *The Politics of Twentieth-Century Novelists*, ed. George A. Panichas (New York: Hawthorn Books, 1971), p. 323.

2. Radford, p. 13.

3. Norman Mailer, *The Deer Park* (New York: G. P. Putnam's Sons, 1955), p. 311. All further references to this book will be noted in parentheses in the text.

4. Diana Trilling, "The Radical Moralism of Norman Mailer," in Braudy, p. 59.

5. Ihab Hassan, *Radical Innocence: Studies in the Contemporary American Novel* (New York: Harper & Row, 1961), pp. 148, 151.

6. Solotaroff, p. 39.

Chapter 3 (pages 42–50)

1. Norman Mailer, *Barbary Shore* (New York: Grosset & Dunlap, 1963), p. 218. Originally published by Rinehart and Co. in 1951. All further references to the Grosset & Dunlap edition of this book will be noted in parentheses in the text.

2. Norman Mailer, *Marilyn* (New York: Grosset & Dunlap, 1973), p. 30. All further references to *Marilyn* (Mar.) will be noted in parentheses in the text.

3. Variations of this statement recur in Mailer's later work. See *The Deer Park*, p. 200 and *Advertisements for Myself*, p. 163 and p. 477, where he calls it "the best sentence I've ever written."

4. Inexplicably several critics have interpreted McLeod's death as a suicide. See Podhoretz, p. 71, Trilling, p. 51, and Radford, p. 85. For a response to such misinterpretations, see Max F. Schulz's explication of Hollingsworth's killing of McLeod in Adams' collection, pp. 53–54.

Chapter 4 (pages 51–68)

1. Norman Mailer, *The Executioner's Song* (Boston: Little, Brown and Co., 1979), p. 18. All further references to this book will be noted in parentheses in the text.
2. See Merrill, pp. 53, 55.
3. Merrill, p. 55.
4. Merrill, p. 49.

Chapter 5 (pages 69–91)

1. I am using here a modified version of R. W. B. Lewis's well-known image, suggested by Whitman, of "the hero in *space*." Lewis applies the term to Natty Bumppo as the first fully developed example of this hero, stating that he calls "such a figure the hero in *space*, in two senses of the word. First, the hero seems to take his start outside time, or on the very outer edges of it, so that his location is essentially in space alone; and, second, his initial habitat is space as spaciousness, as the unbounded, the area of total possibility. The Adamic hero is discovered as an old stage direction might have it, 'surrounded, detached in *measureless oceans* of space'" (91). I have borrowed the phrase "the old skin" from D. H. Lawrence, *Studies in Classical American Literature* (London: Martin Secker, 1933), pp. 57–58; as quoted by Lewis, p. vi.
2. I have borrowed this phrase from Professor Jack Davis, who has used it to describe Thomas Mann's attitude toward cultural ideals and art.
3. Thomas Mann, "Freud and the Future," in *Essays of Three Decades*, trans. H. T. Lowe-Porter (New York: Alfred A. Knopf, 1947), p. 415.
4. Ralph Waldo Emerson, "Nature," in *Selections from Ralph Waldo Emerson*, ed. Stephen E. Whicher (Boston: Houghton Mifflin Co., 1960), p. 38.
5. Emerson, "The American Scholar," in *Selections*, pp. 68, 70.
6. See Adams, *Existential Battles*, p. 22.
7. See Solotaroff, pp. 82–83.
8. Norman Mailer, *The Fight* (Boston: Little, Brown and Co., 1975), p. 38. All further references to *The Fight* (F) will be noted in parentheses in the text.

Chapter 6 (pages 92–115)

1. Norman Mailer, *An American Dream* (New York: The Dial Press, 1965), p. 2. All further references to this book will be noted in parentheses in the text.
2. Elizabeth Hardwick, "A Nightmare by Norman Mailer," in Lucid, p. 146.
3. Philip Rahv, "Crime Without Punishment," in *The Myth and the Powerhouse* (New York: Farrar, Straus & Giroux, 1968), p. 236.

4. Rahv, p. 237.

5. Rahv, p. 238.

6. Leo Bersani, "The Interpretation of Dreams," in Braudy, pp. 123–24.

7. Trilling, p. 64.

8. Bersani, p. 124.

9. Adams, *Existential Battles*, pp. 78–79. For another description of the novel as a dream-vision, see Radford, p. 101. For other allegorical interpretations, see Donald L. Kaufman, *Norman Mailer: The Countdown/The First Twenty Years* (Carbondale: Southern Illinois University Press, 1969), pp. 41–43; and Barry H. Leeds, *The Structured Vision of Norman Mailer* (New York: New York University Press, 1969), p. 126.

10. John W. Aldridge, "The Energy of New Success," in Braudy, p. 118.

11. Nathaniel Hawthorne, *The Scarlet Letter, The Centenary Edition of the Works of Nathaniel Hawthorne*, gen. ed. William Charvat, Roy Harvey Pearce and Claude M. Simpson, vol. 1 (Columbus, Ohio: Ohio State University Press, 1962), p. 36.

12. Poirier, *Norman Mailer*, p. 123.

13. Poirier, "Morbid-Mindedness," in Lucid, p. 164.

14. Robert J. Begiebing, *Acts of Regeneration: Allegory and Archetype in the Works of Norman Mailer* (Columbus: University of Missouri Press, 1980), p. 6.

15. Begiebing, pp. 5n, 62, 64, 67, 69, and 77.

16. Begiebing, p. 62.

17. Adams, "Existential Aesthetics: An Interview with Norman Mailer," *Partisan Review*, 42 (Summer 1975), 200–01.

18. Begiebing, p. 8n.

19. Begiebing, p. 9.

Chapter 7 (pages 116–38)

1. Norman Mailer, *Why Are We in Vietnam?* (New York: G. P. Putnam's Sons, 1967), pp. 24, 152. All further references to this book will be noted in parentheses in the text.

2. Rusty's shooting of the bear vividly recalls a central incident of Sam Croft's youth when his father stepped in and shot a deer that Sam had been tracking. The incident enforced in Croft's mind a lesson of ruthless opportunism summed up in his father's triumphant remark that the "one that wins is the one that gits it" (158).

3. Emerson, *Selections*, p. 135.

4. For critics who consider the novel's conclusion to be ambiguous, see Tony Tanner, "On the Parapet," in Adams' collection, pp. 143–47; and Merrill, pp. 82–84. For a critic who believes that D. J. and Tex are opposed to the war in Vietnam despite the fact that they exult over the idea of going there, see Aldridge, "From Vietnam to Obscenity," in Lucid, pp. 180–92. For critics who strangely view D. J.'s and Tex's participation in the war as representing either the fulfillment of God's will or an instinctual necessity, see Adams, *Existential Battles*, p. 119; Bufithis, p. 81; and Ehrlich, pp. 97, 111. For a critic who

argues that the god that the boys encounter is actually demonic, see Begiebing, pp. 109–10.

5. Solotaroff, p. 200. For Solotaroff's interpretation of the novel's conclusion, with which I am in substantial agreement, see pp. 197–202. For a similar argument, see Gutman, p. 158.

Chapter 8 (pages 139–63)

1. Hassan, p. 55.

2. As Matthew Grace notes, "the hippies' apparel indicates profound psychic dislocation and disorientation. They march towards the Pentagon wearing American Indian costumes and the uniforms of the Foreign Legion, Wehrmacht, the Confederate and Union Armies. Masquerading as a millennium of history, they have divested their minds of the symbolic and historical perspective their clothing represents." "Norman Mailer at the End of the Decade," in Adams' collection, p. 13.

3. Poirier, *Norman Mailer*, p. 27.

4. See "The Argument Reinvigorated" in CC 95–103.

5. Solotaroff, p. 230.

6. For example, Merrill's essay on *The Armies of the Night* is subtitled "The Education of Norman Mailer." See also Adams, *Existential Battles*, pp. 121–37, especially pp. 135–36.

7. Raymond A. Schroth, "Mailer and His Gods," in Adams' collection, p. 41.

Chapter 9 (pages 164–93)

1. Norman Mailer, *Miami and the Siege of Chicago* (New York: New American Library, 1968), p. 12. All further references to this book will be noted in parentheses in the text.

2. Solotaroff, p. 238.

3. Solotaroff, p. 238.

4. Norman Mailer, *Of a Fire on the Moon* (Boston: Little, Brown and Co., 1970), p. 4. All further references to this book will be noted in parentheses in the text.

5. Many critics have noted striking resemblances in purpose and attitude between Mailer in both *Armies* and *Fire* and Henry Adams in *The Education*. See especially Gordon O. Taylor, "Of Adams and Aquarius," *American Literature*, 46 (March 1974), 68–82. One strikingly suggestive similarity not to my knowledge mentioned concerns the two writers' paradoxical identification of their philosophical orientations. Mailer, of course, refers to himself as a left conservative, while Adams describes himself as a conservative Christian anarchist.

6. Begiebing, p. 176.

7. Poirier, *Norman Mailer*, pp. 4, 5.

8. Norman Mailer, "St. George and the Godfather," in *Some Honorable Men: Political Conventions 1960–1972* (Boston: Little, Brown and Co., 1976),

pp. 351, 352. All further references to this book will be noted in parentheses in the text.

9. Joyce Carol Oates, "Out of the Machine," in Adams' collection, p. 216.

10. The obvious exception is, of course, Seymour M. Hersh. See *The Price of Power: Kissinger in the Nixon White House* (New York: Summit Books, 1983).

Chapter 10 (pages 194–216)

1. Norman Mailer, *Genius and Lust: A Journey Through the Major Writings of Henry Miller* (New York: Grove Press, 1976), p. 86.

2. Norman Mailer, *Existential Errands* (Boston: Little, Brown, and Co., 1972), p. 4. All further references to this book (EE) will be noted in parentheses in the text.

3. Joan Didion, "'I want to go ahead and do it,'" *New York Times Book Review*, 7 October 1979, pp. 26–27.

4. This phrase is taken from the title of Barry Farrell's article for *New West* magazine (20 December 1976).

5. Earl Rovit, "True Life Story," *The Nation*, 229 (20 October 1979), 376.

Chapter 11 (pages 217–36)

1. Norman Mailer, *Ancient Evenings* (Boston: Little, Brown and Co., 1983), p. 3. All further references to this book will be noted in parentheses in the text.

2. Mark Twain, *The Mysterious Stranger*, ed. William M. Gibson (Berkeley and Los Angeles: University of California Press, 1970), p. 405.

3. Norman Mailer, *Tough Guys Don't Dance* (New York: Random House, 1984), p. 6. All further references to this book will be noted in parentheses in the text.

Bibliography

Adams, Laura. "Existential Aesthetics: An Interview with Norman Mailer." *Partisan Review*, 42 (Summer 1975), 197–214.

————. *Existential Battles: The Growth of Norman Mailer*. Athens: Ohio University Press, 1976.

————, ed. *Will the Real Norman Mailer Please Stand Up?* Port Washington, N.Y., and London: Kennikat Press, 1974.

Aldridge, John W. "The Big Comeback of Norman Mailer." *Life*, 58, No. 11 (19 March 1965), 45–47. Reprinted in expanded form as "The Energy of New Success," in Braudy, pp. 109–19.

————. "From Vietnam to Obscenity." *Harper's Magazine*, 236 (February 1968), 91–92, 94–97. Reprinted in Lucid, pp. 180–92.

Alter, Robert. "The Real and Imaginary Worlds of Norman Mailer." *Midstream*, (January 1969), pp. 24–35. Reprinted as "Norman Mailer (1923–   )," in *The Politics of Twentieth-Century Novelists*. Ed. George A. Panichas. New York: Hawthorn Books, 1971, pp. 321–34.

Baldwin, James. "The Black Boy Looks at the White Boy." *Esquire*, 55 (May 1961), 102–06. Reprinted in Lucid, pp. 218–37; and in Braudy, pp. 66–81.

Begiebing, Robert J. *Acts of Regeneration: Allegory and Archetype in the Works of Norman Mailer*. Columbus and London: University of Missouri Press, 1980.

Bersani, Leo. "The Interpretation of Dreams." *Partisan Review*, 32 (Fall 1965), 603–08. Reprinted in Lucid, pp. 171–79; and in Braudy, pp. 120–26.

Bloom, Harold. "Norman in Egypt." *New York Review of Books*, 28 April 1983, pp. 3–5.

Bourjaily, Vance. "Return of the Ancient Mailer." *Esquire*, 100 (July 1983), 116–17.

Braudy, Leo, ed. *Norman Mailer: A Collection of Critical Essays*. Englewood Cliffs, N.J.: Prentice-Hall, 1972.

Bufithis, Philip H. *Norman Mailer*. New York: Frederick Ungar Pub. Co., 1978.

Cowan, Michael. "The Americanness of Norman Mailer," in *Norman Mailer: A Collection of Critical Essays*. Ed. Leo Braudy. Englewood Cliffs, N.J.: Prentice-Hall, 1972, pp. 143–57. Reprinted in Adams' collection, pp. 95–112.

Didion, Joan. "'I want to go ahead and do it.'" *New York Times Book Review*, 7 October 1979, pp. 1, 26–27.

Durczak, Joanna. "Norman Mailer's *Why Are We in Vietnam?* As an Epilogue to William Faulkner's *Big Bottom Woods.*" *Studia Anglica Posnaniensia: An International Review of English Studies*, 11 (1979), 183–200.

Ehrlich, Robert. *Norman Mailer: The Radical as Hipster.* Metuchen, N.J., and London: The Scarecrow Press, 1978.

Eisinger, Chester. *Fiction of the Forties.* Chicago: University of Chicago Press, 1963.

Emerson, Ralph Waldo. *Selections from Ralph Waldo Emerson.* Ed. Stephen E. Whicher. Boston: Houghton Mifflin Co., 1960.

Foster, Richard. *Norman Mailer.* Minneapolis: University of Minnesota Press, 1968.

Geismar, Maxwell. "Frustrations, Neuroses & History." *Saturday Review of Literature*, 26 May 1951, pp. 15–16.

Gordon, Andrew. *An American Dreamer: A Psychoanalytic Study of Norman Mailer.* Rutherford, N.J.: Fairleigh Dickinson University Press, 1980.

Grace, Matthew. "Norman Mailer at the End of the Decade." *Etudes Anglaises*, 24 (January–March 1971), 50–58. Reprinted in Adams' collection, pp. 10–22.

Gutman, Stanley T. *Mankind in Barbary: The Individual and Society in the Novels of Norman Mailer.* Hanover, N.H.: The University Press of New England, 1975.

Hardwick, Elizabeth. "Bad Boy." *Partisan Review*, 32 (Spring 1965), 291–94. Reprinted as "A Nightmare by Norman Mailer" in Lucid, pp. 145–50.

Harper, Howard M. *Desperate Faith: A Study of Bellow, Salinger, Mailer, Baldwin and Updike.* Chapel Hill: University of North Carolina Press. 1967.

Hassan, Ihab. *Radical Innocence: Studies in the Contemporary American Novel.* New York: Harper & Row, 1961.

Hersh, Seymour M. *The Price of Power: Kissinger in the Nixon White House.* New York: Summit Books, 1983.

Howe, Irving. "Some Political Novels." *The Nation*, 172 (16 June 1951), 568–69.

Hux, Samuel Holland. "American Myth and Existential Vision: The Indigenous Existentialism of Mailer, Bellow, Styron, and Ellison." Ph.D. diss., University of Connecticut, 1965.

Irwin, John T. *American Hieroglyphics: The Symbol of the Egyptian Hieroglyphics in the American Renaissance.* New Haven: Yale University Press, 1980.

Johnson, Michael L. *The New Journalism: The Underground Press, the Artists of Nonfiction, and Changes in the Established Media.* Lawrence: University Press of Kansas, 1971, pp. 64–84. Selection reprinted as "Norman Mailer," in Adams' collection, pp. 173–94.

Kaufman, Donald L. *Norman Mailer: The Countdown/The First Twenty Years.* Carbondale: Southern Illinois University Press, 1969.

Lawrence, D. H. *Studies in Classical American Literature.* London: Martin Secker, 1933.

Leeds, Barry H. *The Structured Vision of Norman Mailer.* New York: New York University Press, 1969.

Lewis, R. W. B. *The American Adam: Innocence, Tragedy, and Tradition in the Nineteenth Century*. Chicago and London: University of Chicago Press, 1955.

Lucid, Robert F., ed. *Norman Mailer: The Man and His Work*. Boston: Little, Brown, and Co., 1971.

Mann, Thomas. "Freud and the Future," in *Essays of Three Decades*. Trans. H. T. Lowe-Porter. New York: Alfred A. Knopf, 1947, pp. 411–28.

Manso, Peter. *Mailer, His Life and Times*. New York: Simon and Schuster, 1984.

Marcus, Steven. "The Art of Fiction XXXII: Norman Mailer, an Interview." *The Paris Review*, 8, No. 31 (Winter–Spring 1964), 28–58. Reprinted as "An Interview with Norman Mailer" in Braudy, pp. 21–41.

Maud, Ralph. "Faulkner, Mailer, and Yogi Bear. *Canadian Review of American Studies*, 2 (Fall 1971), 69–75.

Merrill, Robert. *Norman Mailer*, Boston: Twayne Publishers, 1978.

Mills, Hillary. *Mailer: A Biography*. New York: Empire Books, 1982.

Oates, Joyce Carol. "Out of the Machine." *The Atlantic*, July 1971, pp. 42–45. Reprinted in Adams' collection, pp. 216–23.

Pearce, Richard. "Norman Mailer's *Why Are We in Vietnam?*: a Radical Critique of Frontier Values." *Modern Fiction Studies*, 17 (Autumn 1971), 409–14.

Podhoretz, Norman. "Norman Mailer: The Embattled Vision." *Partisan Review*, 26 (Summer 1959), 371–91. Reprinted in Lucid, pp. 60–85.

Poirier, Richard. "Morbid-Mindedness." *Commentary*, June 1965, pp. 91–94. Reprinted in Lucid, pp. 162–70.

———. *Norman Mailer*. New York: The Viking Press, 1972.

———. *The Performing Self*. New York: Oxford University Press, 1971.

———. "The Ups and Downs of Mailer." *New Republic*, 164, No. 4 (23 January 1971), 23–26. Reprinted in Braudy, pp. 167–74.

Radford, Jean. *Norman Mailer: A Critical Study*. New York: Barnes & Noble Books, 1975.

Rahv, Philip. "Crime Without Punishment." *New York Review of Books*, 25 March 1965, pp. 1–4. Reprinted in *The Myth and the Powerhouse*. New York: Farrar, Straus & Giroux, 1968, pp. 234–43.

Rolo, Charles J. "A House in Brooklyn." *The Atlantic*, 187 (June 1951), 82–83.

Rovit, Earl. "True Life Story." *The Nation*, 229 (20 October 1979), 376–78.

Schrader, George Alfred. "Norman Mailer and the Despair of Defiance." *The Yale Review*, 51, No. 2 (December 1961), 267–80. Reprinted in Braudy, pp. 82–95.

Schroth, Raymond A. "Mailer and His Gods." *Commonweal*, 90 (9 May 1969), 226–29. Reprinted in Adams' collection, pp. 34–42.

Schulz, Max F. "Norman Mailer's Divine Comedy," in *Radical Sophistication: Studies in Contemporary Jewish-American Novelists*. Athens: Ohio University Press, 1969, pp. 69–109. Reprinted in Adams' collection, pp. 43–79.

Solotaroff, Robert. *Down Mailer's Way*. Urbana: University of Illinois Press, 1974.

Stern, Milton R., and Seymour L. Gross, eds. *American Literature Survey.* Vol. 1. New York: The Viking Press, 1962.

Tanner, Tony. "On the Parapet (Norman Mailer)," in *City of Words: American Fiction 1950–1970.* New York: Harper & Row, 1971, pp. 344–71. Reprinted in Adams' collection, pp. 113–49.

Taylor, Gordon O. "Of Adams and Aquarius." *American Literature*, 46 (March 1974), 68–82.

Trilling, Diana. "Norman Mailer." *Encounter*, 19, No. 5 (November 1962), 45–56. Reprinted in Braudy, pp. 42–65.

Wenke, Joseph. "Norman Mailer," in *Dictionary of Literary Biography, The Beats: Literary Bohemians in Postwar America.* Ed. Ann Charters. Vol. 16. Detroit: Gale Research Company, 1983, 361–71.

Index